Contesting Clio's Craft:
New Directions and Debates in
Canadian History

Contesting Clio's Craft:
New Directions and Debates in Canadian History

Edited by
Christopher Dummitt and Michael Dawson

INSTITUTE FOR THE STUDY OF THE
AMERICAS

UNIVERSITY OF LONDON · SCHOOL OF ADVANCED STUDY

The Institute for the Study of the Americas (ISA) promotes, coordinates and provides a focus for research and postgraduate teaching on the Americas – Canada, the USA, Latin America and the Caribbean – in the University of London.

The Institute was officially established in August 2004 as a result of a merger between the Institute of Latin American Studies and the Institute of United States Studies, both of which were formed in 1965.

The Institute publishes in the disciplines of history, politics, economics, sociology, anthropology, geography and environment, development, culture and literature, and on the countries and regions of Latin America, the United States, Canada and the Caribbean.

ISA runs an active programme of events – conferences, seminars, lectures and workshops – in order to facilitate national research on the Americas in the humanities and social sciences. It also offers a range of taught master's and research degrees, allowing wide-ranging multi-disciplinary, multi-country study or a focus on disciplines such as politics or globalisation and development for specific countries or regions.

Full details about the Institute's publications, events, postgraduate courses and other activities are available on the web at *www.americas.sas.ac.uk*.

© Institute for the Study of the Americas, 2009

British Library Cataloguing-in-Publication Data
A catalogue record for this book is available
from the British Library

ISBN   978 1 900039 88 8

INSTITUTE FOR THE STUDY OF THE
A M E R I C A S
UNIVERSITY OF LONDON · SCHOOL OF ADVANCED STUDY

University of London
Senate House
Malet Street
London
WC1E 7HU
Telephone: 020 7862 8870
Fax: 020 7862 8886
Email: americas@sas.ac.uk
Web: www.americas.sas.ac.uk

Contents

		Page
Acknowledgements		vii
Notes on Contributors		viii
Introduction		ix
Debating the Future of Canadian History: Preliminary Answers to Uncommon Questions		
Christopher Dummitt and Michael Dawson		
1.	Reflections on the Place of Quebec in Historical Writing on Canada	1
	Magda Fahrni	
2.	Sharing Authority in the Writing of Canadian History: The Case of Oral History	21
	Steven High	
3.	Persistence and Inheritance: Rethinking Periodisation and English Canada's 'Twentieth Century'	47
	Michael Dawson and Catherine Gidney	
4.	Canadian Progress and the British Connection: Why Canadian Historians Seeking the Middle Road Should Give 2½ Cheers for the British Empire	75
	Andrew Smith	
5.	After Inclusiveness: The Future of Canadian History	98
	Christopher Dummitt	

6.   Nation, Empire and the Writing of History in Canada   123
      in English
      Adele Perry

7.   Transnational Intentions and Cultural Cringe: History Beyond   141
      National Boundaries
      Katie Pickles

8.   Canada in the Age of Revolutions: Rethinking Canadian   162
       Intellectual History in an Atlantic Perspective
      Michel Ducharme

Acknowledgements

First and foremost our thanks go to the contributors to this volume for their enthusiastic dedication to this project. We also thank those in attendance at the Rethinking Canadian History conference (held in London in May 2007) where original versions of these chapters were presented. The thought-provoking questions and suggestions offered by audience members, session chairs, and commentators were extremely valuable and are greatly appreciated. James Dunkerley, the former Director of the Institute for the Study of the Americas, was incredibly supportive at all stages of the project. Logistical support for the conference came in many forms and for their assistance we would like to thank Karen Perkins, Olga Jimenez, Mark Murphy, Richard Dennis, Phillip Buckner, and Malcolm and Rita Dawson.

As the project moved from conference to book, it benefited from the comments of the peer-reviewers as well as the dedicated staff at the press including Karen Perkins and Emily Morrell.

Financial support for this project was provided by the British Academy; the Institute for the Study of the Americas; the London Conference for Canadian Studies; the Canadian High Commission, London; the Foundation for Canadian Studies; and St. Thomas University. We thank all of these institutions for making the conference and book possible.

Juliet Sutcliffe and Catherine Gidney contributed enormously to both the success of the conference and the completion of this book. For this, and so much else, we are very grateful.

Christopher Dummitt & Michael Dawson

Notes on Contributors

Michael Dawson is Chair of the History Department at St. Thomas University in Fredericton, New Brunswick. He is the author of *The Mountie from Dime Novel to Disney* (1998) and *Selling British Columbia: Tourism and Consumer Culture, 1890–1970* (2004). His current research examines the British Empire/Commonwealth Games and explores the connections between national identity in Canada, Australia and New Zealand.

Michel Ducharme is an Assistant Professor in the History Department at the University of British Columbia. His research focuses on the intellectual, cultural and political debates in Canada between 1760 and 1867.

Christopher Dummitt is an Assistant Professor in the Department of History at Trent University. He is the author of *The Manly Modern: Masculinity in Postwar Canada* (University of British Columbia Press, 2007). He is currently writing a book about how Canadians have come to remember former prime minister William Lyon Mackenzie King.

Magda Fahrni is an Associate Professor in the Department of History at the Université du Québec à Montréal. She is the author of *Household Politics: Montreal Families and Postwar Reconstruction* (University of Toronto Press, 2005), recipient of the Canadian Historical Association's Clio-Québec Prize in 2006. She also co-edited, with Robert Rutherdale, *Creating Postwar Canada: Community, Diversity, and Dissent, 1945–75* (University of British Columbia Press, 2008).

Catherine Gidney is an Adjunct Professor in the Department of History at St. Thomas University. She is the author of *A Long Eclipse: The Liberal Protestant Establishment and the Canadian University, 1920–70* (Montreal and Kingston: McGill-Queen's University Press, 2004), winner of the Canadian History of Education Association's Founders' Prize, 2004–2006. Her current research focuses on youth, health and the making of the modern self.

Steven High is Canada Research Chair in Public History at Concordia University. He is also co-director of the Centre for Oral History and Digital Storytelling and the lead investigator of the Life Stories Community-University Research Alliance (CURA).

Adele Perry teaches history at the University of Manitoba where she is Canada Research Chair in Western Canadian Social History. Her current project is a study of kinship, intimacy and empire in one nineteenth-century transnational family.

Katie Pickles teaches history at the University of Canterbury, Christchurch, New Zealand. She has edited three books, written a variety of journal articles and essays, and is the author of *Transnational Outrage: The Death and Commemoration of Edith Cavell* (Palgrave 2007), and *Female Imperialism and National Identity: Imperial Order Daughters of the Empire* (Manchester University Press, 2002), which will be released in paperback in Spring 2009.

Andrew Smith is an assistant professor of history at Laurentian University. His research interests centre on nineteenth-century political, business, and constitutional history.

Introduction
Debating the Future of Canadian History:
Preliminary Answers to Uncommon Questions

Christopher Dummitt and Michael Dawson

There is a familiar, perhaps even tired, ring to many of the questions that dominate debate about Canadian history in the first decade of the twenty-first century. Why is the public so ignorant of Canadian history? And who is to blame? Is Canadian history 'dead'? And, if so, who killed it? Are we naively clinging to empirical ideas about truth and a knowable past in the face of poststructuralism, discourse analysis and our postmodern condition? Over the past 20 years these have been among the most commonly asked questions about history in Canada and abroad. One of the things that is so striking about these questions is their persistence. The same questions continue to be asked but there are few new answers. While each of these questions produced highly charged debates about the nature of historical research, they now seem overused, even stale. What will replace them? Are there new debates on the horizon that will open up and reshape Canadian history?

One of the problems faced by those who want to see a vigorous debate about the nature of Canadian history today is an absence of wide-ranging discussion. This current absence may even be related to the ways in which older debates about Canadian history tended to shut down genuine communication. As in Australia, the United States and elsewhere, debates over the truth of history or the importance of 'national' history invited interventions that were largely polemical and polarising. The ignorance of the opposing side was asserted, its ignominy assumed, and the path to enlightenment revealed. This tended to be true whether the discussants were academic historians writing in scholarly monographs or politicians and journalists involved in public commemoration. To a great extent, it was the manner in which these debates were initially framed, or responded to, that limited their efficacy and overall contribution to the development of a healthy and dynamic exchange of ideas about the future of Canadian history.

One of the most public examples of this process in Canada centred around the Dominion Institute's annual Canada Day Quiz and the accompanying reports and editorials lambasting the public's ignorance of their 'national history'. Inaugurated in 1997, the yearly quizzes provide the Institute and media pundits with an excuse to secure space on newscasts and in newspapers to display their horror at the failures of historical knowledge displayed by huge swathes of Canadians.[1] In the first quiz, for example, the Institute noted – and journalists picked up on – the finding that 'just below a third (31 per cent) knew that the battle of Vimy Ridge was an important allied victory in WWI.'[2] That a labelling of Vimy as 'an important allied victory' is debatable is not, in such a quiz, to be acknowledged. That is not the point; one is supposed to already agree with the premises behind the quiz: i.e., it is a travesty that less than a third of Canadians know the basic facts about what is presented as a key piece of national history. A more recent version of this exercise was, in fact, the commemoration of the ninetieth anniversary of Vimy Ridge in April 2007. At least one programme (CBC Radio's *The Current*) did, in that instance, give some airtime to a military historian who suggested that the battle was not as important as it is typically presented.[3] But this was a lonely contrarian viewpoint. The commemoration was largely an exercise in attempting to eradicate the ignorance that the Dominion Institute had ostensibly shown to be so prevalent over the previous decade. In this latter instance the scope of the debate was quite limited, but as with the Dominion Institute quizzes, the original orientation of the debate remained the same: the call to eradicate ignorance framed the issue in such a way that it left little room for nuance, sustained reflection and a constructive exchange of ideas.

A similarly polarising debate emerged largely in response to Michael Bliss's 1991 suggestion that Canada's past was being 'sundered' and, especially, to J.L.

---

[1]   See, for example, M. Campbell, 'Nationalism dips at dawn of global era,' *Globe and Mail*, 1 Jul. 1997, A1, A6; R. Griffiths, 'Heritage Day, but not Ottawa's way', *Globe and Mail*, 16 Feb. 1998, A19; R. Griffiths, 'The death of history', *Globe and Mail*, 23 Sept. 2000, A16; S. McCarthy, 'Political history not our forte', *Globe and Mail*, 11 Jan. 2002, A4; S. Adrangi, 'The latest Canada Day quiz shows many of us are in the dark about war and peace', *Globe and Mail*, 1 Jul. 2003, A3; R. Griffiths, 'To chart a future, we need a map', *Globe and Mail*, 1 Jul. 2003, A11; J. Simpson, 'A particularly Canadian affliction: historical memory loss', *Globe and Mail*, 22 Dec. 2007, A23.

[2]   The results for all of the institute's quizzes can be viewed online at www.dominion.ca/polling.htm.

[3]   The original programme on 6 Apr. 2007 and can be listened to at www.cbc.ca/thecurrent/2007/200704/20070406.html. The book under discussion was G. Hayes, A. Iarocci, M.Bechthold, *Vimy Ridge: A Canadian Reassessment* (Waterloo, Ontario, 2007).

Granatstein's 1998 accusation that Canadian history was 'dead'.[4] In *Who Killed Canadian History?* Granatstein argued that interest in Canadian history had been largely destroyed by a combination of the academy's infatuation with social history and a lack of will among provincial education bureaucracies to insist on making Canadian history mandatory for the nation's youth. What was required, he argued, was a return to 'national' history so that the ignorance imposed upon students by their professors and high-school teachers and administrators could be eradicated.[5] The end result was a spirited and tempestuous exchange that pitted defenders of Canadian social history against Granatstein and media commentators who sympathised with his position.[6]

As a rhetorical strategy, Granatstein's call to eradicate ignorance proved an alluring method of rallying public support for his cause. However, as a way of opening up reflective discussion and debate, this campaign, like the one waged by the Dominion Institute, has been less fruitful. Often these campaigns were waged with the built-in assumption that everyone (or at least those who are up to speed and in the know) already agreed on the basic principles of how we should proceed. The major questions to be asked, stories to be told and lessons to be learned were presented as self-evident rather than open to debate.

It was easy to identify this limitation in the public outcry around the Dominion Institute Canada Day Quiz. But a similar kind of dynamic also seemed to be at work in the academy. This may not have been obvious initially. On the surface, there seems to have been some vigorous debate over the very meaning of Canadian history in response to the 'sober second thoughts' that Bliss and Granatstein aired in the 1990s. Both historians questioned the costs of social history's rise to prominence, linking these new developments to the travails of the Canadian nation itself. In both cases, other historians responded vigorously to defend the profession and to champion the new approaches these two historians attacked. It should not be necessary to rehash the various interventions in this debate to point out one important feature: this was largely a debate between *two historians* and most of the rest of the historical profession. Bliss and Granatstein were, in the academy if not in the larger society, isolated and quite quickly

---

[4]   M. Bliss, 'Privatizing the Mind: The Sundering of Canadian History, the Sundering of Canada', *Journal of Canadian Studies*, vol. 26, no. 4 (1991) and J.L. Granatstein, *Who Killed Canadian History?* (Toronto, 1998).

[5]   For an important exploration of the continuing, and restrictive, influence of 'national' thinking among historians, see Adele Perry's chapter in this volume.

[6]   Editorial opinion and media coverage were largely supportive of Granatstein's arguments. See, for example, D. Frum, 'Lack of history teaching is national suicide', *London Free Press*, 25 Apr. 1998, F4; I. Urquart, 'It's time to send history back to school', *Toronto Star*, 30 Jun. 1998, A15; J. Reaney 'Historian-warrior Jack Granatstein battles on', *London Free Press*, 15 Apr. 1999, C1.

dismissed as out of step with modern historiographical and political trends.[7] In other words, although they may have questioned the main priorities of the profession, the profession itself largely went ahead unimpeded by their critique. In retrospect, this is hardly surprising given the way in which Granatstein, in particular, put forward his case. The opening salvos (and several of the defensive responses) were hardly conducive to sustained and productive discussion and, in the end, the potential for substantive debate about how and why Canadian history ought to be studied quickly evaporated.[8] But with Bliss and Granatstein so easily sidelined within the profession, other historians continued with their own particular projects, rarely discussing Canadian history writ large.

While these two debates attracted some significant public attention, one cannot overlook a third, less public, exchange about the nature of historical knowledge that also dominated discussions about Canadian history. Throughout the late 1980s and 1990s, whether it was in scholarly conferences, graduate methodology classes or coffee shops, Canadian historians spent a good deal of energy arguing about their ability to truly know the 'truth' of the past.[9] Here too was a debate that quickly became polarised, with historians finding themselves divided into camps that championed the importance of 'class' over 'gender' or even gender history over women's history – an indication that the tendency to polarise debate was not a characteristic monopolised by those on the right of the political spectrum. This debate, like the other two, seems to have faded in recent years and the profession has largely adopted the notion that categories like race, gender and sexuality work together, are socially constructed, and that sources always need to be read 'against the grain'.

---

[7] For the response of historians, see the various rejoinders to Bliss published in *Journal of Canadian Studies*, vol. 27, no. 2 (1992); and the three main responses to Granatstein, A.B. McKillop, 'Who Killed Canadian History? A View from the Trenches', *Canadian Historical Review*, vol. 80, no. 2 (1999) pp. 269–99; B. Palmer, 'Of Silences and Trenches: A Dissident View of Granatstein's Meaning', *Canadian Historical Review*, vol. 80, no. 4 (1999) pp. 676–86; and T.J. Stanley, 'Why I Killed Canadian History: Conditions for an Anti-Racist History in Canada', *Histoire sociale/Social History*, vol. 33, no. 65 (2000), pp. 79–103.

[8] Attempts to bridge the two sides were quite limited. For concrete suggestions on the way forward see G. Friesen, *Citizens and Nation: An Essay on History, Communication, and Canada* (Toronto, 2000) and I. McKay, 'The Liberal Order Framework: A Prospectus for a Reconnaissance of Canadian History', *Canadian Historical Review*, vol. 81, no. 4 (Dec. 2000), pp. 617–45.

[9] The debate about the cultural or linguistic turn involved much more than Canadian historians, of course, but some of the more frequently cited Canadian interventions in this debate included B. Palmer, *Descent into Discourse: The Reification of Language and the Writing of Social History* (Philadelphia, 1990); M. Valverde, 'Gender History/Women's History: Is Feminist Scholarship Losing its Critical Edge?', *Journal of Women's History*, vol. 5, no. 1 (1993), pp. 89–128; M. Valverde, 'Some Remarks on the Rise and Fall of Discourse Analysis', *Histoire sociale/Social History*, vol. 33, no. 65 (2000), pp. 59–77; J. Sangster, 'Beyond Dichotomies: Reassessing Gender History and Women's History in Canada', *Left History*, vol. 3, no. 1 (1995), pp. 109–121.

As these three debates have begun to recede from view, the absence of sustained debate across subfields of Canadian history is increasingly striking. That these three debates still remain reasonably common reference points in public and academic discourse is due not so much to their continuing relevance but, we think, to the fact that alternative and more relevant reference points have not yet been championed sufficiently. Indeed, the idea for this book emerged out of the editors' frustration that there did not seem to be either a publication or even a venue in which current ideas about the future direction of Canadian history could be found or aired.[10] As we thought about ways to introduce our students to the current state of the profession we searched largely in vain for suitable published material that reflected current trends. For the reasons outlined above it did not seem logical to trot out Bliss and Granatstein and their critics yet again or even the exchanges about the cultural or linguistic turn. Another possibility could have been an anthology that gathered together readings representing a variety of emerging subfields (Canadian environmental history, the history of sexuality in Canada, etc.). But such a book would mainly give examples of some fine research from new and developing fields. It would not necessarily offer discussion and debate *across* those fields or about Canadian history itself.

We wanted a work of discussion and debate, not an anthology. And if it did not exist, we decided that we ought to facilitate its creation. But where should we look for material to include in such a project? There are certainly some signs of a growing desire to understand and debate Canadian history writ large in the attention given to Ian McKay's 'Liberal Order Framework'. The original essay published in 2000 has been followed up by McKay's 2005 book, *Rebels, Reds, Radicals: Rethinking Canada's Left History*, and the 2006 conference held to discuss and debate the liberal order framework at the McGill Institute for the Study of Canada. The book that comes out of that conference will offer one important window onto an increasingly popular approach to Canadian history.[11] McKay's work is popular for a variety of reasons, but one of those reasons surely is because it so neatly blends together various streams of thought about the Canadian past into a singular framework. It provides a way of linking together the study of race, class and gender along with the burgeoning subfield on the history of liberal state formation and other areas of keen interest including Aboriginal and Quebec history. We appreciate the way this work has allowed for a conversation across subfields, but our purpose was not to provide a framework

---

[10]   One very worthwhile exception is the 'Forum' section in the *Canadian Historical Review*, which has, *for particular subfields*, offered a refreshing chance for new historiographical debates to be aired.

[11]   McKay, 'The Liberal Order Framework'; McKay, *Rebels, Reds, Radicals: Rethinking Canada's Left History* (Toronto, 2005) and M. Ducharme and J.F. Constant (eds.), *The Liberal Order Framework in Canadian History* (Toronto, forthcoming 2009).

itself. Our aim was to provide a forum for a variety of views about how Canadian history can be rethought and transformed. The trick, we came to believe, was to provide relatively new voices with an opportunity to ask original questions that spoke to the profession as it currently exists.

This book does not purport to have uncovered *the* way forward for Canadian history. Its aim, rather, is to cultivate discussion. The discussion element was built into this project from the very beginning. In the spring of 2007 nine historians of Canada who are – very roughly defined – in the early stages of their careers, met at the Institute for the Study of the Americas at the University of London, England. Each had been invited to write and present a paper that spoke to the current and future state of the profession. The subjects covered in this book are not a representative sample of all the current fields and subfields. Instead, we invited a selection of scholars who roughly covered many of the various fields, time periods and regions.[12] They all took on subjects related to their own research, but they also went far beyond this specific focus to ask broad questions about the discipline itself. After a great deal of (sometimes heated) discussion, questioning and, after the conference, revision, these papers are presented now in this book. The questions that they pose and the challenges they take on suggest some of the directions in which established scholars in the early stages of their career are taking the study of Canadian history.

The historians in this collection do not all agree. Our desire as editors was to create a book that offered genuine alternatives, and even serious disagreement, while highlighting emerging trends and underscoring the necessity of asking difficult and challenging questions that could open up new and productive debates. We think the chapters that follow offer an alluring glimpse into the kinds of issues and ideas that Canadian historians will be grappling with for years to come.

Many of these essays ask direct and unsettling questions about the way Canadian history is currently studied. This is one of the elements that the papers have in common: they force us to explicitly address historiographical issues that have been largely (and perhaps even strategically) ignored. In the opening chapter Magda Fahrni takes an old issue – the relation between French and English Canada and their historiographies – and adds an important new twist. 'What explains the increasing reluctance of English-Canadian scholars to study

---

[12]   The range of the profession represented in this current volume was meant to be greater but due to some unforeseen circumstances several of the contributors could not attend the meeting in London. It was a shame that these tended to be those whose work covered the eighteenth and early nineteenth centuries, which means that this earlier period of Canadian history is not as well covered as we would have liked.

Quebec?' she wonders. And 'is there anything that gives "English Canada" coherence as an object of study other than being "not Quebec"?' From this starting point Fahrni gives an up-to-date account of the institutional and intellectual linkages and cleavages between English-Canadian and Quebec historiography and makes the case for non-Quebec historians to factor Quebec into their studies on the grounds that a comparative approach would provide a more comprehensive understanding of the Canadian past.

Other essays in the collection take on similarly unsettling questions. In his contribution, Steven High asks Canadian historians to think again about the way in which they derive their authority as experts. He encourages us to 'think deeply about narrative voice, memory, authority' and 'the public's role in the historical process' while daring us to 'share authority' with the subjects we study. To make his case he examines the uneasy relationship between oral history, public history and Canadian academic historians. In their chapter, Michael Dawson and Catherine Gidney tackle the issue of periodisation. How do the seemingly prosaic and innocuous decisions we make when framing our studies (centuries, decades and 'postwar' eras) shape – or even distort – our version of the past? In taking these 'demarcations of convenience' for granted, they ask, do we risk losing sight of long-term cultural patterns?

For Andrew Smith it is Britain's imperial legacy that Canadian historians need to rethink and re-examine. Why is it, Smith asks, that Canadian historians so rarely address the fact that Canada is seen internationally as a success story? Could it be that to do so would mean writing a history of empire that goes against recent trends and assumptions? Smith does not definitively answer the question of the link between Canada's imperial past and its current status, but he does offer provocative questions and a window onto a way of writing about empire that is rarely seen in the literature on Canada today. With Christopher Dummitt, the unsettling questions stem from the unacknowledged legacy left by the rise since the 1960s of a more 'inclusive' history – an approach which is centred on, but goes beyond, social history. The inclusive history has become the common sense of the profession. Writing as someone whose own work is part of this approach, Dummitt nonetheless argues that the inclusive history has left the discipline with some rarely discussed gaps, distortions and unanswered questions. The future of Canadian history, he suggests, must surely focus not on the problems of the inclusive history's predecessors (as is often the case now), but rather on the prejudices of inclusive history itself. Dummitt's essay, like the other chapters, challenges us to survey the status quo and ask sometimes provocative questions about how we study Canadian history.

The second key commonality among the essays is their focus on comparative and transnational approaches to history. This is perhaps fitting given that the original conference was held outside Canada, but there is surely much more to this than the location of a conference venue. All of the chapters, to varying degrees, draw upon international and comparative examples to contextualise their examinations of Canadian history. A number go further and offer alternative models for comparative and transnational studies. These models sometimes overlap, but the authors' rationales are quite distinct. Adele Perry, for instance, argues for a postcolonial and transnational approach to history and calls upon Canadian historians to realise just how often we continue to fall back on the comfortable 'fiction' of the nation. By encouraging us to break free from *a priori* assumptions about the importance of national boundaries she calls for a more global approach to Canadian history – one that recognises Canada's imperial links with the outside world and that will allow Canadian historians to draw more fully upon, and contribute to, international historiography. In her chapter, Katie Pickles also champions transnational and postcolonial history but in doing so she highlights the difficulties she has encountered and the barriers that remain in place for historians determined to adopt this approach. Like Smith, Perry and others, Pickles emphasises the importance of examining imperial and colonial linkages. But hers is a more personal assessment of the speedbumps one is likely to encounter along the way. Chief among her concerns is the continued influence of a 'cultural cringe' or inferiority complex among historians in Canada (and New Zealand) that limits opportunities for genuine transnational and comparative history.

Michel Ducharme also calls for a more comparative approach to Canadian history – but he is more specifically focused upon trying to rescue Canadian intellectual history from its current marginalised and isolated existence within Canadian historiography. And rather than focusing on a 'British world', Ducharme champions an Atlantic framework – a framework that he believes 'would help to put Canadian history on the global historiographical map' and allow for the integration of French and English scholarship along the lines of what Fahrni calls for in her chapter. The future of Canadian history, it would seem, will require a comparative and transnational approach. But just how such an approach can best be put into practice remains open to debate.

A third key theme of this book concerns the process by which Canadian history is both created and consumed. Many of the contributors argue that Canadian history needs to broaden its base; they offer a critique of the relative isolation of Canadian history and historians from other academic fields and from the general public at large. For example, both Steven High and Katie Pickles address the issue of historical authority. High argues that a determined effort to share authority with our historical subjects through oral history projects – to bring historical subjects into the very creation of historical knowledge – is a promising way forward. For Pickles the key issue is to address and dismantle the institutionalised barriers that discourage 'outsiders' from studying Canada. Others such as Michel Ducharme, Magda Fahrni and Adele Perry champion the possibilities of new interpretive frameworks that will encourage Canadian historians to take a more comparative approach. The possibility here is that such approaches could, in turn, provide greater opportunities for international scholars to incorporate Canadian examples into their studies. Christopher Dummitt offers two suggestions: he champions historical narratives that can blend analysis with popular forms of storytelling, and he suggests that the way in which we write history needs to be reinvigorated, that we ought to adopt a more artful and even holistic style. All of these suggestions are plausible but they are not all easily reconcilable. In the coming years we will undoubtedly learn a great deal about just how effectively these approaches can be combined or, alternatively, whether they are positioned in opposition to one another. With competing suggestions come choices and differences of opinion.

Finally, all the chapters include an explicit or implicit evaluation of social history's legacy for the study of Canadian history. To a certain extent this is unavoidable. Over the past 40 years social history has redefined Canadian history in enormously positive ways. But as readers will quickly see, in asking demanding questions of the status quo the chapters that follow often note that for all its influence, social history as it has been practised in the Canadian field to date has left some important questions unasked. These deal with issues such as the efficacy of a 'national' framework, periodisation, legacies of empire and ongoing divisions between Quebec and 'English Canada', and the source of historians' authority to speak about the past. Fittingly, it may well be on this very point that the contributors to this volume are most divided. The most pronounced division emerges between Dummitt and Perry. Dummitt argues in his chapter that social history's clarion call for an ever more inclusive history, whatever its political attractions, no longer maintains the same intellectual originality that it did in the 1970s or even the 1990s. Hence, his insistence on a more introspective and less defensive debate about the merits and prejudices of inclusive history, one that will find ways to inspire future historians. Perry argues that 'the case that inclusion has been achieved has not been conclusively made' and was, in fact, 'never the goal of the revisionist historiography in the first place'. Instead, she explains, the task is to rethink 'the past through the categories of race, ethnicity, class, gender, region, sexuality and colonisation'. There is, then, within this book, no consensus on the extent to which the ways forward require a break with past practice. And that is as it should be.

What this book does offer is a re-engagement with discussion itself. It provides a forum in which preliminary answers are provided to uncommonly asked questions. Our hope is that both the questions raised and the answers offered serve to promote new directions of study and new debates about Canadian history. Collectively the essays in this book promise to open up a series of overlapping debates premised on the understanding that for the dialogue to be substantive and productive the initial call to discussion should tolerate, and indeed encourage, disagreement. What, then, are the new developments in thinking that should inspire historians in the future? What are the new fissures of intellectual thought that divide us? Is the very notion of 'Canadian history' now passé? Or, if not, how might historians of Canada capitalise upon current trends towards transnational, global, and comparative history without losing sight of 'national', regional or local developments? Some readers will embrace some arguments presented here more than others; and all readers, we imagine, will weigh the relative importance of each chapter differently. But all of you, we hope, will feel that your contributions to future discussions on these and other issues are welcome and, indeed, expected, as the historical study of Canada moves forward in new and quite possibly unexpected directions.

Chapter 1
Reflections on the Place of Quebec in Historical Writing on Canada

Magda Fahrni

In 1945, novelist Hugh MacLennan borrowed the expression 'two solitudes' from the poet Rainer Maria Rilke in order to describe the two Canadas, French and English – two nations conceived of today as Quebec and English Canada.[1] In popularising Rilke's metaphor, MacLennan provided future scholars with an analytical framework and an efficient shorthand for dealing (and, sometimes, a convenient excuse for not dealing) with one of the central cleavages in Canadian history and historiography. To some extent, the 'two solitudes' metaphor remains relevant today, in terms both of the institutional structures of the his-torical discipline and the intellectual content of the history that is being written.

This chapter originated in a certain frustration with what one of my colleagues calls an 'implicit separatism' visible in much of the Canadian historiography – that is, what appears to be the increasing number of accounts of the history of 'Canada' that are really accounts of English Canada (and often, not even all of English Canada) – as though Quebec had already left the federation and therefore need not be taken into account. But I wanted this chapter to be more than a complaint. And I also didn't want to give the impression that Quebec history is generally neglected: within Quebec, the historiography is in fact flourishing. So I begin by noting that Quebec historiography is alive and well. There are journals, scholarly associations and conferences devoted to Quebec history; historical stud-ies of Quebec are published regularly, in French and in English. The vast major-ity of these studies, however, are carried out by historians working in Quebec. The second part of the chapter demonstrates and interrogates the institutional, intellectual and often methodological divide separating scholars of Quebec and students of English Canada. Why is it, I ask, that fewer and fewer studies written outside Quebec take Quebec into account? What explains the proliferation of

---

[1] H. MacLennan, *Two Solitudes* (Toronto and New York, 1945).

studies of family, culture, politics, religion, etc., 'in English Canada'? Is there anything that gives 'English Canada' coherence as an object of study other than being 'not Quebec'?[2] What explains the increasing reluctance of English-Canadian scholars to study Quebec – a reluctance that did not seem to exist thirty years ago, when almost all large history departments in English Canada included a specialist in New France or French Canada, and when Quebec was an integral part of textbooks, syntheses, anthologies and course offerings in English-Canadian universities? One could evoke a number of possible responses, including the language barrier, a lack of political will, the fear of doing Quebec history badly, and perhaps a hostility to nationalism, particularly on the left, rooted in assumptions that nationalist sentiment is inherently reactionary.[3]

The third section of my chapter explores an alternative explanation for the current lack of dialogue between historians of English Canada and those interested in Quebec: namely, that regional and local studies better serve contemporary historians' methodological and intellectual objectives, and that there is at present little interest in syntheses or pan-Canadian studies, with or without Quebec. Finally, I offer thoughts on the ways in which seeking to understand Quebec's history could enrich our understanding of English-Canadian history and allow Canadian historians to participate in international historiographical currents. Practitioners of the new imperial history, for instance, could look to the Quebec case as a rare example of a double European colonisation and succeeding European metropoles.[4] Likewise, the many historians currently interested in transnationalism would find a ready-made case study within Canada's borders. Two principal arguments run through this chapter: first, that the historiography of Canada would benefit from increased scholarly attention to Quebec, and second, that historians of Canada might fruitfully analyse Quebec history using

---

[2]   Analyses of the divide between the two historiographies include J.-C. Robert, 'La recherche en histoire du Canada' and J. Burgess, 'Exploring the Limited Identities of Canadian Labour: Recent Trends in English Canada and in Quebec', both in *International Journal of Canadian Studies/Revue internationale d'études canadiennes*, no. 1–2 (Spring–Fall/printemps–automne 1990).

[3]   In the Canadian context, this hostility to nationalism might be seen as a 'Trudeauvian' current, a current adopted by much of the English-Canadian intelligentsia. Historian Ramsay Cook, for example, shared Pierre Elliott Trudeau's discomfort with nationalism, although this never prevented Cook from studying and attempting to understand Quebec nationalisms. See the most recent collection of Cook's essays entitled *Watching Quebec: Selected Essays* (Montreal, 2005). On the English-Canadian left's difficulties with the national question in Quebec, see S. Mills, 'When Democratic Socialists Discovered Democracy: the League for Social Reconstruction Confronts the "Quebec Problem"', *Canadian Historical Review*, vol. 86, no. 1 (Mar. 2005), pp. 53–81.

[4]   Another example of a double colonisation would be Puerto Rico: see A.A. Barreto, *Language, Elites, and the State: Nationalism in Puerto Rico and Quebec* (Westport, 1998). My thanks to José Igartua for this reference.

the tools of comparative history and *histoire croisée*.[5] Indeed, I would argue that thinking historically about Quebec leads almost automatically to the practices of comparative history and *histoire croisée*.

To interrogate the place of Quebec in current historical writing on Canada is to presuppose another, more normative question: namely, what ought to be the place of Quebec in current historical writing on Canada? While the answers to this second question no doubt vary widely among potential respondents, I would argue that it is important that historians integrate an understanding of Quebec's history into their histories of Canada. In part, this is because the place of Quebec within Canada today remains highly contested (both within and outside Quebec) and historical analysis can help us understand the reasons that this is so. It is also because Quebec's particular history helps to explain a considerable array of past developments on a Canada-wide scale, such as federal politics (we might think of longstanding Prime Minister Mackenzie King, who never made an important decision without considering how it might affect his electoral success in Quebec) and policies (such as the launching of official multiculturalism by antinationalist Prime Minister Pierre Elliott Trudeau in the 1970s). Most importantly, perhaps, it is because attention to the historical place of Quebec within Canada would allow Canadian historians to engage with some of the most exciting international historiographical tendencies, namely transnational, borderland, 'new imperial' and comparative studies.

One could use any number of indicators to measure the current place of Quebec in historical writing on Canada: textbooks and manuals; the articles published in Canada's premier scholarly historical journal, the *Canadian Historical Review*; the papers given at the annual conference of the Canadian Historical Association, along with the proceedings of that conference; recent monographs; recent and ongoing theses; prize-winning books; and course offerings in Canadian universities. In this chapter, I shall draw on recent monographs and works of synthesis, but also on recent issues of the *Revue d'histoire de l'Amérique française*, the *Canadian Historical Review* and the *Journal of the Canadian Historical Association*, among other sources, in order to assess the place of historical writing on Quebec within the larger body of historical writing on Canada.

Although this chapter is critical of certain contemporary trends in the writing of Canadian history, it attempts to go beyond sermonising and pious platitudes about the necessity of bridging the two solitudes in order to seriously explore the reasons why Quebec is not more often studied by historians working in English Canada, as well as the real theoretical and empirical insights that might result from increased attention to Quebec's historical place within Canada.

---

[5] For a good analysis of the differences between comparative history and *histoire croisée*, see J. Kocka, 'Comparison and Beyond', *History and Theory*, vol. 42, no. 1 (2003), pp. 39–44.

Quebec Historians and Historiography Today

The historiography of Quebec is a flourishing field, as testified by the regular publication of books and articles in both French and English and by the success of the annual congress of the Institut d'histoire de l'Amérique française and numerous smaller conferences throughout the year.[6] Almost all of these conferences on Quebec history take place within Quebec; the authors of most of these books and articles work in Quebec. There are a few recurrent exceptions: a small number of historians of Quebec working at English-language universities outside the province are regular attendees at these conferences and publish extensively in the field;[7] the same can be said of historians of Quebec teaching in francophone universities outside the province (Ottawa, Moncton, Hearst) and of a small smattering of European scholars who keep up with developments in the field.[8]

In the themes and tendencies prevalent in recent years, Quebec historiography in many ways resembles recent English-Canadian historiography. An examination of the premier Quebec history journal, the *Revue d'histoire de l'Amérique française*, shows that since 2000, the journal, which is published four times a year, has published extensively in the fields of cultural history (16 articles),[9] the history of ideas and ideologies (nine articles) and the history of New France (nine articles). Special theme issues devoted to Amerindian history (six articles), public history (10 articles), the history of women and gender (seven articles), the history of consumerism and consumption (five articles) and the history of the environment (eight articles) have focused particular attention on these historical questions. Since 2000, few to no articles have been published in the fields of economic history, military history or the history of immigration and ethnicity. Another indication of trends in recent work in the history of Quebec are the 18 books submitted for the 2007 Clio-Quebec prize, awarded by the Canadian Historical Association. Ten of these books were written in French; eight in English. Five deal with a historical period prior to the nineteenth century, nine with the nineteenth century and eleven with the twentieth century. The books focus on themes such as the family, the law, women, youth, public health and urban infrastructures, religion, immigration, nationalism, the union

---

[6]   For one controversial examination of Quebec historiography, see R. Rudin, *Making History in Twentieth-Century Quebec* (Toronto, 1997). One of the many vigorous responses provoked by Rudin's analysis is Y. Gingras, 'Making Up History', *Literary Review of Canada*, vol. 7, no. 10 (Summer 1999), pp. 19–22. A less controversial analysis of Quebec historiography is S. Gagnon, *Le passé composé: de Ouellet à Rudin* (Montreal, 1999).

[7]   I think, for instance, of Bettina Bradbury, Colin Coates, Bruce Curtis, Allan Greer and Jack Little.

[8]   For instance, Belgian historian Serge Jaumain and Italian historian Luca Codignola.

[9]   Including three articles on the history of religion and the Catholic Church.

movement, and consumerism and mass consumption. The subjects of these books, and the fact that we see here a preponderance of studies dealing with the twentieth century, echo tendencies also prevalent in recent English-Canadian historiography.

In Quebec, as in English Canada and elsewhere, there has in recent years been a reaction to the longstanding (that is, since the 1970s) predominance of social, and particularly socioeconomic, history. In the 1970s and 1980s, socioeconomic history was perhaps even more important in Quebec than in English Canada: we have only to think, for instance, of the work of Gilles Paquet and Jean-Pierre Wallot, Fernand Ouellet, Normand Séguin, Serge Courville, and Gérard Bouchard.[10] Some critics have recently called for a return to the study of the intellectual, the ideological and the cultural; others have appealed for the revitalisation of political history.[11] The journal *Mens: Revue d'histoire intellectuelle de l'Amérique française* was founded in 2000 by a group of doctoral students and recent PhDs based at Laval University as an explicit challenge to what these young historians perceived to be the domination of the *Revue d'histoire de l'Amérique française* and social history in Quebec. As they wrote in the first issue of the new journal, 'nous estimons que, bien qu'elle fasse l'objet d'un traitement occasionnel dans certaines publications, l'histoire intellectuelle au Québec ne bénéficie pas d'une visibilité à la mesure de l'importance qu'elle devrait prendre dans le paysage historique.'[12] Several years earlier, in 1992, another new journal, the *Bulletin d'histoire politique*, had criticised what its founders perceived as the marginalisation of political history in Quebec, a history '[l]ongtemps repoussée aux marges d'une histoire dite "scientifique" ... .'[13] The *Bulletin d'histoire politique* is still active, well over a decade later, and it attracts and publishes a large number of submissions from graduate students in particular, drawn to the journal's emphasis on studies of nationalism, political ritual, the military, and memory and

---

[10] G. Paquet and J.-P. Wallot, *Patronage et pouvoir dans le Bas-Canada, 1794–1812: Un essai d'économie historique* (Montreal, 1973); F. Ouellet, *Histoire économique et sociale du Québec, 1760–1850: structures et conjonctures* (Montreal, 1971); N. Séguin, L. Verreault-Roy and R. Hardy, *Statistiques de l'évolution de l'agriculture en Mauricie: 1850–1950* (Trois-Rivières, 1979); S. Courville, *Entre ville et campagne: l'essor du village dans les seigneuries du Bas-Canada* (Sainte-Foy, 1990); G. Bouchard, *Quelques arpents d'Amérique: population, économie, famille* (Montréal, 1996).

[11] For analyses of these debates, see M. Pâquet, 'Histoire sociale et histoire politique au Québec: esquisse d'une anthropologie du savoir historien', *Bulletin d'histoire politique*, vol. 15, no. 3 (printemps 2007) pp. 83–102; J. Burgess, 'L'histoire du Québec: tendances récentes et enjeux', in Denise Lemieux (ed.), *Traité de la culture* (Quebec, 2002).

[12] M. Beausoleil, Y. Bégin, D.-C. Bélanger, D. Foisy-Geoffroy and M. Lapointe, 'Présentation de la revue *Mens*', *Mens*, vol. 1, no. 1 (automne 2000).

[13] J.-M. Fecteau, 'Manifeste,' *Bulletin de l'Association québécoise d'histoire politique*, vol. 1, no. 1 (automne 1992), p. 4.

commemoration. Yet proponents of political history, including those involved in producing the *Bulletin d'histoire politique*, still appear to feel that political history receives short shrift in Quebec: witness, for instance, the op-ed published in *Le Devoir* in January 2007 by historians Jacques Rouillard, of the Université de Montréal, and Robert Comeau, of the Université du Québec à Montréal. Rouillard and Comeau deplore what they see as 'la tendance chez les historiens de profession dans les universités à discréditer l'histoire politique depuis les années 70 au profit de l'histoire sociale. Cette dernière spécialisation en est venue à détenir une position tellement dominante qu'elle occupe une large part de la recherche parmi les historiens francophones des universités québécoises.' Political history is all the more important, they argue, given that Quebec constitutes a minority society within Canada and that 'c'est à travers nos institutions politiques que le combat pour notre survie s'est affirmé avec force.'[14]

The Great Divide

If the recent evolution of Quebec historiography in some ways resembles that of its English-Canadian counterpart, there remain a number of institutional, intellectual and methodological divides between the two fields.

There are, for instance, differences in both the historiographical influences and the methods used by francophone historians of Quebec. Not surprisingly, the latter are influenced by the historiography of France to a much greater extent than are most English-Canadian historians. This is particularly evident in cultural history, where the French historiography is abundant and flourishing. The cultural history practised by most francophone historians of Quebec owes little to cultural studies approaches developed in the United States, and much more to historians of France such as Pascal Ory.[15] Quebec historians interested in questions of collective memory and commemoration, for instance, look for

---

[14]   J. Rouillard and R. Comeau, 'La marginalisation de l'histoire politique dans les universités francophones', *Le Devoir*, 13 Jan. 2007. The main purpose of this op-ed was to critique the changes recently proposed to the high-school history curriculum in Quebec. For a critique of Rouillard's and Comeau's op-ed, see M. Dagenais and C. Laville, 'Le naufrage du projet de programme d'histoire "nationale". Retour sur une occasion manquée accompagné de considérations sur l'éducation historique', *Revue d'histoire de l'Amérique française*, vol. 60, no. 4 (printemps 2007), p. 546.

[15]   P. Ory, *L'histoire culturelle* (Paris, 2004). For a few examples of recent work on cultural practices in Quebec, see the special issue of the *Canadian Historical Review* edited by Colin Coates (volume 88, number 1, Mar. 2007). Note that the editors of this issue defined 'cultural history' very broadly; some of the articles included in the issue could be considered 'old-fashioned' social or intellectual history.

inspiration to Pierre Nora and Maurice Halbwachs; those interested in the history of cultural practices such as reading, writing and correspondence look to Roger Chartier; and those interrogating the cultural meanings of war to Stéphane Audoin-Rouzeau and Annette Becker.[16] Alongside different sources of historiographical inspiration are differences of method: quantitative analysis maintains a certain importance in Quebec history,[17] while poststructuralist approaches, as we shall see, have made relatively little headway among francophone historians practising in Quebec.

The divide between English-Canadian and Quebec historiography generally is echoed by similar divides within historiographical subfields. As Denyse Baillargeon has noted, for instance, a tangible divide separates women's history in Quebec and that practised in the rest of Canada. Although on either side of the divide the twin fields of women's history have taken 'des voies parallèles', sometimes evolving in intellectually and methodologically similar ways, the barrier between the two remains very real, and exceptions – those scholars who explore the history of women in both national contexts – remain just that.[18] Despite the fact that research in Quebec women's history over the past 20 years has tended to emphasise the commonalities between the experiences of women in Quebec and those of their counterparts in English Canada and other western societies, few historians have undertaken explicitly comparative studies, or even studies that take both collectivities into account. The synthesis *Canadian Women: A History*, often used as a textbook in undergraduate history classes, is an important exception, although ironically, it is not always easy to teach the two histories in lockstep. My own teaching experience in Quebec women's history has forced me, for instance, to considerably rethink the generally accepted periodisation of the history of Canadian feminism. In English Canada, it has

---

[16]   P. Nora (ed.), *Les lieux de mémoire*, 3 vols. (Paris, 1984); M. Halbwachs, *La mémoire collective* (Paris, 1950); R. Chartier, *Lectures et lecteurs dans la France d'Ancien régime* (Paris, 1987); S. Audoin-Rouzeau et A. Becker, *14–18 Retrouver la guerre* (Paris, 2000). For a recent analysis of cultural history in Quebec and Canada, see C. Bouchard, 'L'histoire culturelle au Canada', in Philippe Poirrier (ed.), postface de R. Chartier, *L'histoire culturelle, un tournant mondial de l'historiographie?* (Dijon, 2008).

[17]   Recent examples include G. Paquet and J.-P. Wallot, *Un Quebec moderne 1760–1840. Essai d'histoire économique et sociale* (Montreal, 2007); J. Brun, *Vie et mort du couple en Nouvelle-France. Québec et Louisbourg au XVIII' siècle* (Montreal , 2006); and the significant amount of quantitative analysis in D. Fyson, *Magistrates, Police, and People: Everyday Criminal Justice in Quebec and Lower Canada, 1764–1837* (Toronto, 2006). It is nonetheless certain that interest in quantitative history has declined since its heyday in the 1970s.

[18]   D. Baillargeon, 'Des voies/x parallèles. L'histoire des femmes au Québec et au Canada anglais (1970–1995)', *Sextant*, no. 4 (1995), pp. 133–68. Such divides are also evident in other fields, e.g. labour history and economic history.

long been standard practice to teach that so-called first-wave feminism ended around 1920, that feminist efforts receded into the background in the interwar period and the immediate post-Second World War era, and that so-called second-wave feminism emerged toward the end of the 1960s.[19] But in Quebec, where women achieved the provincial vote in 1940 and where efforts to reform the Civil Code were just as important to first-wave feminists as attempts to secure the vote, this schema simply doesn't work: the 1920s and 1930s witnessed dozens of feminist campaigns to obtain political and civic rights and were hardly a period of 'recession' for the feminist waves.

Not only do scholars rarely study the women of both national collectivities, but English-Canadian historians of women in particular appear reluctant to incorporate studies in the history of Quebec women into their work. Perhaps this is due to the language barrier; perhaps, as Baillargeon suggests, it is because many English-Canadian historians of women assume that the Quebec experience was so different as to be irrelevant for the English-Canadian case. The converse is less true, as most francophone historians of women have been engaged in explicit attempts to understand Quebec women's history in the broader North American context.[20]

While the study of women per se has evolved in somewhat similar directions in both Quebec and English Canada, there has until recently been little interest in Quebec in gendered histories of men and masculinity. To be sure, sociologists such as Germain Dulac have been publishing in the area of masculinity studies for years.[21] Recently, historians of Quebec such as Jarrett Rudy, Louise Bienvenue and Christine Hudon have undertaken stimulating explorations of masculinity in Quebec's past.[22] And there are certainly graduate theses on the

---

[19] I am well aware that the 'waves' metaphor has been challenged by a number of historians of North America over the past 15 years. Indeed, my own work demonstrates that women were far from absent from the public and political spheres in the 1940s. See J. Meyerowitz (ed.), *Not June Cleaver: Women and Gender in Postwar America, 1945–1960* (Philadelphia, 1994); S. Murray, *The Progressive Housewife: Community Activism in Suburban Queens, 1945–1965* (Philadelphia, 2003); M. Fahrni, *Household Politics: Montreal Families and Postwar Reconstruction* (Toronto, 2005). On the different chronologies of women's history in English Canada and Quebec respectively, see Baillargeon, 'Des voies/x parallèles', pp. 157–8.

[20] Baillargeon, 'Des voies/x parallèles', pp. 166–8.

[21] G. Dulac, *Penser le masculin: Essai sur la trajectoire des militants de la condition masculine et paternelle* (Quebec , 1994).

[22] J. Rudy, 'Unmaking Manly Smokes: Church, State, Governance, and the First Anti-Smoking Campaigns in Montreal, 1892–1914', *Journal of the Canadian Historical Association*, no. 12 (2001), pp. 95–114; L. Bienvenue and C. Hudon, '"Pour devenir homme, tu transgresseras ... ." Quelques enjeux de la socialisation masculine dans les collèges classiques québécois (1880–1939)', *Canadian Historical Review*, vol. 86, no. 3 (Sept. 2005), pp. 485–511.

history of masculinity underway.[23] Moreover, a special issue of the *Revue d'histoire de l'Amérique française* on gender published in 2004 included several articles that dealt specifically with masculinity, through topics such as boarding-school friendships between young men, marital sexuality and fatherhood.[24] Yet by and large, this is an area that has been submitted to less investigation than in English Canada. Historian Jeffery Vacante has argued, somewhat controversially, that this is owing to the fact that 'the study of masculinity threatens to unravel the narrative of Quebec's evolution as a modern and liberal society'. According to Vacante, the 'new study of masculinity, which is part of the drift within the historical profession away from the materialist past and toward the study of discourse, threatens to shine a light on precisely those illiberal discourses that supposedly marked Quebec society as different.'[25] Whether or not Vacante is right (and I personally don't think that he is), it is certain that poststructuralist approaches have made few inroads into women's and gender history in Quebec. As recently as 2001, for instance, Micheline Dumont, one of Quebec's best-known historians of women, wrote that gender history informed by poststructuralist analysis 'n'en est encore qu'à ses premiers balbutiements, tant la force des anciennes conceptions continue de prévaloir'.[26] Perhaps, as Denyse Baillargeon suggests, this is because such approaches, emphasising the multiplicity and contingent nature of social identities, call into question the unity of a society that is, after all, a minority within North America and that many feel cannot afford to be divided.[27]

Alongside the historiographical and methodological cleavages between English-Canadian and Quebec historiographies – and possibly even more

---

[23] For example, M.-J. Béchard, 'Les hommes en transformation? Une analyse des représentations des hommes au Québec à travers le magazine *Actualité*, 1960–1976' (Mémoire de maîtrise, Université du Québec à Montréal, 2003); S. Roy, 'Le célibat masculin à Montréal (1870–1920)' (PhD thesis, McGill University, in progress).

[24] See the articles by Louise Bienvenue and Christine Hudon, Isabelle Perreault, Vincent Duhaime, and Cynthia Fish in *Revue d'histoire de l'Amérique française*, vol. 57, no. 4 (printemps 2004).

[25] J. Vacante, 'Liberal Nationalism and the Challenge of Masculinity Studies in Quebec', *Left History*, vol. 11, no. 2 (Fall 2006), pp. 107, 109.

[26] M. Dumont, *Découvrir la mémoire des femmes. Une historienne face à l'histoire des femmes* (Montreal, 2001), p. 142.

[27] Baillargeon, 'Des voies/x parallèles', pp. 164–5. One could legitimately ask to what extent poststructuralist approaches have made inroads into English-Canadian historiography. Beyond such classics as J. Parr's *The Gender of Breadwinners: Women, Men, and Change in Two Industrial Towns 1880–1950* (Toronto, 1990) and M. Valverde's *The Age of Light, Soap, and Water: Moral Reform in English Canada, 1885–1925* (Toronto, 1991), which incorporate some of the insights of Joan Scott and others, the influence of poststructuralism on English-Canadian historiography seems limited to historians' recognition of the shifting nature of identities and the multiplicity of possible narratives.

significant – is the institutional divide. Quebec historians have their own universities, francophone and anglophone; their own major granting agency, the Fonds québécois de la recherche sur la société et la culture; their own learned society, the Institut d'histoire de l'Amérique française; and their own journals, notably the ones mentioned above: the *Revue d'histoire de l'Amérique française*, the *Bulletin d'histoire politique*, and *Mens*. What this means, in part, is that Quebec historians are less likely to participate in the annual meetings of the Canadian Historical Association and to publish in such pan-Canadian, but predominantly English-language, journals as the *Canadian Historical Review*. Many historians of Quebec find that French-language sessions at the Canadian Historical Association attract few audience members and that French-language articles published in the *Canadian Historical Review* are infrequently read or cited by English-Canadian historians. It thus makes more sense for them to present the results of their research to their 'natural' audience, that is, an audience that functions in French and that is largely concentrated in Quebec. An analysis of the *Journal of the Canadian Historical Association* over the past 10 years (the 1996 to 2005 issues), for instance, shows that only 15 of the 102 articles published deal with Quebec (14.7 per cent). It is worth noting that four of these 15 articles are to be found in the 2001 issue, drawn from the Quebec City Congress, and five of the 15 from the 1999 issue, drawn from the Congress held in Sherbrooke, Quebec. An analysis of the *Canadian Historical Review* over the past 10 years reveals that it has a somewhat better record: of the 152 articles or 'forums' published between 1997 and 2006, 36 (almost 24 per cent) deal with Quebec. It seems clear to me that the problem is not that the *Canadian Historical Review* doesn't want to publish studies of Quebec or studies written in French: on the contrary. Rather, the problem is surely that it doesn't receive enough submissions about Quebec, particularly submissions written in French. I suspect that the same goes for the Canadian Historical Association and thus for the *Journal of the Canadian Historical Association*. Both the Canadian Historical Association and the *Canadian Historical Review*, conscious of their pan-Canadian mandates, are, I imagine, receptive to research on Quebec, but many (francophone) historians of Quebec choose not to present or publish there, for the reasons mentioned above.

In contrast to the relatively little space occupied by studies of Quebec in these pan-Canadian journals, the textbooks used in introductory Canadian history courses and the (few) syntheses of Canadian history recently published continue to accord a fair amount of attention to Quebec. H.V. Nelles's *A Little History of Canada* is one of these, although after the conquest of New France, Quebec occupies little space until the Quiet Revolution of the 1960s, the FLQ activity of the 1960s and 1970s, and the constitutional battles of the 1980s and 1990s. Nelles claims that in the 1960s, 'Quebec had awakened as if from a long sleep': this contentious opinion is certainly reflected in the structure of his book, where, apart from appearances at the Rebellions of 1837-8 and the Canadian Confederation of 1867, Quebec appears to have been largely dormant between 1760 and 1960.[28] The 2006 edition of Desmond Morton's *A Short History of Canada* is better at integrating Quebec's history throughout the book, from the arrival of Jacques Cartier in North America to the early twenty-first-century Gomery Commission.[29] I have already alluded to *Canadian Women: A History*, edited by Alison Prentice et al., as another synthesis that takes care to include material on Quebec; the second edition of Bryan D. Palmer's *Working Class Experience* and Desmond Morton's *Working People* also give a fair bit of attention to Quebec.[30] 'Older' political histories of Canada tended to see the Quebec question as central to their narratives of Canada's birth, progress and threatened break-up.[31] English-Canadian political scientists writing today continue to interrogate Canada-Quebec relations, both past and present[32] – although some of them rely upon an outdated historiography of 'French Canada' rather than on the most recent studies of Quebec.[33] Where Quebec is absent, in fact, is not in the textbooks and syntheses, but in the monographs published by the vast majority of Canadian historians working in social and cultural history. Some of these

[28] H.V. Nelles, *A Little History of Canada* (Don Mills, 2004). The quotation is on page 222.

[29] D. Morton, *A Short History of Canada*, 6th edition (Toronto, 2006).

[30] Prentice et al., *Canadian Women: A History*; B.D. Palmer, *Working-Class Experience: Rethinking the History of Canadian Labour, 1800–1991*, 2nd edition (Toronto, 1992); D. Morton, *Working People* (Toronto, 1990).

[31] See, for instance, W.L. Morton, *The Kingdom of Canada: A General History from Earliest Times*, 2nd edition (Toronto, 1969 [1963]).

[32] G. Stevenson, *Parallel Paths: the Development of Nationalism in Ireland and Quebec* (Montreal and Kingston, 2006); K. McRoberts, *Misconceiving Canada: the Struggle for National Unity* (Don Mills, 1997).

[33] For example, R. Whitaker and G. Marcuse, *Cold War Canada: The Making of a National Insecurity State, 1945–57* (Toronto, 1994). The history of Quebec and the history of 'French Canada' are two rather different things. In the 1970s, many academic historians began consciously writing the history of Quebec, as defined by territory, so as to include the history of all those who lived within its boundaries. See, e.g., P.-A. Linteau, R. Durocher, J.-C. Robert and F. Ricard, *Histoire du Québec contemporain*, vol. II, *Le Québec depuis 1930*, revised edition (Montreal, 1989), p. 5, where the authors state that 'Le Québec que nous étudions ici est défini comme un territoire plutôt que d'après l'appartenance ethnique. ... Nous n'écrivons donc pas l'histoire des Canadiens français, bien qu'ils tiennent tout naturellement une grande place dans cette étude.' The history of French Canada, on the other hand, is defined by ethnicity; it is the history of a particular ethnic group, Catholic and French-speaking, wherever they might be found: in New Brunswick, Ontario or Manitoba, for instance, as well as in Quebec. See, e.g., Y. Frenette in collaboration with M. Pâquet, *Brève histoire des Canadiens français* (Montreal, 1998). The distinction between the two terms also reflects political choices: since the 1960s and 1970s, francophone Quebecers rarely define themselves as French-Canadian but rather as Québécois — underlining their commitment to the nation that is Quebec.

historians have chosen to examine their objects of study in the context of what they call 'English Canada';[34] others claim to be studying Canada but in fact exclude any consideration of francophone Quebec.[35] Still other Canadian historians, like their counterparts elsewhere, have tended over the past 20 years to focus on particular regions and to undertake microanalyses and microhistory. It is, in part, this focus on the local and the regional that has allowed for an easy neglect of Quebec and the lack of communication between the two historiographies.

One Explanation for the Divide: the Lure of the Local

The 1970s saw the publication of a host of fascinating, detailed microhistories, particularly in Europe: histories that were in some ways a rebuke to sweeping structuralist analyses and those founded on the constitution of long series of statistics. As Carlo Ginzburg and Carlo Poni argued at the beginning of the 1980s, microhistory, viewed from one angle, was an acknowledgement of the loss of faith in macrohistorical processes and a universal master narrative.[36] But it was also a historiographical movement born of optimism: the conviction that a sixteenth-century Italian miller, or the thirteenth-century inhabitants of Montaillou, a village in southwest France, could be of interest to historians of other people, periods and places.[37] The historian's lens was deliberately narrowed to focus on a village, a family, an individual; such a narrow lens permitted him or her to grasp phenomena that might not otherwise be visible, several centuries later. As Emmanuel Le Roy Ladurie argued in his now classic study, the village of Montaillou was, among other things, 'l'amour de Pierre et de Béatrice, et c'est le troupeau de Pierre Maury':[38] implicit in his observation was the assumption that such things were historically significant.

In Canada, as elsewhere, historians were captivated by the methodological and narrative potential of microhistories and case studies. At the same time, the 1970s and 1980s witnessed the desire on the part of many Canadian historians to call into question established pan-Canadian narratives – narratives that all too often

---

[34]   For one example among many, see N. Sutherland, *Growing Up: Childhood in English Canada from the Great War to the Age of Television* (Toronto, 2000).

[35]   Again, for one example among many, see L.B. Kuffert, *A Great Duty: Canadian Responses to Modern Life and Mass Culture, 1939–1967* (Montreal and Kingston, 2003).

[36]   C. Ginzburg and C. Poni, 'La micro-histoire', *Le débat*, no. 17 (1981), pp. 133, 134.

[37]   C. Ginzburg, *The Cheese and the Worms: the Cosmos of a Sixteenth-Century Miller* (Baltimore, 1980); E. Le Roy Ladurie, *Montaillou, village Occitan de 1294 à 1324* (Paris, 1975).

[38]   Le Roy Ladurie, *Montaillou*, p. 625.

took central Canadian experiences to be the norm – and to explore the histories of particular regions: Atlantic Canada, the Prairies, British Columbia, the north.[39] The result of these twin forces – one international, one specifically Canadian – was an increased focus on the small scale, the local and the regional – and a greatly enriched knowledge of the communities that make up Canada. This development is now firmly entrenched in Canadian historiography and, despite what appears to be a growing tendency to undertake comparative and transnational studies, remains the dominant model for theses and monographs. A focus on the local, on its own, doesn't mean a neglect of Quebec: there are plenty of microstudies and case studies of Quebec localities and particular regions.[40] But what it does mean is that historians whose primary interests are other parts of Canada are less likely to adopt a comparative perspective or to include Quebec in their analyses. Moreover, within Quebec, some (perhaps isolated) voices feel that a focus on microhistory and local studies has caused Quebec historians to lose sight of the larger Quebec collectivity and of its political and cultural specificities.[41]

Let me be clear here: I think that local and regional studies are a good thing, and I'm not necessarily advocating a return to synthesis. In any event, I'm not sure that there is sufficient interest for synthesis among historians today, as either writers or readers, to warrant such a return. Producing a meaningful synthesis of Canadian history in 2007 would be, at best, challenging, given the abundance of studies of Canada published over the past 30 years, examining a multiplicity of localities, themes, and topics. It is also a project that is epistemologically fragile: as Ian McKay points out, 'the ambition of "rethinking Canada" in one great social or political synthesis' is 'a procedure that often takes for granted the very boundaries of the "Canada" to be rethought'.[42] Synthesis also raises the spectre

---

[39]   There are numerous examples of Canadian historians who have worked extensively on the history of particular regions, for instance E. Forbes, *Challenging the Regional Stereotype: Essays on the 20th Century Maritimes* (Fredericton, 1989); J. Fingard, *The Dark Side of Life in Victorian Halifax* (Porters Lake, Nova Scotia, 1989); A. Artibise, *Winnipeg: An Illustrated History* (Toronto, 1977); R.A.J. McDonald, *Making Vancouver: Class, Status, and Social Boundaries, 1863–1913* (Vancouver, 1996).

[40]   For instance, P. Gossage, *Families in Transition: Industry and Population in Nineteenth-Century Saint-Hyacinthe* (Montreal and Kingston, 1999); C. Hudon, *Prêtres et fidèles dans le diocèse de Saint-Hyacinthe, 1820–1875* (Sillery, 1996); B. Bradbury, *Working Families: Age, Gender, and Daily Survival in Industrializing Montreal* (Toronto, 1993). See also the series of regional histories of Quebec published by the Institut québécois de la recherche sur la culture (IQRC).

[41]   Rouillard et Comeau, 'La marginalisation de l'histoire politique'.

[42]   McKay advocates, instead of synthesis, a strategy of 'reconnaissance' that would allow historians to examine 'the implantation and expansion over a heterogeneous terrain of a certain politico-economic logic — to wit, liberalism.' Ian McKay, 'The Liberal Order Framework: A Prospectus for a Reconnaissance of Canadian History', *Canadian Historical Review*, vol. 81, no. 4 (Dec. 2000), p. 618.

of historiographical traditions that have fallen into disuse, or at least under suspicion: master narratives, particularly narratives scaffolded on nation-building political histories. As Harold Bérubé pointed out not too long ago in the journal *Mens*, even two very recent examples of synthesis – Jocelyn Létourneau's *Le Québec, les Québécois. Un parcours historique* and H.V. Nelles's *A Little History of Canada* – are 'des œuvres somme toute assez traditionnelles, plus intéressées à raconter qu'à expliquer', and this despite '[la] volonté affichée [des auteurs] de ne pas faire d'histoire nationale ou d'échapper aux schémas trop linéaires'.[43] Létourneau himself has stated that the ideal narrative of Canadian history would be neither 'un récit unitariste (une seule vision du pays d'un océan à l'autre) ni non plus atomisant (autant d'histoires du pays pour autant de visions), mais plutôt [...] un niveau d'articulation historiographique, d'ordre factuel et narratif, qui permette de conceptualiser et de se représenter le Canada dans ses maillages dissonants et ses équilibres oscillants, dans ses proximités distantes et ses interdépendances orageuses.'[44] In other words, a level of analysis somewhere between a single unified vision and a plurality of narratives: one that would allow for dissonance as well as consensus, and also for interdependencies.

What Might be Gained from Bridging the Divide?

In writing this chapter on the place of Quebec in historical writing on Canada, I at times wondered whether this was in fact a question worth pursuing. The relative importance of Quebec in historical writing on Canada was an important issue 30 years ago. At that moment, both within and outside Quebec, historians, politicians and ordinary citizens were struggling to understand the historical and contemporary place of Quebec within Canada and to devise other, more workable political and constitutional arrangements for the future. Today, in 2007, many English-Canadian historians appear to practise what I refer to above as a 'séparatisme implicite'. For their part, many francophone historians prefer to focus their intellectual energies and inquiries into the past on the nation that is Quebec, defined by territory, language, culture, and, until the mid twentieth century, religion, rather than exploring Quebec's links with other parts of Canada or its membership in a larger political entity. With a few exceptions – I think, for instance, of Jocelyn Létourneau's exploration of 'canadianité' and of scholars such as Michèle Dagenais and Nadia Fahmy-Eid, each of whom has

---

[43]   H. Bérubé, 'La mémoire mise à jour: l'histoire (a)nationale sous le signe du pragmatisme', *Mens*, vol. 7, no. 1 (automne 2006), p. 129.

[44]   J. Létourneau, 'L'avenir du Canada: par rapport à quelle histoire?', *Canadian Historical Review*, vol. 81, no. 2 (Jun. 2000).

undertaken comparative studies – English Canada plays a very small part in most historical writing on Quebec.[45]

Perhaps this is as it should be: an accurate reflection of the two nations that currently co-exist within the political structures of Canada. After all, it isn't necessarily a unique situation: other multinational countries such as Belgium have also produced two historiographical solitudes.[46] And perhaps to argue that we ought to be writing books that include both Canada and Quebec is to imply adherence to an older, celebratory, pan-Canadian nation-building philosophy that doesn't actually interest me that much. Yet I would argue that the historiography of Canada has much to gain from taking Quebec into account, and that a fruitful way to do this is to adopt the techniques of comparative history and *histoire croisée*. Moreover, thinking historically about Quebec would allow historians of Canada to participate in some of the more exciting international historiographical developments afoot at the moment.

In some ways, the moment seems ripe for renewed interest in Quebec on the part of English-Canadian scholars. If it is indeed the case that there is a move away from local studies and microhistories toward examinations of the Atlantic world, borderlands, empire and imperial networks, such broader transnational frameworks provide ample space for an examination of Quebec. Quebec, structured in many ways around the St. Lawrence River, the maritime highway between the Atlantic Ocean and the interior of the continent, was since its inception an important part of the Atlantic world.[47] Catherine Desbarats's current work on the Jesuit Pierre-François-Xavier de Charlevoix's writings on the history of the New World is but one example of recent studies that examine the migration of people, and especially ideas, throughout the French Atlantic world (one of the Atlantic worlds evoked in Michel Ducharme's chapter in this book).[48] Moreover, Quebec's relationship with the northeastern United States

---

[45]   J. Létourneau, *Que veulent les Québécois?* (Montreal, 2006); M. Dagenais, *Faire et fuir la ville. Espaces publics de culture et de loisirs à Montréal et Toronto aux XIXe et XXe siècles* (Quebec, 2006); N. Fahmy-Eid, A. Charles, J. Collin, J. Daigle, P. Fahmy, R.Heap and L. Piché, *Femmes, santé et professions: histoire des diététistes et des physiothérapeutes au Quebec et en Ontario, 1930–1980: l'affirmation d'un statut professionnel* (Montreal, 1997). José Igartua, a longtime specialist in the history of Quebec, has recently published an examination of English-Canadian national identities: Igartua, *The Other Quiet Revolution: National Identities in English Canada* (Vancouver, 2006).

[46]   See, e.g., P. Van Den Eeckout and P. Scholliers, 'Social History in Belgium: Old Habits and New Perspectives,' *Tijdschrift voor sociale geschiedenis*, no. 23 (1997), pp. 147–81; J. Puissant, 'L'historiographie du mouvement ouvrier belge', *Revue de l'Université Libre de Bruxelles* (1981), pp. 175–92.

[47]   We have only to think of Donald Creighton's classic *The Commercial Empire of the St. Lawrence, 1760–1850* (Toronto, 1937).

[48]   M. Ducharme, 'Canada in the Age of Revolutions: Rethinking Canadian Intellectual History in an Atlantic Perspective', in this volume. The French Atlantic History Group, an interuniversity research group, was recently established at McGill University.

has always been important, and has been examined, for instance, by historians interested in transnational migration, particularly French-Canadian migration, between rural and urban Quebec and the industrial towns and cities of New England.[49] Scholars of First Nations groups have also examined the cross-border migrations that occurred between Quebec and the northeastern United States. Allan Greer's work on 'colonial saints' likewise demonstrates the potential of transnational studies of the colonial 'Americas'.[50] Historians have also examined the implantation of American settlers in the 'buffer zone' or 'borderland' that was Quebec's Eastern Townships. J.I. Little has in fact shown that the Townships permit us not only to examine 'the dynamics of contact between distinct cultures', but also 'how a common culture became differentiated on either side of an international boundary line'.[51] Finally, Quebec provides a case study of choice for those interested in empire. In contrast to what Adele Perry and Katie Pickles have observed here for the English-Canadian historiography,[52] the question of empire has never really been absent from the historiography of Quebec. Home to competing Amerindian empires, it was a key outpost of the French Empire for two centuries.[53] Conquered by the British in 1760, it became one more of Britain's North American colonies for 200 years. Most recently, scholars interested in Americanisation, and especially *américanité*, have examined Quebec's place in the orbit of the American economic and cultural empire.[54]

Furthermore, if it is true that we are seeing a resurgence of the political and the cultural, along with a historical interest in memory and identity, these too provide epistemological frameworks favourable to the study of Quebec. A number of Quebec historians have recently examined these questions in fascinating studies of memory and commemoration: I think particularly of Patrice

---

[49]   B. Ramirez, *On the Move: French-Canadian and Italian Migrants in the North Atlantic Economy, 1860–1914* (Toronto, 1991); B. Ramirez with Y. Otis, *Crossing the 49th Parallel: Migration from Canada to the United States, 1900–1930* (Ithaca, NY, 2001); Y. Roby, *Les Franco-américains de la Nouvelle-Angleterre: rêves et réalités* (Sillery, 2000); Y. Roby, *Histoire d'un rêve brisé? Les Canadiens français aux États-Unis* (Sillery, 2007).

[50]   A. Greer and J. Bilinkoff (eds.), *Colonial Saints: Discovering the Holy in the Americas, 1500–1800* (New York, 2003); A. Greer, *Mohawk Saint: Catherine Tekakwitha and the Jesuits* (New York, 2005).

[51]   J.I. Little, *Borderland Religion: The Emergence of an English-Canadian Identity, 1792–1852* (Toronto, 2004), p. xi.

[52]   See their chapters in this book.

[53]   B. Trigger, *The Children of Aataentsic: a History of the Huron People to 1660* (Montreal and Kingston, 1976); J.S. Pritchard, *In Search of Empire: the French in the Americas, 1670–1730* (Cambridge; New York, 2004).

[54]   Y. Lamonde, *Ni avec eux ni sans eux: le Québec et les États-Unis* (Quebec, 1996); G. Bouchard, *Québécois et Américains: la culture québécoise aux XIXe et XXe siècle* (Saint-Laurent, 1995).

Groulx's *Pièges de la mémoire. Dollard des Ormeaux, les Amérindiens et nous* and of Colin Coates's and Cecilia Morgan's *Heroines and History*.[55] Interestingly, when historians who work primarily on English Canada choose to study commemoration, they too focus on Quebec – we have only to think of H.V. Nelles's prize-winning *The Art of Nation-Building*, translated into French as *L'histoire-spectacle*.[56]

Most promising, it seems to me, is the potential of comparative history and *histoire croisée*. Indeed, I would argue that serious consideration of Quebec's historical place within Canada leads almost inevitably to comparative history and *histoire croisée*. The goal of *histoire croisée* (what some have translated as 'entangled histories') is not simply the systematic comparison of two societies on a certain number of points, but rather, the study of 'the processes of mutual influencing, in reciprocal or asymmetric perceptions, in entangled processes of constituting one another'. As historian Jürgen Kocka writes, 'the history of both sides is taken as one instead of being considered as two units for comparison'.[57] Taking Quebec into account renders a comparative or 'entangled' approach unavoidable – suggesting to historians a range of questions and interpretive possibilities that might not otherwise have occurred to them.

Comparison, I would argue, is an inherent good for historians: as the adage goes, 'Qui ne connaît qu'une société n'en connaît aucune.'[58] Knowing the other – or *an* other – helps one to understand oneself. Comparison is inherently destabilising ('un dépaysement', in French), rendering the familiar unfamiliar, forcing us to re-examine what we thought we knew in light of the other.[59] As Kocka remarks, comparison allows us to interrogate supposed historical specificities (we might think here of the old clichés, propagated in English-Canadian writing for decades, of the 'backwardness' of a certain 'priest-ridden province'). Quebec historian and sociologist Gérard Bouchard also notes that comparison renders historians less likely to claim false exceptionalisms, arguing that comparative history 'fournit [...] des moyens de récuser les fausses singularités auxquelles donne aisément naissance une perspective trop ethnocentrique et dont se nourrissent volontiers les entreprises identitaires, tout particulièrement les représentations de la nation.'[60]

---

[55] P. Groulx, *Pièges de la mémoire. Dollard des Ormeaux, les Amérindiens et nous* (Hull: Vents d'Ouest, 1998); C. Coates and C. Morgan, *Heroines and History: Representations of Madeleine de Verchères and Laura Secord* (Toronto, 2002). Another example would be R. Rudin, *Founding Fathers: the Celebration of Champlain and Laval in the Streets of Quebec, 1878–1908* (Toronto, 2003).

[56] Published in English by the University of Toronto Press in 1999 and in French by Boréal in 2003.

[57] Kocka, 'Comparison and Beyond', p. 42.

[58] Quoted in G. Bouchard, *Genèse des nations et cultures du Nouveau Monde. Essai d'histoire comparée* (Montreal, 2001), p. 47.

[59] Kocka, 'Comparison and Beyond', pp. 40, 41.

[60] Bouchard, *Genèse*, p. 47.

Quebec, of course, is not the only possible point of comparison. Comparing Canada with other parts of the British Empire or with other parts of North America is likely to enrich our understanding of the choices made by those who inhabited this territory in the past. It seems to me, however, that overlooking the very obvious opportunity for internal comparison would be foolish, not least because historians of Canada can take advantage of the substantial and rich historiography that exists for Quebec. Tracing Quebec's evolution helps us to understand that of Canada generally and that of English Canada in particular. Comparing English Canada's history with that of Quebec is inherently interesting: why did two societies co-existing within a single political state sometimes evolve in different ways? How important are these differences when one considers that both societies participated in larger changes (industrialisation, urbanisation) taking place throughout the western world? More specifically, a consideration of Quebec could allow historians of Canada insight into such topics as empire, religion, and the welfare state. With regard to empire, for instance, taking Quebec into account would allow historians of Canada to demonstrate the ways in which this country evolved differently from other parts of the British Empire or other white settler societies. Canada was not Australia, or New Zealand, or India, or the United States ... and the co-existence of, and occasional conflict between, the descendents of two major European powers was one reason for its difference. Likewise, while there is no need to exaggerate the influence of the Catholic Church in Quebec, the key role played there (until relatively recently) by religious orders in providing educational, health and social services does force historians of English Canada to reconsider easy generalisations about the secularisation of Canadian society.[61] Christopher Dummitt, in his contribution to this volume, notes a decline in the practice of religious history in English Canada. This has certainly not been the case in Quebec; on the contrary, religious history has experienced a renaissance of sorts in recent years.[62] Finally, examining the ways in which some Quebecers resisted the federal welfare-state measures of the 1940s and 1950s would force historians of English Canada to rethink what has become a rather whiggish narrative of Liberal benevolence and the rise of the welfare state.[63]

[61]   Interventions in the secularisation debate include R. Allen, *The Social Passion: Religion and Social Reform in Canada 1914–1928* (Toronto, 1971); C. Berger, *Science, God and Nature in Victorian Canada* (Toronto, 1983); R. Cook, *The Regenerators: Social Criticism in Late Victorian English Canada* (Toronto, 1985).

[62]   Christopher Dummitt, 'After Inclusiveness: The Future of Canadian History', in this book. For a good recent historiographical discussion of Catholicism in Quebec, see R. Hardy, 'Regards sur la construction de la culture catholique québécoise au XIXe siècle', *Canadian Historical Review*, vol. 88, no. 1 (Mar. 2007), pp. 7–40 and especially 8–10.

[63]   On Quebec and the postwar federal welfare state, see Y. Vaillancourt, *L'évolution des politiques sociales au Québec, 1940–1960* (Montreal, 1988); D. Marshall, *Aux origines sociales de l'État-providence. Familles québécoises, obligation scolaire et allocations familiales, 1940–1955* (Montreal, 1998).

More extensive attention given to Quebec could also help us to better under-
stand English Canada in and of itself, and not simply its interactions with Quebec.
Too many studies of English Canada adopt a presentist perspective and take
Toronto as the centre of their study,[64] when in fact, Toronto's economic, political and cultural preeminence at the heart of 'English Canada' is a relatively recent
phenomenon, dating back only to the 1960s. For two centuries before that,
Montreal was the 'first city' of English Canada (as well as the metropolis of French
Canada); it was here that could be found the country's financial and social elite.
Studies of the values of this Anglo-Canadian elite also call into question reigning
analyses of Canadian Protestantism: in a city where leading Anglo-Canadians
were Anglicans and not Methodists, for example, social and cultural mores were
perhaps more flexible than analyses of a rigid Puritanism have assumed.[65]

Furthermore, comparison with English Canada would help to do away with
some longstanding beliefs in Quebec exceptionalism. For instance, studying the
importance of Catholicism in the Maritimes, or the crucial role, both economic
and symbolic, played by agriculture on the Prairies, would call into question
hoary old chestnuts regarding the uniquely religious or uniquely rural nature of
Quebec. Likewise, examining the ways in which western Canadian provinces
attempted to repatriate a certain number of federal measures in the 1960s would
call into question the uniqueness of Quebec's Quiet Revolution.[66]

A number of comparisons between Quebec and predominantly English-
speaking societies have already been undertaken. Gérard Bouchard, for example,
has carried out an examination of Quebec within the context of other 'collectivités neuves' such as Australia, New Zealand and the United States.[67] Garth
Stevenson has recently examined the 'parallel paths' of nationalism in Quebec
and Ireland.[68] Sylvie Lacombe has compared French-Canadian and English-
Canadian nationalisms, while Michèle Dagenais has compared municipal services
in Montreal and Toronto.[69] Nadia Fahmy-Eid and her collaborators have examined female health professionals in Quebec and Ontario while, over 20 years ago,
Marta Danylewycz, Beth Light and Alison Prentice undertook a similar exercise

---

[64]   For instance, Valverde, *The Age of Light, Soap, and Water*. My thoughts on this matter owe much
to conversations with Suzanne Morton.

[65]   On this Anglican Tory elite, see Brian Young's studies of the McCord family, for instance: 'The
Meaning of Death and Burial to a Patrician Family' in Bettina Bradbury and Tamara Myers (eds.),
Negotiating Identities in 19th and 20th Century Montreal, (Vancouver, 2005). See also M. Westley,
Grandeur et déclin: l'élite anglo-protestante de Montréal 1900–1950 (Montreal, 1990).

[66]   J. Richards and L. Pratt, *Prairie Capitalism: Power and Influence in the New West* (Toronto, 1979).

[67]   Bouchard, *Genèse*.

[68]   Stevenson, *Parallel Paths*.

[69]   S. Lacombe, *La rencontre de deux peuples élus: comparaison des ambitions nationale et impériale au
Canada entre 1896 et 1920* (Quebec, 2002); Dagenais, *Faire et fuir la ville*.

for female teachers in the same two provinces.[70] Yet the potential for further comparative research is huge.

To conclude, then, pan-Canadian, implicitly nation-building syntheses are not the only ways in which historians of Canada can take Quebec into account. Studies of empire, of networks and of borderlands are all alternative ways of keeping in mind the historical diversity within Canada. Moreover, it isn't necessary to abandon the local studies and microhistories that, to many of us, remain among the most stimulating ways of interrogating the past. The key, rather, is that we be conscious of the make-up of the particular localities that we study – and conscious of the ways in which these localities differed from others with which they co-existed in Canada. What I'm asking for here is not 'inclusiveness', as described in Christopher Dummitt's chapter in this book, but rather, comparison and contrast. Inclusiveness is about belonging, about who is recognised to be part of the polity or the country, and I think it's a worthwhile project. A comparative approach, however, is a different kind of intellectual exercise: assessing a given society, as it is, in light of an 'other'.

In sum, I would argue that we should aim to achieve some degree of (implicit or explicit) comparative history within a Canadian setting, along with an understanding of the fundamentally 'entangled' nature of the histories of Quebec and Canada. Ideally, this approach should incorporate elements of *histoire croisée*, as defined by Jürgen Kocka, and also, in the words of Jocelyn Létourneau, rethink 'l'expérience historique canadienne dans ses dissonances structurantes'.[71] Without necessarily returning to synthesis, such a solution would explore particular localities in their broader contexts, keeping in mind their links with other localities, the ways in which they were structured by conflict and what Létourneau calls 'dissonance', and finally the ways in which these localities participated in networks of communication and exchange – borrowing, lending, and sometimes excluding, people, goods and ideas.

Acknowledgements

I would like to thank the editors of this anthology for inviting me to take part in the Rethinking Canadian History conference, for allowing me to participate by teleconference when I was not able to be in London in person, and for their detailed comments on the original version of this chapter. I would also like to thank Christophe Horguelin and, especially, my colleague José Igartua for reading this chapter and for their very useful suggestions.

[70]   Fahmy-Eid et al., *Femmes, santé et professions*; M. Danylewycz, B. Light and A. Prentice, 'The Evolution of the Sexual Division of Labour in Teaching: a Nineteenth-Century Ontario and Quebec Case Study', *Histoire sociale/Social History*, vol. 16, no. 3 (May 1983), pp. 81–109.

[71]   Létourneau, 'L'avenir du Canada'.

Chapter 2
Sharing Authority in the Writing of Canadian History: The Case of Oral History

Steven High

> The distance between academic and popular history will not be bridged 'by historians reaching out to "the public"', but rather by their reaching in to discover the humanity they share.
>
> David Glassberg, *Sense of History*[1]

> We need projects that will involve people in exploring what it means to remember, and what to do with memories to make them active and alive, as opposed to mere objects of collection.
>
> Michael Frisch, 'The Memory of History'[2]

Historian Michael Frisch coined the phrase 'shared authority' in 1990 to describe the collaborative work of the oral history interview.[3] The dialogic nature of the interview – researcher's questions and narrator's responses – produces a unique source, the authority of which is derived from the academic training and professional distance of the university researcher and from the life experience and storytelling ability of the community narrator. The old distinctions between the researcher and subject are thus blurred, as is the once clearly drawn line between the past and present. Sharing authority is about much more than speaking to new audiences; it requires the cultivation of trust, the development of collaborative relationships, and shared decision-making. It cannot be rushed. As a result, 'a commitment to sharing authority is a beginning, not a destination – and the beginning of a necessarily complex, demanding process of social and self discovery'.[4]

[1] David Glassberg quoted in K.T. Corbett and H.S. Miller, 'A Shared Inquiry into Shared Inquiry', *The Public Historian*, vol. 28, no. 1 (Winter 2006), pp. 32–3. D. Glassberg, *Sense of History: The Place of the Past in American Life* (Amherst, 2001), p. 210.

[2] M.H. Frisch, 'The Memory of History', in Susan Porter Benson, Stephen Brier and Roy Rosenzweig (eds.), *Presenting the Past: Essays on History and the Public* (Philadelphia, 1986), p. 17.

[3] M. Frisch, *The Shared Authority: Essays on the Craft and Meaning of Oral and Public History* (Albany, 1990).

[4] M. Frisch, 'Sharing Authority: Oral History and the Collaborative Process', *Oral History Review*, vol. 30, no. 1 (2003), pp. 111–2.

The shared authority found in the oral interview runs counter to how university-trained historians have traditionally derived their authority. When I went to grad school in the 1990s, most historians continued to find their authority in distance. The more distance we put between ourselves and our subjects the better. To that end, we were required to adopt third-person language in our texts and to avoid references to the present – to speak of 'today' was sometimes to be found guilty of 'presentism'. Anybody with first-hand experience of the past being studied was considered suspect, even tainted.[5] Those who claimed experiential authority did not have the requisite distance (nor training) to interpret the past. Such strategies to monopolise historical interpretation, whether consciously adopted or not, provided historians with the confidence to act as gatekeepers of the past. The invisible hand of the historian in turn made our narratives appear authoritative and objective.[6]

The rise of the 'New Social History' in the 1970s and 1980s did not fundamentally change our relationship to our pasts or to our publics. If anything, we became more inward-looking than ever. Historians sought to write history from the bottom up, including heretofore marginalised groups as subjects of study and the recovery of new qualitative and quantitative sources. The subject matter changed, but not the research process or our authorial voice. No one speaks of 'truth' or 'objectivity' any more, but the perspective we take in our writing remains essentially unchanged. With the exception of a few innovative projects discussed below, the research process itself is predicated on achieving 'objective neutrality'. Movement historian James Green, one of those who challenged the canon of objectivity in the United States, found his work dismissed as 'too subjective to be considered "real history".'[7] The ascendancy of social history thus represented only a half-revolution.[8]

---

[5] In an influential essay, Joan Scott notes that 'experience' comes to stand in for 'fact'. The authority of the witness, like that of the expert, produces a discourse that buffers the subject from critique — naturalising one person's perspective. She calls on us to go beyond facts and a universalised 'experience' to enquire into whose experiences/facts these are, where they come from and how they operate in history. J. Scott, 'The Evidence of Experience,' *Critical Inquiry*, vol. 17, no. 4 (1991).

[6] P. Novick, *That Noble Dream: The 'Objectivity Question' and the American Historical Profession* (Cambridge, 1988). The professionalisation of Canadian historians is likewise treated in D. Wright, *The Professionalization of History in English Canada* (Toronto, 2005).

[7] J. Green, *Taking History to Heart: The Power of the Past in Building Social Movements* (Amherst, Massachusetts, 2000), p. 2.

[8] In recent years, the cultural turn in the humanities and social sciences has challenged all of us to take a more explicitly critical and political perspective. Della Pollock, a US-based theorist in oral history and performance, asks us to consider what it means to represent the past. To what extent is historical writing an exercise in history-making? In response to this crisis in representation, it has become increasingly common for historians to self-consciously place ourselves in our written

The chapter will tackle several fundamental questions about the evolving place of disciplinary authority and the public in Canadian history. How do Canadian historians derive our authority? Do we still find it in distance? Has our relationship to the present changed fundamentally? What role does the public (real or imagined) play in our research? In responding to these questions, I argue that alternative approaches to historical research have largely failed to take root in Canadian historical writing. What is remarkable about this story is the marginality of 'oral', 'public', and 'movement' histories in comparison to the vibrancy of these approaches in the United States, Great Britain and elsewhere. Too often, historians are only vaguely aware of what we are doing and why we are doing it. What I find most compelling about these alternative approaches to the writing of history is not the promise of new audiences for our work, but rather (as Michael Frisch has written) the 'capacity to redefine and redistribute intellectual authority, so that this might be shared more broadly in historical research and communication rather than continuing to serve as an instrument of power and hierarchy'.[9]

The shared authority of the oral history interview can therefore be used as a tool in building research alliances that bridge the university-community divide. What follows is organised into three parts. First, we will look at several efforts to share authority in the United States. We will then turn our attention to oral history in Canada. As we will see, university-based historians responded to the public popularity of oral history in the 1970s with anger and sarcasm. Oral history, they said, was not 'real history' and its 'practitioners' were not 'true historians'. This public assault on oral history, combined with the unique character of the Canadian Oral History Association, worked against the adoption of oral techniques in the academy. Due to its limited appeal to academic historians in Canada, oral history is only now beginning to be used to bridge the community-university divide. In looking at these examples, this chapter hopes to 'rethink Canadian history' in terms of who does the writing.

---

narratives and to examine cultural contexts. The cultural turn, however, has come late to Canada. As a result, this approach tends to unite younger researchers in opposition to an older generation of social historians. If this book is any indication, the cultural turn seems to be at the heart of our efforts to 'rethink Canadian history'. D. Pollock, 'Introduction: Making History Go', in *Exceptional Spaces: Essays in Performance and History* (Chapel Hill, 1998), p. 3. Hayden White has been called the patron saint of the linguistic turn. V.E. Bonnell and L. Hunt (eds.), *Beyond the Cultural Turn: New Directions in the Study of Society and Culture* (Berkeley, 1999), p. 1. See: H. White, 'The Value of Narrativity in the Representation of Reality', *Critical Inquiry*, vol. 7, no. 1 (1980); H. White, *Metahistory: The Historical Imagination in Nineteenth Century Europe* (Baltimore, 1973).

[9]   Frisch, *A Shared Authority*, p. xx.

Historians and the Public in the United States

Public history (which intersects with and overlaps oral history) was first established as a formal discipline at the University of California in Santa Barbara in the 1970s. Its subsequent growth was tied to a double crisis: a jobs crisis for history graduates on the one hand and a crisis in confidence among historians looking for wider audiences on the other.[10] Yet the rise of the public history movement in the United States, and its later development here in Canada, did not necessarily result in a more inclusive or bottom-up approach to the writing of history. Public history, as a modality, was largely a matter of status attainment for historians who found themselves working in museums, archives, historic sites and heritage organisations. Their authority, they claimed, was derived from their specialised training and their expertise speaking to 'the public'.[11] Their credibility thus originated in the same kinds of places as that of university-based historians.

In itself, I never found this narrow notion of public history particularly interesting. For me, it is not enough to 'go public' – the fundamental issue is not the content or even the intended audience, but how one gets there. Museums and government buildings are not inherently more democratic or closer to the people than the ivory tower. The variant of public history that has inspired me most comes in many names: 'people's history', 'community history', 'movement history', 'history workshop', 'progressive public history', the 'new museumology', and 'oral history'. What all of these approaches share is the desire to include ordinary people in the research process and to redistribute the authority and the power that comes with it. Communities would therefore not simply be subject to the academic gaze of university-based researchers but become true partners in research. This is, of course, easier said than done.

In their classic anthology *Presenting the Past*, Susan Porter Benson, Stephen Brier and Roy Rosenzweig noted that 'people's history' generally refers to 'efforts to encourage a progressive, accessible, and frequently oppositional historical vision in a variety of community and organizational contexts.'[12] In effect, they saw history as a catalyst for social change and community-building. The desire to democratise the historical process has also animated some 'progressive

---

[10]   M. Riopel, 'Réflexions sur l'application de l'histoire,' *RHAF*, vol. 57, no. 1 (Summer 2003), p. 6. See his doctoral thesis: 'L'historien et le milieu. Réflexions sur l'application de l'histoire: la publication d'une synthèse historique sur le Témiscamingue' (Doctoral thesis, Laval University, 2001).

[11]   Benson, Brier and Rosenzweig (eds.), 'Introduction,' in *Presenting the Past: Essays on History and the Public*, p. xvi.

[12]   Benson, Brier and Rosenzweig, 'Introduction,' in *Presenting the Past*, p. xvii.

public historians'.[13] Grassroots museums and community history projects sprang up across the United States in the 1960s and 1970s.[14] The living farm movement, for example, sought to communicate a dynamic picture of farm life with interpreters and a lived-in look.[15]

Yet the history workshop movement in the UK, founded by Raphael Samuel, is perhaps the best international example of the desire to create a popular history movement with a political edge.[16] Starting in 1967, Samuel's democratic vision of historical writing led him to organise weekend events for (and by) his working-class students at Oxford's Ruskin College. These activities soon drew a national audience and other workshops appeared in other localities. Building on this success, a pamphlet series was launched in 1970 and the first issue of *History Workshop Journal* appeared in 1976. While there has been some debate about the movement's ability to make history more relevant to ordinary people, few would deny its influence in the academy.[17]

The 1970s saw a number of innovative projects in the United States that encouraged the participation of working people in 'uncovering and presenting their own history'.[18] I would like to briefly describe four such projects before turning to Canada. Each one of the following projects attempted to bridge the divide between gown and town using a combination of oral history interviewing, popular illustrated histories, booklets, newspaper resources and documentary film.

1. From its inception in the late 1970s, the **Southern Oral History Program** represented a collaborative effort to interpret the lived experience of over 300 cotton mill workers. The University of North Carolina-based group committed itself to presenting the research in a storytelling style - 'by allowing

[13] This is a term used by Cathy Stanton to distinguish those public historians seeking to share authority from those who are not. C. Stanton. *The Lowell Experiment: Public History in a Postindustrial City* (Amherst, 2006).

[14] M. Wallace, *Mickey Mouse History and Other Essays on American Memory* (Philadelphia, 1996), p. 21.

[15] *Ibid.*, p. 22. Ultimately, however, Wallace believes that most museums generated ways of seeing that 'lent a naturalism and inevitability' to the authority of elites and thus 'served established power'.

[16] History Workshop in Great Britain provided a model for engaging with the wider community, inspiring similar efforts in other countries such as the United States and South Africa. Green, *Taking History to Heart*, p. 52. P. Bonner, 'New Nation, New History: The History Workshop in South Africa, 1977–1994,' *Journal of American History* (Dec. 1994), p. 978.

[17] D. Russell, 'Raphael Samuel, History Workshop and the value of democratic scholarship', *Popular Music*, vol. 16, no. 2 (1997), p. 217.

[18] J. Brecher, 'The Brass Workers History Project,' in Benson, Brier and Rosenzweig, *Presenting the Past*, p. 267. L. Shopes, 'Oral History and Community Involvement: the Baltimore Neighborhood Heritage Project', in Benson, Brier and Rosenzweig, *Presenting the Past*, p. 249.

millhands' voices to drive the narrative, we hope to reach an audience that makes history but seldom reads it.' In conducting 360 interviews, they learned to trust the 'interpretive authority of ordinary people'.[19] The culmination of the project was the award-winning book, *Like A Family: The Making of a Southern Cotton Mill World*.

2. The **Baltimore Neighborhood Heritage Project** began in 1977 in one of the city's older ethnic neighbourhoods and was later expanded to five others like it. The project team, headed by Linda Shopes, conducted 200 interviews and produced a series of popularly written essays published in the *Maryland Historical Magazine* as well as a picture book and a popular theatre piece called *Baltimore Voices*.

3. The **Brass Workers History Project**, set in the Naugatuck Valley of Connecticut, was initiated in the late 1970s by a video producer, a community organiser, a union education director, and a labour historian. In the end, the project produced a popular history book called *Brass Valley* – a kind of collective family album (1983), a film documentary (1984) and a curriculum guide. Oral narratives were central to the stories being told.

4. **History Workshop** - Inspired by what he saw in Great Britain, historian James Green returned to New England in the 1970s and organised a series of history workshops in Lynn, Lawrence and Boston. Using oral history as the medium, Green sought to engage workers in a living conversation about the past. The success of these efforts ranged widely. The one-time workshop in Lynn worked because it was a 'genuine reunion and party for the elders, who spoke individually and with great power and eloquence ... .'[20] The workshop in Lawrence, however, was poorly attended and met with community cynicism and some criticism for being a fly-by-night operation. James Green left that meeting 'questioning the wisdom of organizing one-time events in industrial cities'. The Boston effort among female office workers was therefore more long-term. The group hired a union activist and produced a booklet based on the oral testimony of working people.

What unites these four projects is their reliance on oral history interviewing to bridge the university-community divide. While each project demonstrated the usefulness of oral history in this regard, obstacles were encountered. Historian Jeremy Brecher, for example, reported that it took a great deal of time

[19]   J. Dowd Hall, J. Leloudis, R. Korstad et al. *Like a Family: The Making of a Southern Cotton Mill World* (Chapel Hill, 1987), p. xiv. Michael Frisch uses the same phrase in 'Working-Class Public History in the Context of Deindustrialization: Dilemmas of Authority and the Possibilities of Dialogue', *Labour/Le Travail* no. 51 (Spring 2003), p. 156.

[20]   Green, *Taking History to Heart*, p. 56.

and effort to gain people's trust and build an informal support network. Sharing authority takes time, and 'plenty of it'.[21] It also requires commitment and a substantial grounding in the communities themselves. For Shopes, these kinds of projects need to be 'firmly rooted in the communities being studied and have well developed links with local institutions and organizations.'[22] Another problem encountered was the tension that exists between community participants who want to validate and celebrate their histories and historians who seek to critically examine the same. While several of the project leaders express frustration with community myth-making, Jeremy Brecher learned to quit worrying and love community history.[23]

Yet there are dangers in this loving embrace of community. The implied commonality and goodness of community hides difference as well as hierarchies of power and privilege.[24] Despite its emotive power, community is difficult to define – whose community is it? Who can speak on its behalf? The positive moral and political cachet of community can also provide ideological cover for the 'safe' recovery of an unequal and racist past. In a recent essay in the *Journal of Social History*, Leon Fink inquires into the politics of community history and heritage in Cooleemee, North Carolina. In doing so, he finds that the local historical association mobilised memory in this deindustrialised mill town as a community-organising tool, yet in doing so it hid class conflict, poor working conditions and Jim Crow racism. The mythologising of pioneer 'milltown heroes' validated white mill workers but contributed to a conservative brand of localism that served to reproduce old inequalities.[25]

In recent years, sharing authority has become something of a mantra in oral history circles in the United States. The phrase resonates with oral historians who constantly grapple with issues of ethics, authority and methodology. The promise of extending this idea outwards towards a 'more broadly democratic cultural practice' has generated enthusiasm but few concrete results.[26] Nonetheless, we must think of public history as dialogue or shared inquiry rather than something that 'we' deliver to 'them'.[27] At its best, sharing authority keeps

---

[21] Brecher, 'The Brass Workers History Project', p.277.

[22] Shopes, 'Oral History and Community Involvement', p.249.

[23] J. Brecher, 'How I Learned to Quit Worrying and Love Community History: A 'Pet Outsider's' Report on the Brass Workers History Project', *Radical History Review* 28–30 (1984).

[24] Community discourse, Mike Wallace notes, risks neglecting larger structures of power and inequality. Wallace, *Mickey Mouse History*, p. 43.

[25] L. Fink, 'When Community Comes Home to Roost: the Southern Milltown as Lost Cause', *Journal of Social History*, vol. 40, no. 1 (Fall 2006), pp. 119–45.

[26] L. Shopes, 'Commentary: Sharing Authority', *Oral History Review*, vol. 30, no. 1 (2003), p. 103.

[27] Corbett and Miller, 'A Shared Inquiry into Shared Inquiry', p. 20.

questions of power and authority at the forefront.[28] To explore these issues further, we will now turn to the emergence of oral and public histories in Canada and look at how they were received by university-based historians.

Oral History in Canada

Despite its popularity in the United States and Great Britain, oral history has remained marginal to the work of university-based historians in Canada. While a growing number of Canadian historians draw on oral interviews as sources of information, very few consider themselves oral historians and fewer still use oral history as a means of political engagement or community empowerment. Except for a brief flurry of activity in the 1970s, the Canadian Oral History Association (COHA) has been largely inactive, publishing an annual journal that few professional historians have ever read. This section will explore the reasons why oral history has failed to take hold in Canadian universities.

A keyword search of the *Globe and Mail* database from 1945 until the present reveals the rise of oral history as an identifiable approach to history. There was very little mention of oral history before the 1970s, except for the occasional reference to the work of the Columbia (University) Oral History Research Office founded by Allan Nevins in 1948 or the oral history interviews conducted by the JFK Library in Boston.[29] Oral history only emerged in Canada in the 1970s.

Technological change was pivotal to the development of oral history. The first recording device was the phonograph, invented in 1877. The development of reel-to-reel magnetic tape recorders and their diffusion in the 1940s allowed large government institutions such as the Smithsonian in Washington or the Museum of Man in Ottawa to record sound heritage. Yet it was the introduction of affordable cassette recorders in the 1960s that launched oral history as a popular hobby or research methodology in North America. Suddenly, archivist Richard Lochead recalled, the tape recorder 'held the possibility of wide scale recording of people's memories'. Now virtually anyone could ostensibly become an oral historian. If the tape recorder made mass oral history possible, it did not lead to fundamental changes in the way professional historians did

---

[28]   *Ibid.*, p.18.

[29]   B. Catton, 'Capturing the voices of people who shape history', *Globe and Mail*, 3 May 1965. The article was reprinted from *THINK* magazine. Revelations about John F. Kennedy's desire to have Cuban leader Fidel Castro assassinated, revealed in oral history interviews opened to the public in 1970, produced headlines and editorials even in Canada. H. Raymont (New York Times Service), 'Kennedy discussed assassination of Castro, papers reveal', *Globe and Mail*, 17 Aug. 1970, A1. Editorial, 'A frank lot', *Globe and Mail*, 20 Aug. 1970.

their research. On the contrary, Canadian historians rose in defence of their disciplinary authority and set out to draw a line between 'historians' on the one hand and 'oral practitioners' on the other. For reasons that will become clear, oral history became synonymous with 'amateur' or 'popular' history in Canada. As a result, it could not easily be used to bridge the gap between university-based historians and our publics.

The 1970s were nonetheless an exciting time for popular oral historians and sound archivists in Canada. The period saw regular national conferences, regional meetings and the birth of the Canadian Oral History Association. The COHA has its organisational roots in the oral history committee of the Archives Section of the Canadian Historical Association, which organised the founding conference of the association at Simon Fraser University in October 1974.[30] Though the conference attracted 170 delegates, including popular oral historians such as Barry Broadfoot and Peter Stursberg, and a handful of university-based historians like Jack Granatstein, archivists predominated. The association's leadership, including its first president, Leo LaClare, was made up of provincial and federal government archivists.[31] In Quebec, meanwhile, the 'Memoire d'une époque' project ran for a number of years wherein hundreds of life histories were recorded each year and submitted to province-wide competition.[32] CBC radio also incorporated oral history into its programming. One of the most popular radio series was Bill McNeil's 'Voice of the Pioneer', a 20-minute weekly set of interviews that ran for more than 20 years.[33]

Canadians were also reading oral history in record numbers. Bestselling oral history books like Barry Broadfoot's *Ten Lost Years* (1973) on the Depression decade 'touched a deep chord in the Canadian psyche'.[34] It was printed 'again and again and again as the book flew out of stores, to become one of Canada's

---

[30] W. MacDonald, 'Some Reminiscences of COHA', *Oral History Forum* 25 (2005), pp. 15–16. The conference witnessed a 'fierce debate' about the name of the new association. It pitted proponents of 'aural history' against those of 'oral history'. Many Western Canadian delegates, led by the Public Archives of British Columbia (PABC), urged delegates to support 'aural history'. The PABC, an early leader in oral history collection, used the term 'aural history', but oral history was in the ascendancy across North America. In typical Canadian fashion, the result was a compromise: 'oral/aural history'. It lasted only one year as aural history was dropped the following year at the association's next meeting at Memorial University in St. John's.

[31] R. Lochead, 'Funding the Good Fight', *Oral History Forum* 25 (2005), p. 46.

[32] R. Labelle, 'Reflections on Thirty Years of Oral History in Canada', *Oral History Forum* 25 (2005), p. 8.

[33] J. Creighton, 'Book honors "pioneers" who closed out an era', *Vancouver Sun*, 3 Jan. 1989, p. C2.

[34] W. French, 'Broadfoot finds gold in the Canadian past', *Globe and Mail*, 10 Jul. 1976.

all-time bestsellers' with well over 300,000 copies sold.[35] Broadfoot's sequel, *Six War Years* (1974), was also a bestseller. *Globe and Mail* columnist William French estimated that Broadfoot cleared $100,000 in royalties from the two hardcover editions alone, bringing the former journalist 'national attention, dramatically confirming the virtues of oral history and [giving] us an acute new sense of our heritage'.[36] *Ten Lost Years* was even transformed into a hit stage musical by George Luscombe and his Toronto Workshop Productions that toured the country.[37] Writing decades later in *The Beaver*, Christopher Moore placed Broadfoot's oral histories 'among the most powerful books anyone has written about Canadian history'.[38] They moved him to tears. To an impressive degree, Barry Broadfoot's books established oral history in the minds of Canadians.[39] It is therefore worth exploring his work more deeply.

Born in Winnipeg in 1926, Broadfoot began his newspaper career at the *Winnipeg Tribune* in 1955 and spent the next 24 years as a reporter and editor at a variety of Western Canadian newspapers, ending his career at the *Vancouver Sun*.[40] His reputation as a legendary newspaper man was cultivated by his editor, Douglas Gibson, who wrote that the 'grizzled books editor' was part of an older generation of newsroom men 'who almost certainly had a bottle stashed within easy reach'.[41] Broadfoot was a war veteran, prankster and 'dyed-in-the-wool newspaperman'. Not surprisingly, nobody believed him when he said that he would quit one day and write a book.[42] Yet the way Broadfoot left the newspaper business became the 'stuff of legend'.[43] One day in March 1972 Broadfoot

---

[35]   D. Gibson, 'A newsman with a nose for Canada', *Globe and Mail*, 6 December 2003, p. R20.

[36]   French, 'Broadfoot finds gold'; see also Lochead, 'Funding the Good Fight', p. 46.

[37]   The Toronto Workshop Productions' (George Luscombe) landmark play *Ten Lost Years* ran for many months in Toronto before touring the country and overseas. 'The testimony of those who survived the Depression was woven through a collage of music and dialogue to evoke with terrible clarity the suffering of so any people.' P. Birnie, 'Arts: Ten Lost Years', *Vancouver Sun*, 21 Aug. 2003, p. C8.

[38]   J. Stoffman, 'Broadfoot told Canada's epic stories', *Toronto Star*, 2 Dec. 2003, p. D6.

[39]   Peter Stursberg has published at least 12 books including two part biographies of Prime Ministers John Diefenbaker and Lester B. Pierson. See for example, *Diefenbaker: Leadership Gained, 1956–1962* (Toronto, 1975) and *Diefenbaker: Leadership Lost, 1962–67* (Toronto, 1976). For his part, Allan Anderson has also published several books including *Roughnecks and Wildcatters* (Toronto, 1981) and *Remembering the Farm: Memories of Farming, Ranching and Rural Life in Canada, Past and Present* (Toronto: Macmillan, 1977). Joan Finnigan has published no fewer than 30 books about the Ottawa Valley, including *Some Stories I Told You Were True* (Ottawa, 1981).

[40]   Editorial, 'Thanks for the memories', *Victoria Times-Colonist*, 2 Dec. 2003, p. A8.

[41]   Gibson, 'A newsman with a nose for Canada'.

[42]   Gibson, 'A newsman with a nose for Canada'.

[43]   A. O'Brian, 'Barry Broadfoot: Renegade reporter compiled nine oral histories of Canada', *Calgary Herald*, 6 Dec. 2003.

decided to quit the business: 'I came in, hung up my coat, took the cover off my typewriter and looked out at the newsroom. Suddenly, it looked like a Russian tractor factory ... . I said "The hell with it." I put 17 years of inter-office memos into a shoebox, liberated the typewriter and walked out.'[44] The typewriter, a 'beat-up black Underwood 5 upright' travelled with him and his tape recorder in his 'beat-up' Volkswagen stopping at donut shops and beer parlours across the country in search of stories of hardship and hurt, courage and resilience. [45]

These early road trips and his oral history technique were mythologised in the many news reports and book reviews of the period. Broadfoot's technique was to drive across the country (actually just to Ontario and back to British Columbia) collecting stories. For each book, Broadfoot would travel from town to town taping dozens of interviews, listening to them as he drove to the next town 'mentally editing to save time later in transcribing' them on his typewriter. These were not full transcripts. 'I wouldn't have the patience,' he admitted. [46] Unlike Studs Terkel, Broadfoot used the tapes over and over again.[47] 'In my naïveté, I stupidly didn't realize their value,' he said later.[48] Broadfoot also claimed poverty: 'I was so broke, travelling across the country, that I kept reusing my tapes. I didn't have the money to buy new tapes for every taping. When I finished the tape, I just erased it – "Oh I don't need this." I wasn't thinking too much of posterity at that time.'[49] In fact, none of the tapes from the *Ten Lost Years* were saved.

In *Ten Lost Years*, Barry Broadfoot did not edit to change meaning or interfere with the rhythm of speech, but rearranged words and abridged the stories to improve their flow: 'Various fragments of the same interview may wind up in different parts of the book, arranged for dramatic effect. Juxtaposition is one of the key techniques of this kind of editing'.[50] According to Broadfoot's longtime editor at Doubleday, Douglas Gibson:

[44] O'Brian, 'Barry Broadfoot'.

[45] G. Fetherling, 'Farewell to Shields, Broadfoot, Kenner', *Vancouver Sun*, 27 December 2003, D16; O'Brian, 'Barry Broadfoot'.

[46] M. Posner, 'A listener to the tale of Canada', *Globe and Mail*, 2 Dec. 2003, R5.

[47] This possibility was made manifest with the publication of Studs Terkel's bestselling books, *Division Street, USA* in 1967 and, especially, *Hard Times: An Oral History of the Depression* in 1969. Terkel was a popular radio personality in Chicago, Illinois who sought, in these first two books, to feel the pulse of the urban community and to capture the human resilience of the Depression years, respectively. He listened to Americans: 'to allow men and women to create themselves out of their own mouths.' For his efforts, he even won a Pulitzer Prize for his 1984 book, *The Good War*. Broadfoot admitted that Terkel inspired him to write *Ten Lost Years*. Yet 'I'm positive I'd have come to the same point on my own,' he contended. French, 'Broadfoot finds gold'.

[48] French, 'Broadfoot finds gold'.

[49] C. Moore, 'Barry Broadfoot talking', *The Beaver* vol. 79, no. 6 (Dec. 1999/Jan. 2000).

[50] French, 'Broadfoot finds gold'.

Before *Ten Lost Years* came out in 1973, Barry and I worked to establish an entirely new book. There had been other oral histories, of course, most notably by Chicago writer Studs Terkel. But this one would be different. Barry's voice would be restricted to a general preface, a summary of events and then to a few paragraphs in italics introducing each chapter, and very occasionally to important explanations to the reader about what was happening to the storyteller, for example, 'he breaks down and cries.' Another difference: the voices would be kept carefully anonymous throughout. There may have been sensible legal reasons for this originally, but the artistic reason proved to be most powerful of all; these anonymous individual voices became blended together in a great chorus where the people of Canada somehow seemed to be speaking, telling what had happened in the real world, not in the archives. [51]

In effect, Barry Broadfoot told Canada's story through the anonymous voices of Canadians – it was a people's history. Out of this 'rich tapestry of history and memoir' he fashioned a national narrative. [52] There was 'something mesmerizing', William French wrote, 'about these authentic Canadian voices, in familiar idiom.'[53] *Ten Lost Years* was a resounding success 'thanks to the graphic and powerful memories of those who suffered through the Depression in Canada'.[54] For a fleeting moment, at least, there was a sense of the transformative potential of oral history.

It would be a mistake, however, to assume that popular oral historians like Barry Broadfoot practised shared authority. The interviewee's role ended once the tape recorder was turned off. This limited role was plainly evident in 1987 when the Public Lending Rights Commission questioned Broadfoot's authorship of *Ten Lost Years*. The commission suggested in a letter to Broadfoot that his books were 'collections of other people's works, introduced and annotated rather than authored by you'.[55] Was he the sole author of his oral history books or the editor of other people's words? The question was important if for no other reason than editors received 80 per cent less in royalties than did authors. Broadfoot was furious. 'By God what an insult', he told the *Globe and Mail*.[56]

[51]   Gibson, 'A newsman with a nose for Canada'.

[52]   Posner, 'A listener to the tale of Canada'; Editorial, 'Barry Broadfoot lives on in his world of our stories', *Vancouver Sun*, 3 Dec. 2003, A18.

[53]   W. French, 'The maestro of tape', *Globe and Mail*, 19 Nov. 1988.

[54]   W. French, 'A personal kaleidoscope. Just right', *Globe and Mail*, 2 Nov. 1974, p. 34.

[55]   W. French, 'Public Lending Right debate takes new twist', *Globe and Mail*, 10 Nov. 1987, D7.

[56]   *Ibid.*

There was no doubt in his mind that he was the sole author of his books. He took the matter up directly with the Minister of Communications and the commission soon relented: 'it was felt that as an oral historian, you recorded the material first ... and you are without doubt the author with copyrights to "your" material'.[57] Stories were, in Broadfoot's words, 'something waiting, literally, to be picked up off the ground and put into my pocket'.[58]

The notion that oral history constituted an informal (democratic) method of writing history, distinct from the more formal method of university professors, nonetheless lived on. Barry Broadfoot, one journalist wrote, 'had scant idea that he might chart new boundaries in the telling of Canadian history'.[59] His work, William French agreed,

> has become an important complement to traditional academic
> histories. He uses his tape recorder as professional historians use
> musty archives; to reveal perceived truth about an event or an era.
> Broadfoot brings to us the raw material of history, the recollections
> of the ordinary people who were involved. Their voices often come
> through with surprising passion and intensity. The historians analyze
> and interpret; the ordinary participants give it to us plain, letting us
> make our own conclusions. There is a danger of exaggeration and
> bias, of course, but historians too have their prejudices.[60]

The comfortable charm of the spoken word conveyed warmth, honesty and the authority of experience. Writing in 1978, *Globe and Mail* columnist Jeffrey Simpson noted that though oral history 'makes academic historians grind their teeth' it was 'much in vogue these days'. [61]

University-based historians resented the public attention and acclaim given to popular oral historians. They were ferocious in their criticism. Jack Granatstein, Ramsay Cook, Peter Neary, Roger Hall and others pounded away at the credibility of Broadfoot and other oral historians. They repeatedly emphasised the loose structure of popular oral histories (a 'curious mishmash' of remembrances[62]), factual errors, tricks of memory, and their maddening subjectivity. The 'simple faith' or 'naïve enthusiasm' of oral historians was invoked to further undermine

---

[57] W. French, 'Making short work of an award dinner', *Globe and Mail*, 8 Dec. 1987, D5.
[58] Moore, 'Barry Broadfoot talking', p. 54.
[59] French, 'Broadfoot finds gold'.
[60] *Ibid.*
[61] Jeffery Simpson, 'Quebec', *Globe and Mail*, 25 Mar. 1978, p. 25.
[62] W.A.B. Douglas, 'War recollections weak history', *The Ottawa Citizen*, 7 Mar. 1992, J8.

their authority.[63] In one devastating review, Jack Granatstein wrote that 'like other enthusiastic amateurs' the author 'fails to realize that sources are not always of equal worth, and oral history, dependent as it is on the memory of the participant about events a quarter century and more in the past, is more fallible than most sources.'[64] He, like other academic reviewers, wanted oral historians to 'cross examine' the sources 'to get near the "truth" '.[65] In raising these concerns, university-based historians openly questioned oral historians' credibility.

Historians also reacted angrily to claims that oral history was a 'new kind of history', arguing instead that oral sources must supplement and not supplant traditional sources. 'Consider Barry Broadfoot', Jack Granatstein wrote in 1976, 'his books were the first in Canada to make effective use of the tape recorder. He gathered his material by trooping across the country, simply talking to ordinary people about their often ordinary experiences. But was he careful about facts or about editing?'[66] In his professional opinion, this was 'just plain bad history'. Some academic book reviewers conceded that oral history was useful, but only in the trained hands of the university historian. Broadfoot's books were little more than 'edited interviews' or 'oral history pastiches', not 'careful scholarship'.[67] As Ramsay Cook wrote, these 'uncorrected and unverified recollections' did 'not constitute anything even approximating history. They are the memoirs, one might say somewhat unkindly, of the politicians who cannot write.'[68]

The academic assault on oral history reached its climax in 1979 when Roger Hall, a historian at the University of Western Ontario, wrote yet another scathing book review. What makes this one stand out is the defiant response of Allan Anderson, a broadcaster and oral historian. The opinions expressed in Hall's column were too much for Anderson, who responded that he was weary of the 'cloddish yammerings' of 'some cheeky historian'. This heated exchange is worth exploring in some detail.

In his review of Bill McNeil's new book, Hall launched a sarcastic broadside on oral history in general, writing:

---

[63] P. Neary, 'The Great War and Canadian Society', *Globe and Mail* (1978); see also R. Cook, 'Lester Pearson and the Dream of Unity', *Globe and Mail*, 14 Oct. 1978.

[64] J. Granatstein, 'Jerky style, Errors galore. Tommy Douglas deserves better — and so does the author', *Globe and Mail*, 18 Oct. 1975, p. 33.

[65] J.L. Granatstein, 'The great virtue of Stursberg's oral history is that the venom and spite show through', *Globe and Mail*, 18 Sept. 1976, p. 39.

[66] Granatstein, 'The great virtue'; see also: J.L. Granatstein, 'A Professor finds that pop history is trivial, hasty, sloppy and demeaning', *Globe and Mail*, 29 Jan. 1977.

[67] Granatstein, 'A Professor finds'.

[68] Cook, 'Lester Pearson and the Dream of Unity'.

Oral history is now in vogue and, to believe its practitioners, it has revolutionized our approach to the past. The mini-tape recorder, like a magic wand, has been credited with the ability to 'democratize' history, to help move it from the chronicle of the great and worthy to the overlooked record of the mere and lowly. In this way it is seen to contribute to the great shift in the writing of history brought about by social science and the computer.[69]

For Hall, the 'absurd notion' that oral history can democratise history and the historian was as 'ridiculous as suggesting anyone who owns a typewriter can be a novelist and anyone with a pistol a marksman.' The 'legion' of 'popular oral practitioners' were, in his mind, not true historians. Unlike professional historians, these amateurs did not evaluate all the evidence and lacked the requisite training to undertake the 'painstaking process of verification' that is needed.[70] In consequence, they 'con themselves as well as the reading public.' Popular oral historians, he added, would have us believe that:

all you have to do is corral some character from the past – great or small – inquire what it was really like to be part of, or present at, X, Y and Z, type it out, and you've captured the truth. Too many granting agencies, publishers and even archives agree. Hence, in this country, we have the varied 'successes' of Barry Broadfoot, Peter Stursberg, Allan Anderson et al. Hearing, according to these gentlemen, is believing. But, of course, it's not. And there is nothing new at all about oral evidence. It has been part of the historian's arsenal from Herodotus to the present. What's new and that which gives it authority and appeal to so many amateurs, is the 'horse's mouth' immediacy of recording tape. The uncritical listener and untrained recorder both are lulled into thinking that they are somehow in touch with the past itself instead of a reminiscence.[71]

In capable hands, Hall conceded, new oral techniques might be useful in adding a 'touch of color and humanity' to the textual record and in popularising the study of the past.[72]

Unlike other reviews of this kind, Hall's stinging words brought a response from Allan Anderson, author of several oral histories. As a professional

[69] R. Hall, 'Popular oral history: caveat emptor', *Globe and Mail*, 16 June 1979.
[70] *Ibid.*
[71] *Ibid.*
[72] *Ibid.*

interviewer with 30 years' experience, he claimed to have the right to write history based on oral sources. Anderson dismissed the facts-based critique of oral history that assumed the objectivity of evidence: 'People are not liars or blowhards by nature, they tend to tell the truth as they saw it, and they usually tell it more accurately and clearly in the stimulation of a good interview than when, laboriously, they sit down to write it.'[73] Clearly on a roll, Anderson then suggested that historians 'indulge in this crazy dichotomy that records a politician's diaries and "documentation"' as history but denies the historicity of the spoken word of ordinary people.[74] Indeed, for Anderson, 'professional historians impale themselves on facts and documentation and current accounts of happenings. An event can be distorted just as much, and perhaps more, five minutes after it happened, as five years later.'[75] History, Anderson wrote, 'essentially boils down to the collective interpretations of individuals of what happened, and one man's or woman's memory, by and large, is as good as anyone else's.'[76] Hall retorted that this idea was 'absolute idiocy' and dismissed Anderson's 'naïve faith in the value of human memory'.[77]

What is interesting in this exchange is that Anderson's definition of history as plural and subjective has aged better than Hall's emphasis on a singular, verifiable history of facts and knowable truth. While it is important to analyse what is being said in an oral history interview and to listen to the silences as well as the words spoken, many of the concerns raised by historians about oral history in the 1970s and 1980s have been effectively countered by a new wave of scholarship that recognises the subjectivity of the oral narrative (these are 'their' truths) and the central place of memory. Both points find voice in Anderson's response. Oral sources tell us 'not just what people did, but what they intended to do, what they believed they were doing, and what they now think they did.'[78] Respected scholars like Alessandro Portelli now urge us to treat the subjective quality of oral narrative as 'unique opportunities rather than the obstacles of historical objectivity and empirical rigor.' Oral sources,

---

[73] A. Anderson, 'Historians seen fit for maintenance work', (letter to the editor). *Globe and Mail*, 3 Mar. 1979, p. 7.

[74] Anderson, 'Historians seen fit for maintenance work'.

[75] *Ibid.*

[76] *Ibid.*

[77] R. Hall, Letter to the editor, *Globe and Mail*, 6 Ap. 1979, p. 7.

[78] A. Portelli, *The Death of Luigi Trastulli and Other Sources: Form and Meaning in Oral History* (Buffalo, 1991). For two good Canadian examples, see: P. Sugiman, 'Memories of Internment: Narrating Japanese Canadian Women's Life Stories', *Canadian Journal of Sociology*, vol. 29, no. 3 (2004); and A. Freund and L. Quilici, 'Exploring Myths in Women's Narratives: Italian and German Immigrant Women in Vancouver, 1947–1961', *Oral History Review*, vol. 23, no. 2 (1996).

however, should not be read as 'iconic renderings of actual sequences of events'.[79]

Yet the damage was done. The message delivered by Hall and the others was clear: only university-trained historians had the right to interpret the past; only they could call themselves historians. This tendency was not lost on journalist Val Clery: 'History is theirs, their attitude seems to suggest, and is exclusively the product of diligent research and verification, scrupulous analysis and synthesis, and objective judgement.'[80] One by one, popular oral historians like Barry Broadfoot, Allan Anderson and the others abandoned the term 'oral history' to describe their work, opting instead for 'living memory' or other terms that lay outside the territorial claims of professional historians. 'The academic historians resent what I do,' wrote Barry Broadfoot, 'because they say it isn't history and somehow I'm taking away from the pool of money that might go toward history books.'[81] The other consequence was that oral history would be all but barred from the course calendars of Canadian history programmes. Until a few years ago, there was not a single centre of oral history research at a Canadian university. In his entry for 'oral history' in the Canadian Encyclopedia, Peter Stursberg suggested that Canadian historians were far more suspicious of oral history than their counterparts in the United States.[82] My research largely supports this conclusion.

In this hostile environment, the Canadian Oral History Association found itself unable to make inroads among university-based historians. Academic interest in the field was 'transient' at best. COHA continued to produce its journal but the association foundered. Longtime members of the association therefore recall the excitement of the 'pioneer period' of the 1970s from the vantage point of an embattled present. 'Times have changed since the heady days of 1974', recalled archivist Richard Lochead, 'and the road has become longer and often uphill, but its legacy is a positive one and its dream still worth pursuing.'[83] James H. Morrison had similarly bittersweet memories in 2005: 'through its highs and lows, the Canadian Oral History Association has persevered. There have always

---

[79] D. James, 'Listening In the Cold: The Practice of Oral History in an Argentine Meatpacking Community', in Alistair Thomson and Robert Perks (eds.), *The Oral History Reader*, 2nd edition (London, 2006), p. 86.

[80] V. Clery, 'For all his humility, Terkel succeeds as a musician or an artist can sometimes inadvertently and instinctively succeed: he reaches in and touches your heart', *Globe and Mail*, 18 Oct. 1980, p. 17.

[81] Posner, 'A listener to the tale of Canada'.

[82] P. Stursberg, 'Oral History', in The Canadian Encyclopedia. www.thecanadianencyclopedia.com.

[83] Lochead, 'Funding the Good Fight', p. 45.

been the faithful few who have appreciated the importance of oral history and committed themselves to the organization and to the Journal and Forum. We are still standing after thirty years and I thank them for that.'[84] This strongly held sense of being under siege was due, in part, to the wars being waged by professional historians, but there were other reasons for the failure to make inroads among the new generation of Canadian social historians.

Oral history in Canada differed from the American movement from the outset. In reflecting on the history of COHA, several longtime members noted that Canadian and American practice differed in several important respects. Canadian practice, they claimed, was far less reliant on transcription. While American oral historians at Columbia University and Berkeley re-used tapes after transcription, Canadians (albeit not Broadfoot) preferred to preserve the original sound recordings. The reason for this divergence was sited in the early influence of folklorists such as Marcius Barbeau at the Museum of Man in Ottawa (folklorists were keenly interested in the voice) and the Canadian Broadcasting Corporation. Richard Lochead, an archivist of sound heritage at the National Archives, noted that CBC radio had long incorporated oral history in its programming. Its desire to preserve sound recordings, rather than transcription, meant that government archivists were brought into the business of preserving sound heritage. CBC archivist John Reynolds could therefore claim to be Canada's only full-time oral historian in 1965.[85] It was only natural then that archivists formed the backbone of the association. For one member, COHA was an 'excellent outreach arm for the National Archives'.[86]

This orientation proved to be a mixed blessing as the Canadian Oral History Association emphasised collection and preservation over activism and scholarship. It therefore differed from its counterparts in the United States and Great Britain where many political and social historians adopted oral history techniques. Ronald Labelle noted the unique character of the Canadian association:

> It remains that archivists have been involved in the COHA from the start, and they have been influential in determining the nature of the

[84]   J.H. Morrison, 'Making Connections: African and Canadian Oral History — A Personal View', *Oral History Forum* 25 (2005), p. 39.

[85]   John Reynolds quoted in B. Lawson, 'The man who helps history break the sound barrier', *Globe and Mail*, 30 Oct. 1965. In 1965, Reynolds travelled the country and collected 150 hours of 'reminiscences' of former members of the Mackenzie-Papineau Battalion — Canadian veterans of the Spanish Civil War. He told the *Globe and Mail* that he was the first person in Canada to attempt the 'systematic' collection of interviews. He was 'not an academic. I'm a Grade 9 dropout who has sort of turned up in this business'.

[86]   Lochead, 'Funding the Good Fight', p. 44.

association. Thus, the COHA Journal and its sequel, the Oral
History Forum, have for the most part published articles presenting
the results of oral history projects, as well as articles of a
methodological nature. There has been little in-depth analysis of
topics related to oral history, and efforts to develop new approaches
to the field have been rare.[87]

For a time, oral history was seen in the public's eye, as well as within the association, as simple acts of memory recovery and not stories that needed to be
interrogated for their meaning. The oral history association's emphasis on
collection and its inattention to theory and analysis thus reinforced the already
negative impression that many Canadian historians had of oral history. It was too
uncritical to be considered legitimate. University-based historians who engaged
in oral history research in the 1970s and 1980s were therefore exceptional.

The Slow Rise of Oral History in Canadian Universities

This began to change in the 1990s, especially among historians specialising in the
histories of immigration, women, Aboriginals, and labour. The shift in temporal
focus of research from the transformative period of industrialisation and urbanisation before the First World War to later decades increased its appeal. Among
the influential books (including several John A. Macdonald prize winners) that
drew extensively on the living memories of interviewees are Joy Parr's *The
Gender of Breadwinners*, Joan Sangster's *Earning Respect*, Julie Cruikshank's *Life
Lived like a Story* and *The Social Life of Stories*, Franca Iacovetta's *Such Hardworking
People*, and Denyse Baillargeon's *Ménagères au temps de la crise*.[88] Each one of these
books has been enthusiastically acclaimed and widely cited. To some degree,
these influential studies made it acceptable again for Canadian historians to draw
on oral history interviews – but usually as one source among many.

That all of these authors are women is not a coincidence: feminist historians
have been central to the development of oral history in Canada. Feminist oral
historians aim to treat interviewees as 'narrators of their own experiences' rather

---

[87]   R. Labelle, 'Reflections on Thirty Years of Oral History in Canada', *Oral History Forum* 25
(2005), p. 12.

[88]   J. Parr, *The Gender of Breadwinners* (Toronto, 1990), J. Sangster, *Earning Respect* (Toronto, 1995),
J. Cruikshank, *Life Lived like a Story: Life Stories of Three Yukon Native Elders* (Vancouver, 1990) and
The Social Life of Stories: Narrative and Knowledge in the Yukon Territory (Vancouver, 1998); F. Iacovetta,
Such Hardworking People (Montreal, 1992), and D. Baillargeon, *Ménagères au temps de la crise* (Montreal,
1991).

than objects of research. According to Susan E. Chase and Colleen S. Bell, 'This subtle conceptual switch – from thinking about women as subjects of their experiences, to thinking about women as narrators of their experiences – preserves the feminist interest in empowerment that underlies the injunction to treat women as subjects. As a narrator, a woman has the power to speak as she chooses; she controls the telling of her experiences.'[89] In her influential article on feminist approaches to oral history, Joan Sangster wrote that listening to women's words will 'help us see how women understood, negotiated and sometimes challenged' dominant ideals.[90] Ruth Roach Pierson has likewise noted that feminist historiography has paid particularly close attention to how scholars negotiate the line between insiders and outsiders.[91]

And yet, Canadian historians have rarely treated oral histories as narrative sources whose form, structure and silences can be interpreted in their entirety. Instead, they are either tapped for information or for bites of emotional 'salsa'.[92] The point of oral history evidence should be something more than adding a 'jolt of emotional and moral authenticity'.[93] A good interview, wrote psychologist Henry Greenspan, 'is a process in which two people work hard to understand the views and experience of one person: the interviewee.'[94] The telling of a story is a dialogical process that is charged, contingent, and reflexive. Life story interviews are an especially rich source for understanding the multiple layers of significance in people's lives. They offer 'a means of making sense and interpreting the experiences of marginalized peoples and forgotten histories', as well as allowing room to explore the contradictions and relations 'between individual memories and testimonies, and the wider public contexts, cultural practices, and forms of representation that shape the possibilities of their telling and their witnessing.'[95] Oral

---

[89]   S.E. Chase and C.S. Bell, 'Interpreting the Complexity of Women's Subjectivity', in Eva M. McMahon and Kim Lacy Rogers (eds.), *Interactive Oral History Interviewing* (Hillsdale, New Jersey, 1994), p. 79.

[90]   J. Sangster, 'Telling Our Stories: Feminist Debates and the Use of Oral History', in Robert Perks and Alistair Thomson (eds.), *The Oral History Reader*, 1st edition (London, 1997), p. 91.

[91]   R. Roach Pierson, 'Experience, Difference, Dominance and Voice in the Writing of Canadian Women's History', in Karen Offen, Ruth Roach Pierson and Jane Rendell (eds.), *Writing Women's History: International Perspectives* (Hampshire, 1991), pp. 79–106.

[92]   M. Frisch, 'Working-Class Public History in the Context of Deindustrialization: Dilemmas of Authority and the Possibilities of Dialogue', *Labour/Le Travail* no. 51 (Spring 2003), p. 160.

[93]   *Ibid.*, p. 163. One of the best examples of the cultural turn in oral history in Canada is the superb essay by Sugiman, 'Memories of Internment: Narrating Japanese Canadian Women's Life Stories', pp. 359–88.

[94]   H. Greenspan, *On Listening to Holocaust Survivors: Recounting and Life History* (New York, 1998).

[95]   K. Lacy Rogers and S. Leydesdorff (eds.), *Trauma: Life Stories of Survivors* (New Brunswick, 2004); see their introduction.

histories are not objects to be picked up and put into our pocket or knapsack, but are memories that have to be put into words. They reconstruct rather than resurrect the past.[96] Life stories are therefore living things, always changing.

In writing this chapter, I struggled to find examples of 'history workshop', 'movement history' or 'progressive public history' in Canada. While the public history movement is 'dynamic and intellectually energetic' in the United States with a major journal (*The Public Historian*), an active association (National Council for Public History) that meets annually, and dozens of graduate and undergraduate programmes in universities, public history is only now taking root in Canadian universities.[97] In 2007, graduate programmes in public history existed at the universities of Western Ontario, Carleton and Quebec (in Montreal) and Canada's first undergraduate programme was launched in September 2006 at Concordia, my own university.

Despite these beachheads, public history continues to be closely associated in Canada with institutional settings such as museums and heritage organisations. 'Public history' and 'academic history' are often treated as mutually exclusive.[98] This opposition is unfortunate as there has been an explosion of interest in memory studies throughout the academy. In recent years, Canadian journals and university library bookshelves have included a large number of studies exploring

[96]   J. Bodnar, 'Generational Memory in an American Town,' *Journal of Interdisciplinary History*, vol. 26, no. 4 (Spring 1996), p. 622.

[97]   See J.R. English, 'The Tradition of Public History in Canada', *The Public Historian*, vol. 5, no. 1 (1983), pp. 47–59; F. Pannekoek, 'Who Matters? Public History and the Invention of Canada's Past', *Acadiensis*, vol. 29, no. 2 (2000), pp. 205–17. In Quebec, scholars have opted to call their discipline applied history (histoire appliquée) rather than public history. For Normand Perron of INRS – Urbanisation, Culture et Société, public history (spelled in English throughout the text) is an American idea, whereas 'histoire appliquée' is the indigenous term. N. Perron, 'Le Chantier des histories régionales et la Public History', *RHAF*, vol. 57, no. 1 (Summer 2003), p. 25. See also M. Riopel, 'Réflexions sur l'application de l'histoire', *RHAF*, vol. 57, no. 1 (Summer 2003).

[98]   In a special issue of RHAF on public history (or 'histoire appliqué'), contributors narrowly defined public history in terms of an intended audience: an abstract 'public' of consumers. A. Mosquin, D. Hamelin and C. Cournoyer, 'La pratique de l'histoire publique et la commemoration contemporaine: aperçu et enjeux', *RHAF*, vol. 57, no. 1 (Summer 2003), p. 79. See also D. Dodd, 'L'histoire appliquée et l'histoire universitaire à Parcs Canada', *RHAF*, vol. 57, no. 1 (Summer 2003), 91–2. One of the clearest examples of this can be found in D.D. Meringolo, 'Capturing the Public Imagination: The Social and Professional Place of Public History', *American Studies International*, vol. XLII, no. 2–3 (Jun./Oct. 2004), p. 86. She writes: 'Public history is an ... often neglected region. Its borders are mobile and permeable. Its population is diverse and diffuse. Dwelling in museums, historic sites, government agencies, and film studios, public historians speak an entirely different language from historians dwelling in colleges and universities. Public historians' sense of professional identity, tools of interpretation and traditions of story-telling are nearly incompatible with those who dwell in the academy.'

collective memory, historic parks and sites, commemorative activity, history and film, historic re-creations, and the heritage industry.[99] Even so, few of these authors would consider themselves public historians. Fewer still have sought to include the public in their research and writing. Canadian historical writing remains a solitary act for the most part.

Unable to identify more than a handful of initiatives in Canada from a search of the scholarly literature, I turned to the subscribers of the H-Canada listserv. In this way, I was directed towards several interesting projects organised around historic sites and material culture. I tend to agree with Lorne Hammond's assertion that most people who are sharing authority simply do so without writing about it for academic publication: 'If you are working with communities it is more of a private conversation with the community, often anchored in regional place, identity and very specific sensitivities, whether it involves First Nations, or a specific ethnic group.'[100] These kinds of relationships, he continued, 'are about trust and respect and the community's power has to be real, not token.' To establish his point, Hammond cited his own experience co-creating the 'Festa Italiana' exhibit with five Italian-Canadian communities. The travelling exhibit contained family and community artefacts and photographic images. To accommodate treasured materials that families did not feel comfortable allowing to travel, the exhibition included four empty cases that were re-created at each community locale – a church hall, lodge, mall, railway station, museums, and recreation centres. Authority was shared at each stop. According to Hammond, 'In one town alone 27 people read my copy to approve it and the communities decided on the exhibit title and what supporting events they would run in conjunction.'

Sharing authority was not always easy. Lorne Hammond recalled being faced with military memorabilia related to the Italian army's campaign against Ethiopia in the 1930s. Should this be included? If so, how? He struggled with this one: 'I

---

[99] There has been a wave of studies exploring memory in Canada. Among the best are the recent books by H.V. Nelles, Ronald Rudin, and Alan Gordon. For historic sites and parks, see: C.J. Taylor, *Negotiating the Past: The Making of Canada's Historic Parks and Sites* (Montreal, 1990); S. Ricketts, 'Cultural Selection and National Identity: Establishing Historic Sites in a National Framework', *The Public Historian*, vol. 18, no. 3 (1996), pp. 23–41; P. Litt, 'Pliant Clio and Immutable Texts: The Historiography of a Historical Marking Program', *The Public Historian*, vol. 19, no. 4 (1997), pp. 7–28; and A. Gordon, 'Heritage and Authenticity: The Case of Ontario's Sainte-Marie-among-the-Hurons', *Canadian Historical Review*, vol. 85, no. 3 (Sept. 2004). One of the best examples of the politics of memory is the debate surrounding 'The Valour and the Horror' documentary in the early 1990s (see Graham Carr's fine essay in the *Canadian Historical Review*). Finally readers would be well served in reading Ian McKay, *The Quest of the Folk* (Montreal, 1994) as well as D. Neufeld and F. Norris, *Chilkoot Trail: Heritage Route to Klondike* (Whitehorse, 1996).

[100] Quoted with permission from a personal communication from Lorne Hammond that is in the author's possession. Mar. 2007.

know the full story and think highly of Haile Selassie. Do I turn it away or work with their objects without personal comment? Now it's getting trickier. The answer is where are my responsibilities, well it's to them, not myself at that moment in time, again, power. I put them in as family artefacts. The case ends up chosen by the local paper for their article illustration ... . Power, community, object.' In surrendering power and process to the community, Hammond discovered that the exhibit developed in a completely different character and direction.

Among the other respondents to my query were university-trained historians working with community groups on local oral history projects and public historians at Parks Canada who work closely with First Nations people on historic sites and monuments.[101] Philip Goldring, for example, related how community involvement grew in Parks Canada projects, in part as a result of the negative consequences that occurred in not doing so in the 1970s and 1980s. There is now a full-fledged policy of involving stakeholders in the preparation of research reports. Goldring points to the collaboration that resulted in *Uqalurait: An Oral History of Nunavut* as evidence of the changes underway at Parks Canada. Another inspiring project involving First Nations peoples culminated in *Pictures Bring Us Messages: Photographs and Histories from the Kainai Nation*, authored by Alison K. Brown, Laura Peers and members of the Kainai Nation.[102] The book is about a visual repatriation project involving a collection of photographs taken on the Blood Reserve in 1925. Throughout the process of interviewing people about the photographs, Brown and Peers worked in close collaboration with the Kainai, formalised in a protocol agreement. The interviews were subsequently played back to the interviewees, edited as requested, and then transcribed. A small team of Kainai read each of the three drafts of the book manuscript. It was 'exhaustively collaborative and very fruitful', noted Laura Peers. Other exciting work is being undertaken outside Canada's universities by Montreal's Musée de la personne, the Ecomusée de Fier Monde, the Workers' Arts and Heritage Centre, and Pier 21 in Halifax. Still more pioneering work is featured in Michael Riordan's book, *An Unauthorized Biography of the World: Oral History on the Front Lines.*

---

[101]   There are a very large number of oral history books in the field of native and Métis history. See, for example, R.J. Preston, *Cree Narrative: Expressing the Personal Meaning of Events* (Montreal, 2003), J. Silman, *Enough is Enough: Aboriginal Women Speak Out* (Ottawa, 1992), M. Evans (ed.), *What it is to be a Metis* (Prince George, 1999), and M. Evans and L. Krebs, *A Brief History of the Short Life of the Island Cache* (Edmonton, 2005). See also P. Airhart, 'Oral Tradition and Oral History: Reviewing Some Issues', *Canadian Historical Review*, vol. 94, no. 3 (1994) and Jennifer Brown and Louis Bird's Omushkego Oral History Project at www.ourvoices.ca.

[102]   A.K Brown, L. Peers and Members of the Kainai Nation, *Pictures Bring Us Messages: Photographs and Histories from the Kainai Nation* (Toronto, 2006).

There are now a number of large collaborative research projects involving university-based historians funded by the Community-University Research Alliance (CURA) programme of SSHRC. This unique programme requires that university-based researchers work in collaboration with community partners. The 'Canadians and their Pasts: Exploring the Historical Consciousness of Canadians' CURA project, led by Jocelyn Létourneau at Laval University, for example, was launched in spring 2006 with seven researchers, 15 collaborators and 12 community partners that range from the Canadian Museums Association to Historica. The project seeks to know how Canadians use the past in their daily lives.[103] Another innovative project is the 'Labour History in New Brunswick CURA', which unites labour historians and various trade unions and heritage organisations in the province. The project's goal is to make labour history more accessible.[104] Oral history is one of the project's principal methodologies. These recent projects need to be studied for what they can tell us about collaboration and the possibilities and pitfalls of sharing authority. What lessons have been learnt? What is lost when historians give up their interpretative monopoly? What is gained in the process?

One of the reasons that I began to write this chapter is that I am leading a new CURA project, called 'Life Stories of Montrealers displaced by war, genocide and other human rights violations'. Our project uses the methodology of oral history to explore the experiences and social memories of Montreal residents displaced by mass violence, ranging from the Holocaust to war and atrocity crime in Rwanda, Cambodia, Latin America, Haiti, and South Asia. Our project was envisioned over a two-year period by a team of 40 university-based researchers and community co-applicants, including 18 community partners representing Montreal's diverse immigrant communities. Through the evidence of individual witness and community testimony, we intend to address three distinct questions: How is large-scale violence experienced and remembered by its victims and perpetrators? How do displaced persons (re)compose and narrate their stories in Montreal, Quebec, and Canada? How can their stories of violence and displacement most effectively be represented to a wider public? Oral history, we believe, has a pivotal role to play in educating ourselves and our communities about the social preconditions, experiences and long-term repercussions of crimes against humanity.

The core research strategy and methodology of the Life Stories project is ideally suited to the CURA mandate because the idea of shared authority is intrinsic to the collaborative work of oral history. As I write these words, the

---

[103] See www.canadiansandtheirpasts.ca.

[104] See www.lhtnb.ca.

project is presently devising strategies designed to share authority beyond the interview stage, enabling interviewees and community partners to help the project interpret interviews and to participate in research production and creative expression.[105] Sharing authority, however, does not mean muzzling scholarly voices. Nor am I saying that sharing authority is always possible or even desirabla. Kathleen Blee's research with women in the Indiana KKK provides a chilling example of the political issues raised when researchers work with communities that they don't identify or empathise with. What I am saying is that it is important for historians to think outside the disciplinary box in terms of how we go about conducting research. If we are successful, the most significant outcome of the Life Stories CURA will be to transform the production of life stories into cultural and historical materials for Montreal's immigrant communities – to preserve within these groups aspects of their history.

Conclusion

To conclude, oral history is built around people. 'It thrusts life into history itself and it widens its scope', wrote Paul Thompson.[106] Yet oral and public history is not necessarily an instrument for social change: 'It depends upon the spirit in which it is used.'[107] At its best, oral history 'can be used to change the focus of history itself, and open up new areas of inquiry; it can break down barriers between teachers and students, between generations, between educational institutions and the world outside; and in the writing of history – whether in books, or museums, or radio and film – it can give back to people who made and experienced history, through their own words, a central place.'[108] What is interesting about the early efforts to share authority in the United States is that, despite their successes, they have not been widely emulated. If remembered at all outside oral and public history circles, they are dismissed as naïve examples of 'enthusiastic populism'.[109]

Oral and public history has been particularly marginal in Canada where there is no obvious equivalent to history workshop, movement history and progressive public history. The hostile response to oral history has meant that efforts to

---

[105]   For more on the project visit http://storytelling.concordia.ca.

[106]   P. Thompson, *The Voice of the Past: Oral History*. Third Edition (Oxford, 2000), p. 23.

[107]   Thompson, *The Voice of the Past*, p. 3.

[108]   *Ibid.*

[109]   R.J. Grele, 'History and the Language of History in the Oral History Interview: Who Answers Whose Questions and Why?' in Eva M. McMahon and Kim Lacy Rogers (eds.), *Interactive Oral History Interviewing* (Hillsdale, New Jersey, 1994), p. 1.

share authority have found expression off-campus in community projects and in the new museums being created. Public history is still viewed by many university-based historians as something other people do. Likewise, Canadian historians using oral sources often have little grounding in the burgeoning international scholarship on oral history theory, ethics and methodology. Oral history is therefore treated as just another source, mined for information or a bit of colour. Relatively few have taken the opportunity to think deeply about narrative voice, memory, authority or the public's role in the historical process. There are signs, however, that this is changing. It is my hope that in rethinking Canadian history, this anthology engages with some of these themes. 'There is a different intellectual tradition that I admire', wrote James Green, 'one of engagement'.[110]

Acknowledgements

I would like to thank my community and university collaborators in the Life Stories CURA (www.lifestoriesmontreal.ca). We have not only talked about sharing authority, we have done our best to practise it over the past two years. Second, I would like to thank my students who have brought the Centre for Oral History and Digital Storytelling to life. They have encouraged me to think creatively about oral and public history. Finally, I would like to thank Michael Dawson and Christopher Dummitt for organising the Rethinking Canadian History conference and for editing this anthology.

---

[110]   Green, *Taking History to Heart*, p. 3–4.

Chapter 3
Persistence and Inheritance:
Rethinking Periodisation and English Canada's 'Twentieth Century'

Michael Dawson and Catherine Gidney

The nineteenth century was the century of the United States. I think that we can claim that it is Canada that shall fill the twentieth century.

Prime Minister Wilfrid Laurier, 1904.[1]

L'esprit d'un siècle ne naît pas et ne meurt pas à jour fixe.
Oscar Wilde, 'The Rise of Historical Criticism.'[2]

Introduction

We are both, in the common parlance of Canadian history, 'twentieth-century' historians. This category shapes our careers, sometimes explicitly, but more often implicitly. We are assigned books to review, invited to conferences or to contribute to edited collections, and were encouraged to apply for academic jobs based upon the perceived unity and functionality of this appellation. It is a convenient and not altogether inaccurate understanding of our research and teaching interests. And, to a certain extent, it is self-imposed. Why, when confronted by a stranger at a conference would one even attempt to hurriedly convey the intricacies of one's study of university health services or municipal store-hour

---

[1] Quoted in N. Hillmer, 'The Twentieth Century Belongs to Canada', *Carleton University Magazine* (2000). http://magazine.carleton.ca/2000_Spring/172.htm (Accessed 7 Mar. 2007).
[2] *Collins Complete Works of Oscar Wilde*, Fifth Edition (Glasgow, 2003), p. 1198. Translated as: The spirit of an age is not born and does not die on a definite day.

regulations when one can instead reach for a more familiar and comfortable reference point – the twentieth century?

There is nothing terribly conspiratorial about this label. The nineteenth-century historians don't necessarily preclude us from their conversations. And we've yet to be cornered by an angry group of eighteenth-century Canadianists eager to settle an old score with their twentieth-century counterparts. But the prevalence of this term, we think, is revealing. It would be tempting to blame Wilfrid Laurier for its continuing use as an adjective – for his oft-misquoted line about Canada being destined to prosper in the twentieth century has surely helped to make it an attractive and comfortable category for those interested in evaluating Canada's political, social and cultural reality. Indeed, the twentieth century acts as a pragmatic 'moral narrative' – to borrow European historian Charles S. Maier's useful phrase. It is a convenient way of taking stock of Canada's 'national' achievements in which contemporary historians compare their assessments of Canada's 'progress' against Laurier's optimism.[3]

Our concern is less with the use of the 'twentieth century' as a moral narrative, than with its use as a structural, or analytical, framework. For the twentieth century shapes our examinations of social, political and cultural processes. To be blunt, the historical examination of Canada in the twentieth century too often looks forward to the present day and underestimates the persistence of what are frequently seen as nineteenth-century social and cultural phenomena: the powerful influence of Protestantism or a close connection to the British world, for example. Moreover, examination of the twentieth century increasingly operates on the assumption that, with the basic temporal structure of the century in place, short-term case studies of already agreed-upon sub-periods are the way forward. One need only look at the significant amount of literature demarcated by the

---

[3]   For explicit examples of such endeavours, see Hilmer, 'The Twentieth Century Belongs to Canada' and J.L. Granatstein, I.M. Abella, D.J. Bercuson, R.C. Brown, and H.B. Neatby, 'Preface' in *Twentieth Century Canada*, 2nd edition (Toronto, 1986). Robert Bothwell and J.L. Granatstein begin with a reference to Laurier's comment – see *Our Century: The Canadian Journey in the Twentieth Century* (Toronto, 2000). For the twentieth century as a framework see also M. Kingwell, C. Moore and S. Borins, *Canada: Our Century* (Toronto, 1999); S.A. Cook, L. McLean and K. O'Rourke (eds.), *Framing Our Past: Constructing Canadian Women's History in the Twentieth Century* (Montreal and Kingston, 2006). Even the *Canadian Historical Review*'s CHR Forum series was partly rationalised on the grounds that the end of the twentieth century was a particularly appropriate moment for historical reflection. See, for example, the editors' comments in *Canadian Historical Review*, vol. 81, no. 4 (2000), p. 616. On 'moral' versus 'structural' narratives, see C.S. Maier, 'Consigning the Twentieth Century to History: Alternative Narratives for the Modern Era,' *American Historical Review*, vol. 105, no. 3 (2000), pp. 807, 826. Twentieth-century events, he argues, are often presented as a story of 'moral atrocity or moral struggle'.

interwar period,[4] the postwar period,[5] or by decade[6] to recognise the prevalence of such categories.

In effect, these smaller units provide the infrastructure which sustains the field of twentieth-century history. And they have come to have a powerful, but largely unexamined, interpretive influence. Who among us has not assigned a textbook that contrasts pre-Second World War attitudes toward immigration or Aboriginal peoples with postwar developments? Or, to take another example, who has not, in the midst of an undergraduate lecture, contrasted the economic prosperity of the 1920s with the trauma of the 1930s, or the conservative social values of the 1950s with the radical departures of the 1960s? To be sure, we attempt to qualify these all-too-convenient distinctions. We note in passing, for example, that the level of economic prosperity varied dramatically by region and was largely a characteristic of the later 1920s rather than the entire decade. But

---

[4] See, for example, S. Hewitt, *Riding to the Rescue: The Transformation of the RCMP in Alberta and Saskatchewan, 1914–1939* (Toronto, 2006); R. Jarvis Brownlie, *A Fatherly Eye: Indian Agents, Government Power, and Aboriginal Resistance in Ontario, 1918–1939* (Toronto, 2003); A. Lévesque, *Making and Breaking the Rules: Women in Quebec, 1919–1939*, trans. Yvonne M. Klein (Toronto, 1994); R.A. Wright, *A World Mission:Canadian Protestantism and the Quest for a New International Order, 1918–1939* (Montreal and Kingston, 1991); J. Struthers, *No Fault of their Own: Unemployment and the Canadian Welfare State, 1914–1941* (Toronto, 1983); V. Strong-Boag, *The New Day Recalled: Lives of Girls and Women in English Canada, 1919–1939* (Toronto, 1988).

[5] See for example, M. Fahrni and R. Rutherdale (eds.), *Creating Postwar Canada: Community, Diversity, and Dissent, 1945–1975* (Vancouver, 2007); C. Dummitt, *The Manly Modern: Masculinity in Postwar Canada* (Vancouver, 2007); M. Fahrni, *Household Politics: Montreal Families and Postwar Reconstruction* (Toronto, 2005); N. Christie and M. Gauvreau (eds.), *Cultures of Citizenship in Post-war Canada, 1940–1955* (Montreal and Kingston, 2003); S.G. Penfold, 'The Social Life of Donuts: Commodity and Community in Postwar Canada' (PhD diss., York University, 2002); P.S. McInnis, *Harnessing Labour Confrontation: Shaping the Postwar Settlement in Canada, 1943–1950* (Toronto, 2001); S. Tillotson, *The Public at Play: Gender and the Politics of Recreation in Post-War Ontario* (Toronto, 2000); J. Parr, *Domestic Goods: The Material, the Moral, and the Economic in the Postwar Years* (Toronto, 1999); M. Gleason, *Normalizing the Ideal: Psychology, Schooling, and the Family in Postwar Canada* (Toronto, 1999); M.L. Adams, *The Trouble With Normal: Postwar Youth and the Making of Heterosexuality* (Toronto, 1997).

[6] See, for example, J. Eayrs, '"A Low Dishonest Decade": Aspects of Canadian External Policy, 1931–1939', in R.D. Francis and D.B. Smith (eds.), *Readings in Canadian History: Post-Confederation*, 6th edition (Toronto, 2002), pp. 347–61; J. Herd Thompson with A. Seager, *Canada 1922–1939: Decades of Discord* (Toronto, 1985); M. Horn (ed.), *The Dirty Thirties: Canadians in the Great Depression* (Toronto, 1972); E.R. Forbes and D.A. Muise, *The Atlantic Provinces in Confederation* (Toronto and Fredericton, 1993); Bothwell and Granatstein, *Our Century*; Kingwell, Moore and Borins, *Canada: Our Century*. On the sixties, for example, see Dimitry Anastakis (ed.), *The Sixties: Passion, Politics, and Style* (Montreal and Kingston, 2008), the 'New World Coming: The Sixties and the Shaping of a Global Consciousness' conference held at Queen's University in June 2007 and the 'Debating Dissent: Canada and the Sixties' conference held at the University of New Brunswick in August 2008.

the very fact that so often our initial reference points are postwar periods and decadal divisions that then require qualification is telling.

Peer-reviewed publications and classroom lectures are obviously quite dissimilar animals. But they are the product of the same historical consciousness and, as we hope this chapter demonstrates, they are affected by the same demarcations of convenience. Like the twentieth century itself, these demarcations contribute to the segmentation of our historical vision. They encourage us to explore *short-term* developments and *short-term* shifts of cultural or social significance. One decade acts as a foil for the next while the prefixes pre, post or inter emphasise the discontinuity brought about by the two world wars. With this infrastructure in place, it becomes more difficult to examine the persistence of social and cultural values over a long period of time, and, by extension, the *process* of social and cultural change. It is, perhaps, a byproduct of our tendency to immerse ourselves in smaller and smaller circles of historiography that we are contributing to a history of Canada in which each of these short time periods has become its own island of time.[7]

We are not, it should be noted, arguing that historians have in any way been unreflective when it comes to thinking about how they study Canadian history. Indeed, we have explored new categories of historical analysis such as gender, race and sexuality.[8] We have debated alternative models of scale: national identity vs. more limited identities such as region and class. We have grappled with the relative merits of political and social history and their concomitant notions

---

[7]   We are not, of course, arguing that no one covers longer time periods that bridge some of these shorter time periods. Indeed, there are some historians who do so consistently: Joan Sangster and Mary Kinnear, for example. But studies framed by demarcations of convenience remain far more common. For examples of works that transgress *some* demarcations of convenience, see Sangster, *Earning Respect: The Lives of Working Women in Small Town Ontario, 1920–1960* (Toronto, 1995) and *Regulating Girls and Women: Sexuality, Family and Deviance in Ontario, 1920–1960* (Toronto, 2001); Kinnear, *A Female Economy: Women's Work in a Prairie Province, 1870–1970* (Montreal and Kingston, 1999) and *In Subordination: Professional Women, 1870–1970* (Montreal and Kingston, 1995); K. McPherson, *Bedside Matters: The Transformation of Canadian Nursing, 1900–1990* (Toronto, 2003); J. Struthers, *The Limits of Affluence: Welfare in Ontario, 1920–1970* (Toronto, 1994); S. Morton, *At Odds: Gambling and Canadians, 1919–1969* (Toronto, 2003); and C. Comacchio, *The Dominion of Youth: Adolescence and the Making of Modern Canada, 1920 to 1950* (Waterloo, 2006).

[8]   K. Dubinsky, R. Frager, F. Iacovetta, L. Marks, J. Newton, C. Strange, M. Valverde, and C. Wright, 'Introduction', in Franca Iacovetta and Mariana Valverde (eds.), *Gender Conflicts: New Essays in Women's History* (Toronto, 1992); J. Sangster, 'Beyond Dichotomies: Re-assessing Gender History and Women's History in Canada', *Left History*, vol. 3, no. 1 (1995), pp. 109–121 and the pointed exchanges that followed in later issues of *Left History*; J. Parr, 'Gender History and Historical Practice', *Canadian Historical Review*, vol. 76, no. 3 (1995), pp. 354–76.

of inclusiveness.[9] And we have argued over the insights of postmodern and poststructuralist theory.[10] We have not, however, interrogated the temporal categories that shape the questions we ask as historians. To put it another way, we have spent very little time thinking about *time*.

Given the current influence of social and cultural history, this is quite surprising. After all, one of the original aims of social history was to encourage new ways of periodising the past.[11] In recent decades social historians of Quebec have consciously reformulated traditional periodisation. Here, a revisionist literature has called into question for Quebec some of the very issues we will be raising in relation to English Canada such as the privileging of particular events and periodising across the wars. In doing so they have engaged in a debate that has focused attention on the political uses of history and the way in which our selection of dates and periods fundamentally shapes interpretation.[12] Yet, in general, and for English Canada more particularly, while social history has changed the way history is written (through new topics and new questions, for example), its impact on the manner in which we periodise history has been rather more

[9] J.M.S. Careless, '"Limited Identities" in Canada', *Canadian Historical Review*, vol. 50, no. 1 (1969), pp. 1–10 and Careless, 'Limited Identities – Ten Years Later', *Manitoba History*, vol. 1 (1980), pp. 3–9. More recently see M. Bliss, 'Privatizing the Mind: The Sundering of Canadian History, the Sundering of Canada', *Journal of Canadian Studies*, vol. 26, no. 4 (1991–92), pp. 5–17, and responses in the issue vol. 27, no. 2 (1992); J.L. Granatstein, *Who Killed Canadian History?* (Toronto, 1998); A.B. McKillop, 'Who Killed Canadian History? A View from the Trenches', *Canadian Historical Review*, vol. 80, no. 2 (1999), pp. 269–99; B.D. Palmer, 'Of Silences and Trenches: A Dissident View of Granatstein's Meaning', *Canadian Historical Review*, vol. 80, no. 4 (1999), pp. 676–86. For a recent rethinking of the concept of region see G. Friesen, 'Space and Region in Canadian History', *Journal of the Canadian Historical Association*, (2005), pp. 1–22. For a new evaluation of the place of 'inclusiveness' in Canadian historiography see Christopher Dummitt's contribution to this volume.

[10] See, for example, M. Valverde, 'As if subjects existed: Analysing Social Discourses', *Canadian Review of Sociology and Anthropology*, vol. 28 (1991), pp. 173–87 and B.D. Palmer, *Descent into Discourse: The Reification of Language and the Writing of Social History* (Philadelphia, 1990).

[11] Indeed, one of the early promises of Canadian women's history was 'to establish new schemes of periodisation'. See R. Pierson and A. Prentice, 'Feminism and the Writing and Teaching of History', *Atlantis*, vol. 7, no. 2 (1982), pp. 41–2.

[12] Significant debate has erupted among historians of Quebec about periodisation and the privileging of events such as the Conquest or the Quiet Revolution. For entry into the debate see, for example, J. Létourneau, 'Le Temps du lieu raconté. Essai sur quelques chronologies récentes relatives à l'histoire du Québec', *International Journal of Canadian Studies*, vol. 15 (1997), pp. 153–65, and J.A. Dickenson and B. Young, 'Periodization in Quebec History: A Reevaluation', *Quebec Studies*, vol. 12 (1991), pp. 1–10. Historians of Quebec have begun to periodise across the wars. Dickenson and Young, for example, have argued that the 1930s to 1960s should be considered a distinct period. See above, page 7. For a more recent use of this period see M. Gauvreau, *The Catholic Origins of Quebec's Quiet Revolution, 1931–1970* (Montreal and Kingston, 2005).

muted.[13] For example, the key dividing points in the three major post-Confederation textbooks continue to emphasise the world wars, decades and, on occasion, the rise and fall of political leaders.[14] This is not a Canadian problem alone.[15] In the international context, Peter Stearns laments that despite early hopes in this regard, 'a decisive sociohistorical periodisation has not replaced more conventional, usually political markers'.[16] Similarly, cultural history has offered important insights into how Canadians experienced time – especially in the context of industrialisation and modernity and the perceived acceleration of daily life. But it too has left traditional categories of periodisation intact.

Our aim in this chapter is not to put forward an overarching new scheme for periodising all of Canadian history, however that might be defined. Instead, our goal is more modest: to initiate a discussion about the common-sense ways in

---

[13] Létourneau notes that in general, syntheses and school texts of either Quebec or English Canada remain remarkably tied to traditional chronologies. Létourneau, 'Le Temps du lieu raconté', p. 159.

[14] The three textbooks are R.D. Francis, R. Jones and D.B. Smith, *Destinies: Canadian History Since Confederation*, 5th edition (Toronto, 2004); M. Conrad and A. Finkel, *History of the Canadian Peoples: 1867 to the Present*, 3rd edition (Toronto, 2002); J.M. Bumsted, *The Peoples of Canada*, 2nd edition (Toronto, 2004). On the lack of 'organizational innovation' in Canadian history textbooks, see Gail Cuthbert Grant's contribution to 'New Wine or Just New Bottles? A Round Table on Recent Texts in Canadian History', *Journal of Canadian Studies*, vol. 30, no. 4 (Winter 1995–96), pp. 175–201. The very notion of Confederation as necessarily *the* dividing point in Canadian history is certainly worthy of sustained discussion and debate. For a brief polemical aside on this issue see M. Dawson, 'A Pox on Canada Day Quizzes,' *Toronto Star*, 28 Jun. 2006, A19.

[15] Indeed, one could ask why periodise (English-) Canadian history at all? Why not a North American or trans-Atlantic or global approach to periodisation? In truth, all of these approaches have merit but none of them necessarily or consistently trumps the others when it comes to explanatory value. Our rationale for focusing here on English Canada is based partly on our observation that historians of English Canada have been less attuned to the issue of periodisation than have their counterparts in Quebec. But it is also based on our contention that there has been and continues to be, on some level, a cultural and social unity among English-speaking Canadians. Identities are complex phenomena and Canadians living in the predominantly English speaking parts of the country today, as in the past, undoubtedly identify with cultural currents, and experience their lives, in relation to local, national and international contexts. Yet a continuously reconstructed notion of 'English Canada' remains a particularly powerful reference point for many Canadians and, as such, it is a worthwhile and productive (but not totalising) reference point.

[16] P.N. Stearns, 'Social History Present and Future', *Journal of Social History*, vol. 37, no. 1 (2003), p. 9. The limited progress on this issue can be seen in the call for papers for the 2008 Berkshire Conference, which asks some of the same questions raised by the first women's historians. For example, it suggests that after 40 years of scholarship, women's historians consider, among other things, 'What are the appropriate markers for change in women's history? Is a traditional timeline of history, periodized by political regimes and cultural revolutions, useful for understanding women's lives? Or should women's historians propose a new periodization for human history?' See www.umass.edu/history/berks/berks.htm [accessed 23 Mar. 2007].

which we periodise history and, in doing so, to highlight important but often overlooked social and cultural continuities between the late nineteenth century and the second half of the twentieth century. We begin by briefly discussing the relationship between periodisation and history. We then examine the problematic nature, and enduring influence, of two common approaches to periodisation often adopted by historians of the twentieth century: 'postwar' eras and decades. These demarcations, we argue, prioritise short-term, segmented and discontinuous time and, in doing so, limit our ability to explore links across longer time periods. We conclude by exploring alternative approaches to periodisation that are better suited to examining both the *persistence* of social and cultural influences and the *process* of social and cultural change.

Periodisation and History

Why should we pay attention to the issue of periodisation? One answer to that question is that it brings order to the past and helps us create narrative structure. It is a necessary, but awkward, component of historical inquiry. There is certainly, in Robert S. Baker's words, a 'museological dimension' to periodisation which appeals 'to our desire for order'. And it is obviously the case that historians' narratives can vary greatly in terms of reflexivity, inclusiveness and subtlety. But we are of the persuasion that periodisation and narratives are unavoidable.[17] Jerzy Topolski notes that without the use of periods 'the only "naturally" coherent narrative would consist of an unlimited flow of factual descriptions without beginning or end and without any distinction between changing structures when a given structure is transformed into another structure.'[18] As a result, if we want to do more than provide a chronicle of past events, periodisation *is* necessary.[19] According to American historian Robert Berkhofer Jr., historians conceive of segments of time as having 'a certain unity so that the time span is not merely arbitrary'.[20] Canadian sport historian Barbara Schrodt similarly argues that 'selected periods' serve a variety of purposes: 'to make the narrative more manageable; to give it unity; to situate the subject of the narrative in a broader

---

[17] R.S. Baker, 'History and Periodization', *Clio*, vol. 26, no. 2 (1997), p. 137.

[18] J. Topolski, 'Periodization and the Creation of Narrative Wholes', *Storia della Storiografia*, vol. 37 (2000), p. 12.

[19] For a similar position see A. Douglas, 'Periodizing the American Century: Modernism, Postmodernism, and Postcolonialism in the Cold War Context', *Modernism/Modernity*, vol. 5, no. 3 (1998), p. 74 and D. Carr, *Time, Narrative, and History* (Bloomington and Indianapolis, 1986).

[20] Quoted in B. Schrodt, 'Problems of Periodization in Canadian Sport History', *Canadian Journal of History of Sport*, vol. 21, no. 1 (1990), p. 65.

context; or to assist in the search for answers to questions posed by the research problem.'[21]

Yet if periodisation is central to the task of historians, the process of choosing periods is not unproblematic. Schrodt notes that 'periods introduce certain assumptions into the search for answers to history problems, and if these assumptions are not carefully examined each time the periods are used, the methodological problem of false periodisation may develop.'[22] The traditional timeline of Canadian sport history, she reveals, was established by four PhD dissertations written in the late 1960s and early 1970s. The authors of these studies essentially established the field of sport history but in doing so they selected beginning and end points for their theses for a number of reasons including the perceived necessity of having their arguments fit into already established political history periods and a more pragmatic, but no less influential, desire to limit the scope of their dissertations. Two decades later their pragmatic choices had become the basis of a common-sense timeline among historians of Canadian sport.[23]

One need not embrace Schrodt's positivist assumptions regarding 'false' and 'true' periodisation to recognise that our decisions regarding periodisation inevitably shape the arguments we make. 'To choose a certain periodisation,' Topolski notes, 'is to choose a certain coherence.'[24] Or, as Charles Maier explains, 'periods stipulate the extension across time of developments that seem to have some relationship to each other and as a group contrast with earlier or later sequences.'[25] But 'to periodise', he argues, 'is to dismiss evidence as much as to gather it.'[26] Perhaps more than that, periodisation can limit the kinds of questions we ask. For as Douglas McCalla reminds us, 'Once established, periodization, like other kinds of categorization, deeply influences what we can think.'[27]

The power of periodisation to silence is eloquently explored in Michel-Rolph Trouillot's trenchant analysis of Columbus's ostensible 'discovery of America'. As the basis for public school lessons and a series of anniversary celebrations, the date 12 October 1492 has dominated historical understanding of the 'discovery'. The result, Trouillot argues, is a date-driven understanding that not only silences

---

[21]   Schrodt, 'Problems of Periodization in Canadian Sport History', p. 65.

[22]   Schrodt, 'Problems of Periodization in Canadian Sport History', p. 65.

[23]   The four theses established the periods 1807–67, 1868–1900, 1900–1920 and 1921–39. See Schrodt, 'Problems of Periodization in Canadian Sport History', pp. 66–7.

[24]   Topolski, 'Periodization and the Creation of Narrative Wholes', p. 16.

[25]   Maier, 'Consigning the Twentieth Century to History', p. 809.

[26]   Maier, 'Consigning the Twentieth Century to History', p. 810.

[27]   D. McCalla, 'The Economic Impact of the Great War', in David MacKenzie (ed.), *Canada and the First World War: Essays in Honour of Robert Craig Brown* (Toronto, 2005), p. 148.

the complex process of European conquest, but also overshadows simultaneous developments ('the prolonged fall of Muslim Granada, the seemingly interminable expulsion of European Jews', for example) that were understood at the time to have much more far-ranging implications.[28] As a demarcation of convenience, 12 October 1492 silences the important developments that occurred before and after the day of 'discovery'. In essence, this date-driven understanding of history hinders our ability to ask the important and awkward historical questions (how? why?) and leaves us focused instead on the comfortably mundane (who? what? where? when?).[29] As Oscar Wilde reminds us, and we believe that with the requisite hindsight Wilfrid Laurier would almost certainly agree, beginning and end points in history are complex and contingent entities and should not be assigned casually. Instead, we need to interrogate demarcations of convenience so that we are more consciously aware of the decisions we make and the periodisations we employ.

Interrogating Common-Sense Demarcations of Convenience: 'Postwar' Periods and Decadal Divisions

Perhaps the most convenient form of periodisation for twentieth-century Canadian historians concerns the use of postwar periods.[30] Indeed, a quick survey of the field's three most popular post-Confederation survey textbooks highlights the extent to which the wars are central to the manner in which the twentieth century is periodised.[31] Fittingly, for a country devoted to ice hockey, these books reach a general consensus on the first three periods: the first ends with the Great War; the second ends with the Second World War; and a third segment encompasses the post-Second World War era. Tellingly, a division

[28] M.-R. Trouillot, *Silencing the Past: Power and the Production of History* (Boston, 1995), p. 113. For date-driven monographs see, for example, P. Berton, *1967: The Last Good Year* (Toronto, 1997) and C. Moore, *1867: How the Fathers Made a Deal* (Toronto, 1997).

[29] As E.H. Carr pointed out many years ago, 'to praise a historian for his accuracy is like praising an architect for using well-seasoned timber.' E.H. Carr, *What is History?* (London, 1961), pp. 10–11. In essence, 12 October 1492 is a convenient reference point but it offers little in the way of explanatory value and, in fact, obscures more than it reveals.

[30] In addition to the monographs outlined earlier in the chapter, a number of textbooks are structured around the 'postwar' period. See R. Bothwell, I. Drummond and J. English, *Canada Since 1945: Power, Politics, and Provincialism*, rev. ed. (Toronto, 1989); A. Finkel, *Our Lives: Canada after 1945* (Toronto, 1997); D. Avery and R. Hall, *Coming of Age: Readings in Canadian History Since World War II* (Toronto, 1996).

[31] Francis, Jones and Smith, *Destinies*, 5th edition (2004); Conrad and Finkel, *History of the Canadian Peoples* 3rd edition (2002); Bumsted, *The Peoples of Canada*, 2nd edition (2004).

emerges only regarding the length of the third period with two of the texts adding an 'overtime' component, roughly the early 1970s to the present, and the other preferring to categorise 1945 to 2003 as a unified period. What emerges here, and in English-Canadian historical writing more generally, is a variation on Eric Hobsbawm's 'short' twentieth century.[32] The Great War provides a convenient (and reasonably sharp) turning point upon which 'traditional' social and cultural influences are impaled, while the rest of the century focuses on the story of modernisation. This story, in turn, is sustained by both the postwar periods and decadal divisions that follow.

Canadianists are certainly not alone in making reference to postwar periods, and the problematic nature of these labels has not gone unnoticed. Speaking at a 1989 roundtable on the suitability of the term 'postwar' for British history, Richard Rose pointed to the problem the idea of *inheritance* poses for strict beginnings and endings. Drawing on his own research on government growth in Britain since 1945, Rose noted 'the enormous importance' of inheritance – namely 'that a government on taking office receives a large legacy of commitments made by administrations in past decades or generations which are carried forward by the force of political inertia.' The policy influences on the postwar era, he explained, were deeply rooted in the prewar and wartime periods. Drawing from his own life, Rose stated, 'I started researching English history 36 years ago. Rationing was on and being September the central heating was off; Mr Attlee and Mr Churchill were in the House of Commons, children of Victorian times whose ideas were shaped in Edwardian times.'[33] In terms of how it affected political leadership, Rose noted, the 'Edwardian' influence persisted into the early years of this ostensibly 'new' period. Rose emphasised both from his research and personal experience the importance of the very elusive idea of inheritance and thus the problem of 1945 as a meaningful start date. And he equally acknowledged the problem of determining what might comprise the end of a postwar period. From the perspective of 1989, he admitted, something had changed significantly since 1945.[34] But what exactly had changed was difficult to discern, in part, he explained, because 'we are not necessarily clear about the

---

[32] E.J. Hobsbawm, *Age of Extremes: the Short Twentieth Century* (London, 1994). The one tangible 'new' period that one might identify with English-Canadian social history, namely the era of industrialisation and transformation from the 1880s to the 1920s, does not fundamentally challenge this division. By the 1920s, the consensus seems to suggest, 'modern' Canada had emerged from this transitional era.

[33] Richard Rose, 'Periodisation in Post-War Britain', *Contemporary Record*, vol. 6, no. 2 (1992), p. 326.

[34] *Ibid.*, p. 326.

consequences of the events of the period.'[35] Hence, Rose asked, 'how do we know what the postwar era is a prelude to? In the year 2100 it's unlikely that we will refer to Britain in the 1990s as the post-war era.'[36] Or, to rephrase this point more forcefully, the use of the term 'postwar' does very little to explain the characteristics of this period, and its capacity to demarcate a period of time will almost certainly decrease dramatically as time passes and distance between the contemporary period and the Second World War grows.

Rose's comments about postwar Britain are apt for both of the postwar periods in the Canadian context. The Great War, for example, is often treated as a rough endpoint to the nineteenth century. We will give two examples here – the first from women's history and the second from religious history. The traditional interpretation of western feminism has focused on a first wave of feminist activism from the late nineteenth century to the 1920s, followed by a period of quiescence and the eventual emergence of a second wave in the 1960s.[37] In Canada, the emphasis on the failings of maternal feminists to sustain collective activism after obtaining the vote at the end of the Great War, as well as the narrow equation of feminism with suffrage, has resulted in historians neglecting mainstream feminism in the period between the 1920s and 1960s.[38] In challenging this approach in his book on British feminism, Brian Harrison notes that one of his main aims is 'to prevent the First World War from artificially separating Edwardian from inter-war feminism. With women's history, as with labour history,' he argues, 'it is misleading to place pre-war and post-war history in separate compartments. Neglect of the Edwardian *inheritance* makes much of what happened between the wars difficult to comprehend'.[39] Indeed,

---

[35] *Ibid.*, p. 327.

[36] *Ibid.*, p. 326.

[37] On the failure of maternal feminists to sustain activism after gaining the vote see C. L. Bacchi, *Liberation Deferred? The Ideas of the English-Canadian Suffragists, 1877–1918* (Toronto, 1983); L. Kealey, 'Introduction,', W. Roberts, '"Rocking the Cradle of the World": The New Woman and Maternal Feminism, Toronto 1877–1914' and V. Strong-Boag, 'Canada's Women Doctors: Feminism Constrained,' all in Linda Kealey (ed.), *A Not Unreasonable Claim: Women and Reform in Canada, 1880s–1920s* (Toronto, 1979), pp. 14, 31, 129.

[38] There are a few exceptions. See, for example the articles in L. Kealey and J. Sangster (eds.), *Beyond the Vote: Canadian Women and Politics* (Toronto, 1989); M. Conrad, '"Not a Feminist, But...": The Political Career of Ellen Louks Fairclough, Canada's First Female Federal Cabinet Minister', *Journal of Canadian Studies*, vol. 31, no. 2 (Summer 1996), pp. 5–28; M. Kinnear, *Margaret McWilliams: An Interwar Feminist* (Montreal and Kingston, 1991); V. Strong-Boag, 'Pulling in Double Harness or Hauling a Double Load: Women, Work and Feminism on the Canadian Prairie', *Journal of Canadian Studies*, vol. 21, no. 3 (Fall 1986), pp. 32–52. Much of the work on the period from roughly 1920 to 1960 tends to focus on individual biographies, an indication that a rethinking of the issue for this period remains at an early stage.

[39] B. Harrison, *Prudent Revolutionaries: Portraits of British Feminists between the Wars* (Oxford, 1987), p. 8. Emphasis added.

as Nancy Forestell points out, in the international context historians have begun to rethink the periodisation of first-wave feminism. They are now extending it into the 1940s and, in doing so, have challenged the notion of the post-First World War period as quiescent. Such work, she notes, has yet to be done in Canada.[40] As a result, the influence of 'first-wave' feminism on 'second-wave' feminism has gone largely unexplored.

In English-Canadian historiography, the Great War has also become a prominent marker that signals the demise of Protestantism's cultural authority and ushers in a modern, and secular, Canada. Historical work does not state the issue so baldly. In *The Regenerators*, which remains the entry point into the 'secularization debate', Ramsay Cook focused attention on the consequences for Protestantism 'of the intellectual transformation that took place in English Canada between Confederation and the Great War'.[41] Though Cook saw the prominent social critics he examined as figures representing the leading edge of what would become a more widespread secularising process, his arguments and the subsequent literature focused attention on the years around the First World War.[42] The result is most starkly seen in one textbook's treatment of Protestantism. The

---

[40]   N. Forestell, 'Mrs. Canada Goes Global: Canadian First Wave Feminism Revisited', *Atlantis*, vol. 30, no. 1 (2005), p. 13. Indeed, she argues that not only is Canadian first-wave feminism due for re-examination but large areas of the history of feminism in Canada have yet to be thoroughly studied. In addition, we note, extending our analysis of the first wave into the 1940s would, conceivably, help to prevent women obtaining the provincial franchise in Quebec being viewed as something of an historical afterthought. An important starting point for historians keen to evaluate just how 'transformative' the Great War really was for Canadians is MacKenzie (ed), *Canada and the First World War*. See also S. Burke, 'Revisiting the Great Divide: World War I and Women's Higher Education in Ontario', in Paul Stortz and E. Lisa Panayotidis (eds.) *Universities and War: Histories of Academic Cultures and Conflict* (University of Toronto Press, in progress).

[41]   R. Cook, *The Regenerators: Social Criticism in Late Victorian English Canada* (Toronto, 1985), p. 229.

[42]   The focus on the Great War as a turning point has been bolstered by a number of monographs. Richard Allen, in *The Social Passion: Religion and Social Reform in Canada, 1914–28* (Toronto, 1971), sees the years prior to 1914 as a period of crest for the social gospel and those after 1918 as one of tension and disintegration. Looking at the context of the university, A.B. McKillop argues that while idealism 'dominated the intellectual life of the pre-War years in Canada', with 'the onset of the First World War, the idealists were on the defensive'. See A.B. McKillop, *A Disciplined Intelligence: Critical Inquiry and Canadian Thought in the Victorian Era* (Montreal and Kingston, 1992), pp. 229–30. For a similar formulation of these arguments slightly later into the twentieth century see D. Marshall, *Secularizing the Faith: Canadian Protestant Clergy and the Crisis of Belief, 1850–1940* (Toronto, 1992). Cook's and McKillop's arguments that in the years after the Great War the reformist impulse within the social sciences gave way to a stance of detached investigation has been reinforced in the work of other historians. See for example, D. Owram, *The Government Generation: Canadian Intellectuals and the State, 1900–1945* (Toronto, 1986) and M. Shore, *The Science of Social Redemption: McGill, the Chicago School, and the Origins of Social Research in Canada* (Toronto, 1987). The first works countering the notion that theological reformulation resulted in a process of secularisation focused roughly on the same time period. See P.D. Airhart, *Serving the Present Age: Revivalism, Progressivism, and the Methodist*

period 1867 to 1918 is framed in terms of 'Religion and Society', while that on interwar culture is revealingly titled 'Protestantism in a Secular Society'.[43] There is now a growing literature showing the dominant cultural influence of Protestantism in English Canada well into the twentieth century.[44] Yet few twentieth-century social and cultural historians, other than those working specifically on the history of religion, tend to incorporate religion into their work in a meaningful way. Gender and labour historians, for example, have provided rich studies of the interconnections between gender, race and class, yet rarely examine the intersection of religion and these other identities.[45] For most English-Canadian historians of the twentieth century, Protestantism's influence was a (welcome?) casualty of the Great War. And, as a result, its continuing influence well into the twentieth century is generally ignored.

Tradition in Canada (Montreal and Kingston, 1992); M. Van Die, *An Evangelical Mind: Nathanael Burwash and the Methodist Tradition in Canada, 1839–1918* (Montreal and Kingston, 1989); B.J. Fraser, *The Social Uplifters: Presbyterians, Progressives and the Social Gospel in Canada, 1875–1915* (Waterloo, 1988). For a slightly longer time period see M. Gauvreau, *The Evangelical Century: College and Creed in English Canada from the Great Revival to the Great Depression* (Montreal and Kingston, 1991).

[43] Conrad and Finkel, *History of the Canadian People: 1867 to the Present*, 3rd edition (2002), pp. 156, 276.

[44] A number of works now highlight its cultural influence well into the twentieth century. M. Gauvreau and O. Hubert (eds.), *Churches and Social Order in Nineteenth- and Twentieth-Century Canada* (Montreal and Kingston, 2006); K. Kee, *Revivalists: Marketing the Gospel in English Canada, 1884-1957* (Montreal and Kingston, 2006); G.R. Miedema, *For Canada's Sake: Public Religion, Centennial Celebrations, and the Re-making of Canada in the 1960s* (Montreal and Kingston, 2005); C. Gidney, *A Long Eclipse: The Liberal Protestant Establishment and the Canadian University, 1920–1970* (Montreal and Kingston, 2004); N. Christie (ed.), *Households of Faith: Family, Gender, and Community in Canada, 1760–1969* (Montreal and Kingston, 2003); M. Van Die (ed.), *Religion and Public Life in Canada: Historical and Comparative Perspectives* (Toronto: 2001); N. Christie and M. Gauvreau, *A Full-Orbed Christianity: The Protestant Churches and Social Welfare in Canada, 1900–1941* (Montreal and Kingston, 1996).

[45] Lynne Marks has argued for some time for the incorporation of the role of religion into both gender and labour history. See, for example, her introduction in *Revivals and Roller Rinks: Religion, Leisure and Identity in Late-Nineteenth Century Small-Town Ontario* (Toronto, 1996). Women's religious experience continues to be overlooked. For example, the collection by V. Strong-Boag, M. Gleason and A. Perry (eds.), *Rethinking Canada: The Promise of Women's History*, 4th edition (Don Mills, 2002), contains no explicit essay on women and religion. Granted, the authors have a limited amount of space but, among other things, the effect reinforces the sense of the twentieth century as secular. Although there are a growing number of articles focusing on the intersection of religion and other categories of identity, scholars who focus on race, class, gender or sexuality rarely include analyses of religious experience. For this new work see, for example, M. Turkstra, 'Constructing a Labour Gospel: Labour and Religion in Early 20th-Century Ontario', *Labour/Le Travail*, 57 (Spring 2006), pp.93–130; T. Block, '"Boy Meets Girl": Constructing Heterosexuality in Two Victoria Churches, 1945–1960', *Journal of the Canadian Historical Association*, no. 10 (1999), pp. 279–96; and Block, '"Families that Pray Together Stay Together": Religion, Gender & Family in Postwar Victoria, British Columbia', *BC Studies*, no. 145 (2005), pp. 31–54.

More questions emerge when one considers the use of the other common war-related division – the Second World War – as a convenient turning point for 'Canada's Century'. There are, to be sure, analytical advantages for emphasising some of the common characteristics of a period (1945 to c.1975) which witnessed relatively sustained economic prosperity. But historians are beginning to question both the separation of the interwar and postwar years and the very definition of postwar itself. Indeed, some recent work points to the continuing links between the postwar period and the pre-1945 period. For example, Michael Dawson's study of tourism in British Columbia argues that the Great Depression and the Second World War were crucial eras in the development of a consumer society in Canada, in contrast to a literature that emphasised the importance of two distinct 'periods' – the 1920s and the postwar era. By documenting the extent to which a tourism-promotion infrastructure was put in place from the 1930s to the 1950s, Dawson's study emphasises the continuities and connections in terms of promoters' activities and, to a lesser extent, consumer behaviour before, after, and during the Second World War.[46] Joy Parr's work on consumption in the postwar years puts forward a very different argument, but one that also highlights continuity by illustrating the lack of access Canadian consumers had to household goods after the war as government policy encouraged expenditures on capital rather than consumer goods.[47] Similarly, Michael Gauvreau and Nancy Christie have recently suggested that Canadian historians might usefully draw on the work of historians in Europe who have argued that as a result of delayed prosperity traditional patterns of consumption survived well into the 1950s.[48]

A growing number of historians are also beginning to challenge the notion of a unitary postwar period. One way they are doing so is by rethinking the timing of the war's social and cultural impact. Barbara Schrodt, for example, notes that Canadian historians in the growing field of sport and leisure have tended to follow the lead of other Canadian historians in assuming that the war was an important 'turning point'.[49] Instead, she argues, 'in Canadian sport, the early postwar years were not substantially different from those immediately preceding the War.'[50] The key postwar changes in Canadian sport, she explains, did not occur

---

[46]   M. Dawson, *Selling British Columbia: Tourism and Consumer Culture, 1890–1970* (Vancouver, 2004).

[47]   Parr, *Domestic Goods*, p. 81. Magda Fahrni's examination of Montreal families after the Second World War provides an important illustration of the limits of consumption during this period. See *Household Politics*, pp. 10–11, chapter 5.

[48]   Christie and Gauvreau, 'Recasting Canada's Post-War Decade', in *Cultures of Citizenship*, p. 5.

[49]   Schrodt, 'Problems of Periodization in Canadian Sport History,' p. 72.

[50]   *Ibid.*, p. 72.

until the early 1960s. It was only then that Canadian sport was transformed by a number of factors including substantial government involvement in promoting sporting activity, a decline in the 'predominant view of sport as a form of idle and useless play', a returning public acceptance of female athletes, and the resolution of the Sunday Sport question.[51] This is not to say that the Second World War was not a factor in any of these transformations. But in viewing sport as a 'conservative and traditional' institution, Schrodt argues that the cultural impact of the war was not really felt until the early 1960s.[52] Instead of emphasising a distinct post-war period, Schrodt argues for the period from roughly 1920 to 1960.[53]

If historians have started to emphasise the links between the interwar and post-war years, so too are they questioning the traditional time period of 1945 to 1975. Nancy Christie and Michael Gauvreau have recently encouraged historians to rethink the parameters of the postwar era.[54] They argue that the years 1943 to 1955 should be seen as a distinct period marked not by 'cultural quiescence, social conformity, and political consensus' but by 'intense cultural and social negotiation' and 'a constant shifting of axes between the elements of tradition and modernity'.[55] Interestingly, in his study of the development of 'postwar' consumption Steve Penfold also sees 1955 as an important turning point after which 'a configuration of mass marketing' emerged to dramatically accelerate the expansion of donut franchises.[56] Historians are also beginning to rethink the traditional endpoint of the postwar era. Penfold, for example, notes that 'the donut shop entered its golden age after 1975' – a development that sits awkwardly with our focus on a postwar period of economic buoyancy that ended in the early 1970s. Both Steven High and Michael Dawson have recently drawn our attention to similarities between the economic realities of the 1945 to 1975 era and the post-1975 period.[57]

To return to the point made by Rose: it is possible that in the long run 'postwar' will be a term that just does not make sense to students of Canadian history. International and European historians are already reconceptualising the second half of the twentieth century. In contrast to Eric Hobsbawm's treatment

[51] *Ibid.*, p. 72.

[52] *Ibid.*, p. 73.

[53] *Ibid.*, p. 74.

[54] Christie and Gauvreau, 'Recasting Canada's Post-war Decade', pp. 6–7.

[55] Christie and Gauvreau, 'Recasting Canada's Post-war Decade', pp. 3, 17.

[56] S. Penfold, *The Donut: A Canadian History* (Toronto, 2008), p. 13.

[57] S. High, 'Capital and Community Reconsidered: The Politics and Meaning of Deindustrialization', *Labour/Le Travail*, vol. 55 (2005), p. 193; M. Dawson, 'Victoria Debates its Postindustrial Reality: Tourism, Deindustrialization, and Store-Hour Regulations, 1900–1958', *Urban History Review*, vol. 35, no.2 (2007), pp. 14–24.

of 1945 to 1973 as one unit (the Golden Age), Arthur Marwick argues for 1958 to 1974 to be seen as a distinct period that he then breaks down into three sub-periods: 1958 to 1963, 1964 to 1968/9, 1969 to 1974.[58] More recently, Tony Judt has argued for 1945 to 1989 (subdivided into 1945 to 1953, 1953 to 1971, and 1971 to 1989) as a unit – 'an interim age: a post-war parenthesis, the unfinished business of a conflict that ended in 1945 but whose epilogue had lasted for another half century.'[59] Whether this periodisation works for North America needs assessment. Judt notes in passing that 'the twentieth century taught rather different and altogether more optimistic lessons' to Americans.[60] And indeed, American historian Ann Douglas believes that the post-Second World War period in American history is best understood culturally as consisting of two eras, an optimistic period from 'roughly 1945 through the early 1960s' and a second period 'from the mid-1960s until the present', which she associates with assassinations, neocolonialism and a considerable decrease in optimism.[61] There are, it would seem, some interesting parallels between these international motivations to break from a periodisation that prioritises a postwar period and the new directions that Canadian historians are exploring. These avenues of exploration need to be encouraged and supported, for they reinforce just how fragile the postwar category is for historians.

The other prominent demarcation of convenience that provides infrastructure for English Canada's twentieth century is the 'decade'. The 1920s, for example, are touted as the 'decisive decade' in the history of Canadian consumerism, the 'first act' in the triumph of mass culture, and the key decade in the redefinition of English-Canadian nationalism.[62] The 1930s are at times a 'low dishonest

---

[58]   Hobsbawm, *Age of Extremes*; A. Marwick, *The Sixties: Cultural Revolution in Britain, France, Italy, and the United States, c.1958–c.1974* (Oxford, 1998), pp. 5, 8.

[59]   T. Judt, *Postwar: A History of Europe Since 1945* (New York, 2005), p. 2.

[60]   Judt, *Postwar*, p. 6. For students of postwar Canadian foreign policy Robert Bothwell points to 1984 as the key transition point. R. Bothwell, *Alliance and Illusion: Canada and the World, 1945–1984* (Vancouver, 2007), p. 393.

[61]   A. Douglas, 'Periodizing the American Century: Modernism, Postmodernism, and Post-colonialism in the Cold War Context', *Modernism/Modernity*, vol. 5, no. 3 (1998), p. 84.

[62]   C. Wright, '"Feminine Trifles of Vast Importance": Writing Gender into the History of Consumption', in Franca Iacovetta and Mariana Valverde (eds.), *Gender Conflicts: New Essays in Women's History* (Toronto, 1992), pp. 237, 239, 243; B.D. Palmer, *Working Class Experience: Rethinking the History of Canadian Labour, 1800–1991*, 2nd edition (Toronto, 1992), pp. 229–236; on nationalism in the 1920s see the work of Mary Vipond, including 'Canadian Nationalism and the Plight of Canadian Magazines in the 1920s', *Canadian Historical Review*, vol. 58, no. 1 (1977), pp. 43–63, and 'The Nationalist Network: English Canada's Intellectuals and Artists in the 1920s', *Canadian Review of Studies in Nationalism*, vol. 7, no. 1 (1980), pp. 32–52, and 'Nationalism and Nativism: The Natives Sons of Canada in the 1920s', *Canadian Review of Studies in Nationalism*, vol. 9, no. 1 (1982), pp. 81–95.

decade' for Canadian foreign policy,[63] and at others the 'dirty thirties' of the Depression.[64] The 1920s and 1930s even share pride of place as 'decades of discord'.[65] The 1950s are seen as a period of domesticity, sometimes equated with conformity and at other times as a period of calm or stability. The sixties, by contrast, represents a period of radical departure and counterculture.[66] And then there are histories written of Canada that take a decade by decade approach – often assigning specific characteristics to each ten-year period.[67] When, to quote Ferdinand Mount, 'did decaditis first strike? When did people begin to think that slicing the past up into periods of ten years was a useful thing to do?'[68] And what, we would add, are the ramifications of this lingering desire to periodise history in this way?

American historian Jason Scott Smith points out that the emergence of the decade as an acceptable, and influential, demarcation of time was itself a contingent product of history in the late 1920s and early 1930s. He argues that two key experiential factors contributed to the rise of the decade as a popular measure of time. One was the sense of nostalgia that emerged in the late nineteenth and early twentieth centuries as a response to the perceived acceleration of modern life. The other was 'the tremendous growth of a culture of "simultaneity".' Together they 'fueled the rise of periodising history by decades, as an ever-increasing sense of confusion and chaos wrought by the currents of modernity led not only to an increased need to understand the present, but also to a need to create historical narratives within which the present could be emplotted.'[69] These factors emerged gradually and became more noticeable following the

---

[63] Eayrs, '"A Low Dishonest Decade": Aspects of Canadian External Policy, 1931–1939'.

[64] Horn, *The Dirty Thirties*.

[65] Thompson and Seager, *Decades of Discord*.

[66] For example, Cyril Levitt notes, 'The child-bearing and child-rearing generation of the fifties was cautious and conformist'. See C. Levitt, *Children of Privilege: Student Revolt in the Sixties. A Study of Student Movements in Canada, the United States, and West Germany* (Toronto, 1984), p. 14. Doug Owram states that 'Ideological debate reasserted itself after the calm of the 1950s'. D. Owram, *Born at the Right Time: A History of the Baby-Boom Generation* (Toronto, 1996), p. 158. Alvin Finkel writes the following about the period from 1963 to 1980: 'State policies continued, for the most part, to pretend that the television "sitcom" model of the family was still prevalent in Canada, and little was done to help working families with childcare, or to aid single-parent and low-income families'. See *Our Lives*, p. 228.

[67] Forbes and Muise, *The Atlantic Provinces in Confederation*; Bothwell and Granatstein, *Our Century*; Kingwell, Moore and Borins, *Canada: Our Century*.

[68] F. Mount, 'The Doctrine of Unripe Time', *London Review of Books* vol. 28, no. 22 (16 Nov. 2006). www.lrb.co.uk/v28/n22/moun01_.html [accessed 8 Apr. 2007].

[69] J. S. Smith, 'The Strange History of the Decade: Modernity, Nostalgia, and the Perils of Periodization', *Journal of Social History*, vol. 32, no. 2 (1998), p. 267.

Great War.[70] As people born in the late nineteenth century came to correlate 'their life histories with the history of the twentieth century itself ... the formative experience of the Great War' reinforced 'an inclination to confuse personal and world history'.[71]

This inclination played a central role in fostering the idea of the decade by the early 1930s. And it was journalists such as Walter Lippmann and Frederick Allen Lewis who played a leading role in legitimising the decade as an acceptable measure of historical time. The 1920s, Smith explains, became the 'first decade truly to legitimate a ten-year span of time as a historic category'.[72] Writing in the 1930s, the influential Lippmann cast the 1920s as representing a shared experience of political lethargy, disillusionment and false hope.[73] For Lippman, as for many of his contemporaries, the arrival of the Great Depression helped to cement the notion of the 1920s as a historical period – one that quickly seemed to be a part of Americans' past rather than present.[74] The emergence of the decade as a common measure of historical time, then, was a product of a specific shared, though not necessarily universal, experience.

But what does decadal thinking mean for historical analysis? Smith makes the point – and we would argue that this holds true for Canada as well – that in the United States 'various trends are said to epitomize an entire decade'. As a result, he argues, 'the concept of the decade represents thinking about time in a punctuated, discontinuous manner. Discontinuous time encourages viewing history not as a seamless web of events, but as discrete, temporally fragmented snapshots.'[75] It does so by encouraging observers to contrast the events or trends of one decade with those of the decade before or after. Such an approach inhibits the examination of social and cultural change over a longer period of time and that, in turn, limits our ability to identify the persistence of social and cultural values.

As Smith notes, decadal analysis also prioritises generational theory. Starting in the late nineteenth century but coming to fruition in the 1920s, contemporaries redefined the meaning of generation, as Smith has nicely phrased it, from 'a

---

[70]   Smith, 'The Strange History of the Decade', pp. 267–8. In this way these were not strictly *post-war* phenomena.

[71]   Smith, 'The Strange History of the Decade', p. 268. For a fascinating analysis of personal and political narratives and their connection to oral history, see A. Portelli, 'The Death of Luigi Trastulli: Memory and the Event', in *The Death of Luigi Trastulli and Other Stories: Form and Meaning in Oral History* (Albany, 2001), p. 1–26.

[72]   Smith, 'The Strange History of the Decade', p. 269.

[73]   Smith, 'The Strange History of the Decade', p. 270–1.

[74]   *Ibid.*, pp. 270, 276.

[75]   *Ibid.*, p. 263.

duration of time' to 'a category of culturally shared experience'.[76] This shared experience, however, has been that of the young, or what Robert Wohl called 'the ideology of youth'.[77] Thus decades have been epitomised not just by a particular trend, but by a particular youth generation. Both contemporaries and later social scientists combined these concepts, resulting in popular categories such as the 'lost' generation of the 1920s, the 'greatest' generation of the 1940s, the 'silent' generation of the 1950s, and the 'baby boom' generation of the 1960s. This focus on youth again steers historians away from long-term trends.

Just as a decadal approach tends to emphasise one particular trend at the expense of others, so the association of a decade with a particular youth generation glosses over the experience of both older individuals and those youth who don't fit the generational trope in question. The decade of the 1960s serves as a useful example.[78] Historians have described 'the Sixties Generation' as a large group of youth united by their reaction against an older generation and through the common experience of new ideas and social mores encompassed in the New Left and the counterculture.[79] Such an interpretation ignores not only the divisions that existed within this generation but also the fact that older individuals accepted, encouraged and sustained the protest and ideals of 'the Sixties Generation'.[80]

[76] *Ibid.*, p. 271. For an analysis of this process see K. Mannheim, 'The Problem of Generations', in Paul Kecskemeti (ed.), *Essays on the Sociology of Knowledge* (London, 1952), pp. 276–322 and R. Wohl, *The Generation of 1914* (Cambridge, 1979). For the literature on generation as applied to the Canadian context see C. Comacchio, *The Dominion of Youth: Adolescence and the Making of Modern Canada, 1920–1950* (Waterloo, 2006), introduction.

[77] Wohl, *The Generation of 1914*, pp. 2–3, 204; Smith, 'The Strange History of the Decade', p. 276.

[78] On the difficulties involved in periodising the sixties, see Anastakis, 'Introduction,' in Anastakis (ed), *The Sixties*, pp. 3–4.

[79] Owram, *Born at the Right Time*, Preface, Chapters 8 and 9; Levitt, *Children of Privilege: Student Revolt in the Sixties*, p. 13; M. Kostash, *Long Way From Home: The Story of the Sixties Generation in Canada* (Toronto, 1980), p. xvii. Owram acknowledges that large numbers of youth were indifferent or opposed to the radicalism and counter-culture of the 1960s. However, these groups' lived reality remains unexplored. For a critique of Owram's use of the concept of generation see R. Wright, 'Historical Underdosing: Pop Demography and the Crisis in Canadian History', *Canadian Historical Review*, vol. 81, no. 4 (2000), pp. 663–5. Berton, *1967*, chapter 4, assumes the existence of a generation gap. For the prominence in the American literature of 'a' seemingly united 1960s youth generation, see R.E. Klatch, *A Generation Divided: The New Left, the New Right, and the 1960s* (Berkeley, 1999), p. 4.

[80] Catherine Gidney makes this argument in 'War and the Concept of Generation: The International Teach-Ins at the University of Toronto, 1965–1968', in Stortz and Panayotidis (eds.), *Universities and War*. On intergenerational cooperation in Quebec see François Ricard, *The Lyric Generation: The Life and Times of the Baby Boomers*, trans. by D. Winkler (Toronto, 1994), pp. 81–2. For the co-existence of different political generations within the women's movement see N. Adamson, 'Feminists, Libbers, Lefties, and Radicals: The Emergence of the Women's Liberation Movement', in J. Parr (ed.), *A Diversity of Women* (Toronto, 1995), pp. 253–6, 271–2.

One specific example highlights the limitations of the current 'generational' approach.[81] From 1965 to 1968 faculty and students at the University of Toronto, supported by the administration, annually hosted an International Teach-In. These events stemmed directly from the first American teach-ins held in spring 1965 to protest heightened involvement in Vietnam. Initiated in October 1965 by Charles Hanly, professor of philosophy at the University of Toronto, the teach-in was organised by both students and faculty.[82] And in examining the organising of the events, as well as reaction to them, what becomes clear is a significant degree of both *inter*generational cooperation and *intra*generational division. In 1965, for example, 70 per cent of the organising committee was over thirty, a rate that rose to 75 per cent with the inclusion of the honorary board. Students, of course, composed the bulk of the audience. Yet they did not hold a unitary view of the teach-in. Some condemned the teach-ins for failing to present the issue in an unbiased manner while others attempted to turn the aims of the forum from education to protest. Faculty, too, were split. Some were prime organisers of the teach-in; others reinforced the view of inter-generational conflict by condemning the event; still others agreed with students on the need for protest. Moreover, key administrators supported the events. In his memoirs, Claude Bissell, President of the University of Toronto in the late 1960s, wrote that 'those of us who worked on the Teach-In had a sense of buoyant satisfaction. We had, so we believed, harnessed the energies of the university in the course of general enlightenment.' Bissell went on to note his satisfaction that a 'potentially disruptive technique' had been turned to academic purpose.[83] The growing view that protest had been submerged into education would, in part, lead to declining interest in the teach-ins by 1968. These events, however, indicate a degree of intergenerational cooperation as well as intragenerational division that has so far been overlooked when English-Canadian historians consider the social and cultural developments of the late 1960s and early 1970s. Our telescopic focus on youth prevents us from seeing connections beyond specific decades and thus longer-term trends.

[81]   The arguments that follow are made at greater length by Gidney in 'War and the Concept of Generation'.

[82]   The topics included 'Revolution and Response', focusing mainly on Vietnam, 'China: Coexistence or Containment', 'Religion and International Affairs', and 'Exploding Humanity: The Crisis in Numbers'.

[83]   C. Bissell, *Halfway Up Parnassus: A Personal Account of the University of Toronto, 1932–71* (Toronto, 1974), p. 125.

Periodising Persistence: Bridging the Nineteenth and Twentieth Centuries

These smaller units – postwar eras and decades – are the building blocks for historians' accounts of the twentieth century. They essentially give the category of the 'twentieth century' a reassuring coherence. And yet just as international historians have criticised these smaller units, so too have they interrogated the usefulness of the larger unit, the century. Indeed, the longevity of the century as a convenient method of periodisation is quite surprising given the ferocity with which it has been attacked. Marc Bloch, for example, railed against the century as wholly arbitrary, irrational and 'insidious'.[84] Centuries, he argued, were no more useful for periodisation than were eras based on the reign of a particular monarch. Both approaches, he emphasised, prioritise convenience over observation. Here is Bloch at his rhetorical best: 'A religious history of the reign of Phillip Augustus? An economic history of the reign of Louis XV? Why not: "Journal of what happened in my laboratory during the second presidency of Grévy," by Louis Pasteur? Or, inversely: "Diplomatic history of Europe from Newton to Einstein"'.[85]

Rather than periodising history by centuries, Bloch encouraged historians to 'look to the phenomena themselves for their proper periods'.[86] D.H. Fischer similarly dismissed the use of centuries by historians and used the term 'hecto-history' to ridicule the assumption that years ending with '00' necessarily serve as important dividing points in history.[87] More recently, Charles Maier has argued that the problematic nature of centuries as measurements of historical time can be seen in the manner in which academic historians struggle to employ them. 'When cited by historians', he explains, 'centuries are like Procrutes' famous bed: the Greek innkeeper either stretched his guests if they were too short or chopped them down if they were too long for the sleeping accommodations that were offered.' Hence, historians have given us the 'long nineteenth century' and, more recently, the 'short twentieth century'.[88] English-Canadian historians, we note, have frequently adopted this approach, with the Great War acting as a key dividing point.

In place of the twentieth century, Maier has championed the notion of territoriality and argued for the unity of the period from roughly the 1840s to the 1960s. Such a period, he suggests, provides the most meaningful framework for

---

[84] M. Bloch, *The Historian's Craft*, trans. P. Putnam (New York, 1953), p. 181.

[85] Bloch, *The Historian's Craft*, p. 183.

[86] Bloch, *The Historian's Craft*, p. 183.

[87] Quoted in Shrodt, 'Problems of Periodization in Canadian Sport History', p. 65.

[88] Maier, 'Consigning the Twentieth Century to History', p. 813.

documenting and contextualising the history of nation states and their relationship to both the once dominant centripetal forces of national economies and
identities and the ascendant centrifugal forces of globalisation and transnational
identities. Within English-Canadian historiography there is no direct equivalent
to Maier's polemic on twentieth-century periodisation. However, it is undoubtedly significant that the two main attempts to rethink Canadian history in recent
years have challenged, at least implicitly, the unity of the twentieth century by
highlighting its links to the nineteenth century. Indeed, both Ian McKay's
'Liberal Order Framework' and Gerald Friesen's *Citizens and Nation* employ a
periodisation quite similar to Maier's framework for territoriality.

For Ian McKay, Canada is best understood as a project of liberal rule that was
initiated in the late 1830s and early 1840s and consolidated though the *process* of
Confederation between the 1860s and 1890s. Never fully secured, the liberal
order was reconfigured in the early decades of the twentieth century to embrace
a 'new liberalism' that allowed for a more organic conception of society and
pacified external challenges to the social and political order. This 'new democracy', McKay argues, remained ascendant until the 1970s when 'classical liberal
individualism' re-emerged in the form of neo-conservatism.[89] Gerald Friesen
offers an interpretive framework for a much longer period. Drawing upon
insights from communications theory and cultural history, Friesen uses the
stories of a handful of ordinary people to illustrate how their lives were historically structured by four different forms of communication: oral-traditional,
textual-settler, print-capitalism and screen capitalism, which he relates roughly to
the cultures of Aboriginal peoples, European arrival to the 1840s, the 1840s to
the 1960s, and the 1960s to the present. In this manner, Friesen uses individual
stories to illustrate the way in which citizenship and nationality are constructed,
and how 'Canada' as a public identity was forged.[90] Tellingly, his third epoch,
like McKay's liberal order framework, bridges the nineteenth and twentieth centuries. Neither McKay's Gramscian-informed neo-Marxist history of liberalism
nor Friesen's history of ordinary Canadians' relationship with communications
technologies relies upon the twentieth century or its supporting infrastructure of
convenient demarcations to frame their arguments. And that, in part, is why
these studies are so innovative.

But there is still much work to be done. Our reliance on postwar periods and
decadal divisions hinders our ability to more fully understand long-term social and

[89]   I. McKay, 'The Liberal Order Framework: A Prospectus for a Reconnaissance of Canadian
History', *Canadian Historical Review*, vol. 81, no. 4 (2000), pp. 617–645.
[90]   G. Friesen, *Citizens and Nation: An Essay on History, Communication, and Canada* (Toronto, 2000).
H.V. Nelles employs a slightly shorter period, 1840–1939, in his *A Little History of Canada* (Don
Mills, Ontario, 2004), p. vii.

cultural patterns. Liberating ourselves from these demarcations of convenience, as we noted earlier, can certainly provide a more accurate understanding of specific short-term developments. But it also would allow us to challenge the comfortable unity of the twentieth century itself as a historical category. And this, in turn, would allow us to pay greater attention to the *persistence* of ideas and values from the nineteenth century well into the twentieth century. Until very recently, for example, historians have ignored the fact that both Protestantism and sympathy for the British connection remained influential well beyond the nineteenth century.[91] In part this is certainly due to historians' political interests and ideological background. Our priorities have been elsewhere: with so many groups excluded as subjects of Canadian history until the 1970s, social historians understandably chose to prioritise their histories rather than those of people more closely connected with traditional centres of power. But our ongoing neglect of these two cultural influences is also, we believe, a product of a 'twentieth century' gaze that is shaped by the postwar periods and decadal divisions and that looks forward from the Great War anticipating change and modernisation while vastly underestimating the persistent cultural inheritance of the nineteenth century.

The few studies documenting the continuing resonance of Protestantism in English Canada buck this trend and offer tangible evidence of cultural influences bridging the nineteenth and twentieth centuries. In her examination of religious discourses on the family, for example, Nancy Christie reformulates the traditional periodisation of Christianity's role in the emergence of the individualist private family. She notes that 'the now standard interpretation of the nineteenth century ... is that it was an era characterized by the rise of the affectional, individualistic family, the ideal of companionate marriage, which emphasized equality between the sexes but in which there were increasingly rigid boundaries between male and female spheres.' This transformation is said to have 'occurred as a result of the expansion of capitalism and the market economy', forged 'by an emerging evangelical middle class'.[92] Christie points to a different configuration of the family within religious discourse. Indeed, among other things, she argues that the family of the nineteenth and early twentieth centuries is better categorised not as an institution that emphasised separate spheres but one that embraced patriarchal domesticity. The ideal of the modern private family, she argues, was articulated, at least by church leaders, not in the nineteenth but in the second half of the twentieth century.[93]

---

[91] One can study these subjects independently, but they are, of course, significantly related.

[92] N. Christie, 'Introduction: Family, Community, and the Rise of Liberal Society', in *Households of Faith*, p. 4.

[93] N. Christie, 'Conclusion: "Patriarchal Piety" and Canada's Liberal Tradition', in *Households of Faith*, pp. 377–81.

While Christie looks at the continuing inheritance of evangelicalism well into the twentieth century, Gary Miedema has taken as his starting point the religious discourse of the 1967 Centennial celebrations. He illustrates the way in which the celebrations point to a new vision of Canada – one that was still substantially Christian but that was beginning to acknowledge religious pluralism, something, he argues, that was 'one of the most significant adjustments in understandings of Canada in the history of the nation'.[94] Yet Miedema also illustrates the continued privileging, even in the 1960s, of the main Christian faiths, as was evident in CBC programming, prime ministers' speeches, the teaching of Christianity in the school system and, perhaps most revealing, the denial of citizenship on the grounds of atheism. An influential Christian Canada was still evident in the 1950s and 1960s, even as its privileged place was already being dismantled, the result of a number of factors, including a more interventionist state, a more diverse society, and changes in public opinion.[95]

The argument for the persistence of Protestant ideals is also key to the work of Catherine Gidney. Starting with the well-established premise of the Protestant nature of many English-Canadian universities in the late nineteenth century, Gidney focuses on a number of denominational and provincial institutions showing that the values and ideals of Protestantism continued to shape university culture into the 1960s. While other historians have focused on the increasing impact within early twentieth century universities of the social sciences and the rise of expertise, and their secularising influence, Gidney examines the public presence of Protestantism through presidents' pronouncements, the moral regulation of residence and campus life, and the prominent place of religious clubs as well as university Christian missions. She argues that even into the second half of the twentieth century a Protestant moral culture pervaded many campuses. Only in the 1950s and 1960s was Protestant hegemony eroded by a number of factors including a loosening of social mores, a more religiously diverse student body, and the ascent of the multiversity.[96]

Neither the limited focus on a particular decade or postwar period, nor the assumption that Protestantism survived only in fits and starts into the twentieth century can explain away such findings. What is required is a reorientation of our gaze away from the internal infrastructure of the historians' twentieth century and its short-term approach to periodisation. In its place we need to embrace a long-term approach that encourages historians to look beyond demarcations of convenience and focus instead on the 'bigger picture'. Only in this

94   Miedema, *For Canada's Sake*, p. xv.
95   Miedema, *For Canada's Sake*, pp. xv, 16–17, 25–30.
96   Gidney, *A Long Eclipse*.

way will we begin to understand the ebb and flow of Protestantism's cultural influence and its significance for Canada during the twentieth century.

A similar case can be made regarding our tendency to downplay and even ignore persistent popular support for Canada's British connection well into the twentieth century. The campaign to acknowledge the persistence of this connection has been waged most extensively by Phillip Buckner, although his consistent calls for historians to take this topic seriously are only slowly bearing fruit.[97] Led by the pioneering work of Carl Berger and Mary Vipond, Canadian historians have generally concluded that while English-Canadian nationalism and British imperialism were easily reconciled in the minds of English Canadians during the late nineteenth century, these two strands of identity began to unwind in the aftermath of the Great War. Examinations of Canada's relationship with Britain after the 1920s have been primarily restricted to the fields of diplomatic and political history. Hence, at the level of popular and political culture, we are left with the comforting but unsubstantiated impression that English Canada's British connection had disappeared by 1930. Like Protestantism, Canada's British connection generally remains on the outside looking in when it comes to twentieth-century historiography.

In his most recent statement on the topic Buckner has traced what he terms English Canada's 'long goodbye' to the British world. And in doing so he makes a strong case for a long-term view of English-Canada's British connection that bridges the nineteenth and twentieth centuries and that acknowledges the impact of the two world wars while emphasising the persistence of pro-British sympathies. He also eschews the decadal focus on generation and youth by noting that while the organisations that most vociferously supported an imperial connection in the 1950s and 1960s had difficulty drawing in new and younger members, their enthusiastic support for the empire was no less genuine and was, perhaps, more influential than we have so far imagined. Indeed, many of these members undoubtedly made up part of the 'establishment' that some Canadian youth found so objectionable.[98]

Slowly but surely, a small body of work is emerging to challenge the assumption that the 1920s witnessed an irreversible shift away from the British connection. For example, studies of English–Canadian cultural critics during the 1950s

[97] P. Buckner, 'Whatever Happened to the British Empire?' *Journal of the Canadian Historical Association*, N.S. vol. 4 (1993), pp. 3–32 and Buckner, 'Was there a "British" Empire? *The Oxford History of the British Empire* from a Canadian Perspective', *Acadiensis*, vol. 32, no. 1 (2002), pp. 110-128. Andrew Smith and Adele Perry offer more optimistic evaluations of the extent to which such an approach is being adopted. See their contributions to this volume.

[98] P. Buckner, 'The Long Goodbye: English Canadians and the British World', in P. Buckner and R. D. Francis (eds.), *Rediscovering the British World* (Calgary, 2005), pp. 181–207.

and 1960s have identified a strong presence of Anglophilia in their pronouncements, while Jonathan Vance's important work on public memory has called
into question the assumption that the Great War forced Canadians to question
their prewar allegiance to Britain.[99] In addition, Michael Dawson's study of the
changing popular imagery of Canada's Mounted Police demonstrates that it was
only in the late 1960s and early 1970s that the RCMP deemed it necessary to
jettison the cultural baggage of its Victorian and imperial imagery in favour of a
more politically correct and inclusive multicultural image. His more recent study
of the 1954 British Empire Games highlights the extent to which imperial sentiment was contested but also effectively reconciled with a wide range of competing political discourses.[100] Similarly, contributors to the edited collection
Canada and the End of Empire provide a number of suggestive case studies that
point to the persistence of popular support for maintaining imperial ties.[101]
Together these case studies suggest that English Canada's British connection persisted into the late 1950s and early 1960s but deteriorated very quickly thereafter.
And yet as one contributor to that collection notes, 'What historians are only
beginning to explain is *how and why* the prestige and attractiveness of symbols
connected to Britain and the empire deteriorated so rapidly'.[102] To answer these
questions a long-term view is required.

It is, perhaps, fitting that Buckner, a 'nineteenth century' historian, is the first
to tentatively map out a long-term analysis of the British connection for the
twentieth century. Our current twentieth-century focus works against such an
approach because it overestimates the ease and speed with which cultural influences such as Protestantism and the British connection lost their pride of place
among English Canadians. Rather than declining precipitously in the wake of
the Great War, these influences continued to shape English-Canadian society

---

[99]   P. Massolin, *Canadian Intellectuals, the Tory Tradition, and the Challenge of Modernity, 1939–1970*
(Toronto, 2001); L.B. Kuffert, *A Great Duty: Canadian Responses to Modern Life and Mass Culture,
1939–1967* (Montreal and Kingston, 2003); J. Vance, *Death So Noble: Memory, Meaning, and the First
World War* (Vancouver, 1997).

[100]   M. Dawson, *The Mountie from Dime Novel to Disney* (Toronto, 1998) — an unfortunate example of cultural history that assumes the demise of Protestantism by the 1920s without engaging
directly with the literature on the subject; Dawson, 'Acting Global, Thinking Local: "Liquid
Imperialism" and the Multiple Meanings of the 1954 British Empire & Commonwealth Games', *The
International Journal of the History of Sport*, vol. 23, no. 1 (2006), pp. 3–27.

[101]   P. Buckner (ed.), *Canada and the End of Empire* (Vancouver, 2005). See also J.E. Igartua, *The
Other Quiet Revolution: National Identities in English Canada, 1945–1971* (Vancouver, 2006) and C.P.
Champion, 'A Very British Coup: Canadianism, Quebec, and Ethnicity in the Flag Debate,
1964–1965', *Journal of Canadian Studies*, vol. 40, no. 3 (2006), pp. 68–99.

[102]   G.A. Johnson, 'The Last Gasp of Empire: The 1964 Flag Debate Revisited', in *Canada and the
End of Empire*, p. 247 (emphasis added).

well into the twentieth century, and their eventual marginalisation was a complicated, and at times conflicted, process. Although they are still necessary, short-term studies of a particular decade or postwar era cannot properly contextualise or illuminate long-term social and cultural change. Researching and writing across traditional temporal boundaries will help to reveal different and equally important historical patterns.

Conclusions

Different research questions require different periodisation schemes, and one must always ask that self-interrogating question: periodisation to what end? What is a logical period or turning point for the history of X may not make sense for a scholar of Y. But given our temporal and topical interests in social and cultural history we think the case for a long-term view – one that frees us from the arbitrary notion of the century and its accompanying infrastructure of postwar periods and decadal divisions – is a worthwhile starting point for a conversation about how and why we periodise Canadian history.

Our current approach to the history of the twentieth century discourages a long-term view that would allow for connections to be drawn between the nineteenth and twentieth centuries. It is as if in our historical unconscious the Great War marks the end of the long nineteenth century and the beginning of the short twentieth century, which, in turn, is neatly divided in half by the Second World War. Within these two postwar periods exist generations as actors soaking up the limelight upon a series of ten-year long stages. There was no great conspiracy to make this so. We do not anticipate uncovering a secret manifesto of the twentieth century in a university archives one day that would allow us to accurately, if in hushed tones, announce 'J'accuse!' The periodisation of Canada's twentieth century emerged piecemeal and largely without debate or discussion. And *that* is why it should be debated and discussed.

Whatever the cause, our understanding of twentieth-century Canada has become strangely disconnected from important themes and developments that are safely assumed to be central to nineteenth-century Canada, but deemed largely passé for the twentieth. Religion and the influence of a British connection are two issues that we have mentioned here, but there are others: rural life, for example. A long-term view which bridges the island-like demarcations that provide the infrastructure for the current approach to the twentieth century allows for a thorough examination of social and cultural continuities between the late nineteenth century and the second half of the twentieth century. And, in doing so, it would allow for a more complex and accurate analysis of

twentieth-century Canada. As Jocelyn Létourneau reminds us, 'Il semble diffi-
cile de sortir des périodisations qui se sont, avec le temps, cristallisées sous la
forme d'axiomatiques historiques et narratives, mémorielles et identitaires'.[103]
But breaking free from comfortable and convenient reference points will help us
to ask new and challenging questions about Canadian history. And that, in turn,
will undoubtedly take us in unexpected, productive and exciting directions.

[103] Létourneau, 'Le Temps du lieu raconté', p. 159.

Chapter 4
Canadian Progress and the British Connection: Why Canadian Historians Seeking the Middle Road Should Give 2½ Cheers for the British Empire

Andrew Smith

On a visit to London in July 2006, Prime Minister Stephen Harper extolled the positive aspects of British imperialism and declared that the 'actions of the British Empire' in Canada 'were largely benign and occasionally brilliant'. Conceding that no part of the world has been unscarred by the 'excesses of empires', he suggested that we discard the currently fashionable view that 'colonialism' was inherently bad. In his speech, Harper traced many features of Canadian society back to Britain. These included a belief in private enterprise, a relatively humane Aboriginal policy and a glorious military heritage that has often involved close cooperation with our American 'cousins'.[1]

Although they came from a politician rather than an academic, Harper's comments help to frame the scholarly debates surveyed in this chapter and to show their political significance. Some academics suggest that the British impact on Canada was generally negative and perhaps something of which British people and their descendents should feel ashamed. Another perspective stresses the positive and calls on us to reject what one Australian historian has labelled the 'black armband' view of the colonial past.[2] My own view is that Harper's view of British imperialism is closer to the truth than the opinions voiced by many Canadian historians. British imperialism brought significant benefits to Canada which are sometimes obscured by the tendency of Canadian historians to focus on the negative aspects of their nation's history. By most statistical measures, Canada is one of the world's most successful countries.[3] It is possible to dismiss

[1] 'Address by the Prime Minister at the Canada–UK Chamber of Commerce', Prime Minister's Office Listserv, 14 July 2006. I would like to thank David Cannadine, Ged Martin, and J. Andrew Ross for their comments on earlier drafts of this paper.

[2] G. Blainey, 'Drawing Up a Balance Sheet of Our History', *Quadrant*, vol. 37, no.7–8 (1993), pp. 10–15.

[3] Canada has the sixth highest entry on the Human Development Index. See United Nations Development Programme, *2006 Human Development Report* (New York, 2006).

statistical indicators such as the Human Development Index as value-laden and culturally specific. Perhaps many Canadian historians will incline to this view. But the ability of Canada to attract immigrants of varied cultural backgrounds suggests that these rankings of countries do indeed reflect reality. In a sense, everyone who gets on a plane to immigrate to Canada or Australia is voting with their feet in favour of nineteenth-century British imperialism.

Understanding how Canada became a success story ought to be a major research focus of the Canadian historical profession. For reasons that include an understandable desire to document their country's shortcomings, Canadian historians have neglected the important task of explaining the reasons for Canada's relative success. Although there is plenty of room to debate the relative importance of other factors, any credible explanation for Canada's success must acknowledge the significant role played by Britain. The great unwritten work of Canadian history is entitled: 'How a land with severe winters became a prosperous and stable G7 country'. If such a book were ever written, it is probable that Britain and its institutions would feature prominently in the first few chapters. This chapter will survey several frameworks for understanding the history of the British Empire and will suggest that Canadian historians can draw on these theories to help explain Canada's achievements.

Much is at stake in the scholarly debate on how we should view Britain's role in Canadian history. Whether we regard the British legacy in Canada as largely positive or largely negative has implications that extend far beyond the comparatively trivial question of whether to retain Canada's current head of state. At issue are our conceptions of social and economic progress, our views of Canada's place in a globalised world and our understandings of the nature of empire. By 'empire', I refer not merely to the British Empire or to the American Empire, but to empire as a generic concept that includes any globe-spanning system of power, trade and allegiance.

This chapter seeks to defend the basic idea that Britain's impact on Canada was largely positive while showing that there are several possible intellectual routes by which one can arrive at this position. It also argues that if Canadian historians are to arrive at a balanced view of the impact of British imperialism, they will need to reconnect with political and economic theory. The chapter begins with an assessment of the recent scholarship on Canada and the British World. It argues that Canadian historians need to engage with the various interpretive frameworks for understanding empire's legacies that have recently been advanced by social scientists. The available frameworks range from Marxian world-systems theory to the New Institutional Economics to the latest ways of thinking about economic culture. No single interpretive framework can fully describe the Anglo-Canadian connection. However, if taken together, these competing frameworks can guide future research on Britain's relationship with the lands that became Canada. The makers of these overarching theories would also benefit from engagement by Canadian historians because Canada's past provides a vast amount of empirical data for testing, refining and, if necessary, falsifying general statements about the nature of imperialism.

Assessing the impact of British imperialism in Canada requires us to think about two separate but related issues. First, we need to consider the ways in which British imperialism contributed to the emergence of the Canadian nation-state (the obvious counterfactual alternative being absorption into the United States). Luckily, military and political historians have written extensively on such topics as the War of 1812 and the Alaska boundary dispute. Indeed, the British Empire is central to the major meta-narratives in Canadian constitutional and diplomatic history (e.g., colony to nation, empire to umpire).[4] Anyone remotely familiar with Canadian political and military history knows that Britain played a crucial role in laying the foundations of a separate nation on the northern half of the North American continent. The second, and perhaps more interesting, set of questions relates to the internal life of the polity that was cobbled together in the nineteenth century from what remained of Britain's North American Empire. Unfortunately, the impact of the British connection on the evolution of Canadian society has been the object of much less study. Perhaps this is because the rise of social history after 1970 coincided with a decreasing level of interest in the role of Britain in Canadian history.

Saying that the British Empire had a positive impact on Canada is understandably controversial. Today, few would try to justify the dispossession of indigenous peoples by land-hungry settlers. Recent comparative histories have underscored the fact that the experiences of Canadian First Nations were part of a global pattern of oppression by the British that manifested itself on other continents, including Australia.[5] Moreover, the British and their descendents mistreated people of other European ethnicities (the Acadian deportation comes to mind). Indeed, we are increasingly aware of the costs that empire imposed even on Canadians of British descent. Today, few would suggest that Canada's national interest was at stake in the First World War or that the sending of Canadian conscripts to the trenches of Flanders was one of the country's proudest moments. Nevertheless, all of these negatives need to be weighed against the many good things that Britain did for Canada.

---

[4] N. Hillmer and J.L. Granatstein, *Empire to Umpire: Canada and the World to the 1990s* (Toronto, 1994).

[5] K.S. Coates, *A Global History of Indigenous Peoples: Struggle and Survival* (London, 2004); J.C. Weaver, *The Great Land Rush and the Making of the Modern World, 1650–1900* (Kingston, 2003).

The Historiography of Canada and the British World: Strengths and Limitations

Evaluating the thesis that the British Empire laid the foundations for Canada's subsequent success is complicated by the many lacunae in the historiography. These lacunae are a function of the fact most historians lost interest in the imperial dimensions of Canadian history around 1960. In his 1993 presidential lecture to the Canadian Historical Association, Phillip Buckner bemoaned the estrangement of Canadian history from British imperial history. Buckner condemned the fact that Canada had largely disappeared from the historical writing in Britain on the history of empire. Whereas the constitutional evolution of Canada and the other colonies of settlement had once dominated historical writing on the British Empire, the 1960s and 1970s had witnessed a shift in focus to the British imperial experience in Africa and India.[6] Buckner called for Canada to be reintegrated into the story as told in Britain. At the same time, he appealed to Canadian historians 'to place the imperial experience back where it belongs, at the centre of nineteenth-century Canadian history'. Buckner was not calling for a return to the days when constitutional history was king, but he was asking historians to investigate Britain's manifold impact on Canada's politics, economy and society.[7]

Buckner's remarks came after several decades in which the British role in Canadian history had been largely ignored. The most obvious reason for the de-emphasis of the British connection by historians was English Canada's redefinition of itself after 1945. During the formative years of the Baby Boom generation, Canada shed many symbols of its British heritage, including the Red Ensign.[8] The increasing irrelevance of Britain to Canada was especially pronounced in the economic sphere: after 1963, the British option ceased to be seriously considered by Canadian policymakers seeking to limit trade dependence on the United States.[9] The lack of interest in Britain's role in Canadian history was also a function of the shifting interests of historians. During the

---

[6]   One imperial historian who swam against this current was Ged Martin at the University of Edinburgh.

[7]   Later printed in P.A. Buckner, 'Whatever Happened to the British Empire?' *Journal of the Canadian Historical Association*, vol. 3, no. 1 (1993), pp. 3–32.

[8]   J.E. Igartua, *The Other Quiet Revolution: National Identities in English Canada, 1945–71* (Vancouver, 2006).

[9]   B.W. Muirhead, *The Development of Postwar Canadian Trade Policy: the Failure of the Anglo-European Option* (Kingston, 1992), pp. 163–177. Perhaps the academic debate over the precise causes of British economic decline that raged in this period made it difficult for historians to envision the days of British economic supremacy. D. Edgerton, 'The Decline of Declinism', *Business History Review*, vol. 71, no.2 (1997), pp. 201–6.

heyday of narrative political history, debates about the nature of the British impact on Canada had preoccupied Canadian historians, as Anglophile scholars[10] clashed with those who stressed the need for Canadian autonomy from Britain.[11] Because they eschewed broad narratives, the newer forms of history that came to the fore in the 1970s and 1980s (e.g., women's history, gay history, labour history) refrained from making broad 'macro' statements about the British impact on Canada, although they illuminated particular facets of this topic (e.g., the social history of British sailors in Canadian ports).[12] Similarly, while the 'cliometric revolution' in Canadian economic history illuminated particular aspects of the Anglo-Canadian relationship, it did not produce any grand statements about whether Canada's close association with Britain fostered or hindered Canada's overall economic development.[13]

One historian who ventured to make general statements was Jack Granatstein. In 1988, he argued that Britain's economic decline in the twentieth century made Canada's drift into the American sphere virtually inevitable. His aim was to defend the conduct of the Liberal governments that had presided over Canada's deeper integration into the continental economy after 1945. Granatstein, however, did not grapple with the question of how this diplomatic reorientation influenced the internal life of the country.[14] He might have looked at questions of business culture, secularisation and social policy. Indeed, aside from the First Nations historians who argued that European colonialism was immoral and unjustified,[15] few historians after 1970 made broad generalisations about the British impact on Canadian society. Quebec academic historians de-emphasised the Conquest by stressing that French Canada was a 'normal' western society. As a result, the British impact on French Canada's social structure, a topic once debated vigorously by historians of eighteenth-century Canada, became less central.[16]

[10]   D. Creighton, *The Forked Road: Canada, 1939–1957* (Toronto, 1976); W.L. Morton, *The Kingdom of Canada* (Toronto, 1963).

[11]   A.R.M. Lower, *Colony to Nation: a History of Canada* (Toronto, 1946); R.D. Francis, 'Historical perspective on Britain: the ideas of Canadian historians Frank H. Underhill and Arthur R.M. Lower', in P. Buckner and R.D. Francis (eds.), *Canada and the British World: Culture, Migration and Identity* (Vancouver, 2006), pp. 309–21.

[12]   J. Fingard, *Jack in Port: Sailortowns of Eastern Canada* (Toronto, 1982).

[13]   Perhaps this is because cliometric economic history was focused on points of detail, such as charting the annual fluctuations in Canada's balance of payments. The field of economic history was revolutionised in the 1960s, when the older qualitative approach was supplanted by a much more quantitative approach known as cliometrics. T.J.O. Dick and J.E. Floyd, *Canada and the Gold Standard: Balance-of-Payments Adjustment, 1871–1913* (Cambridge, 1992).

[14]   J.L. Granatstein, *How Britain's Weakness Forced Canada into the Arms of the United States* (Toronto, 1989).

[15]   K.S. Coates, *A Global History of Indigenous Peoples: Struggle and Survival* (London, 2004).

[16]   R. Rudin, *Making History in Twentieth-Century Quebec* (Toronto, 1997), pp. 171–218.

But since 1993, historians on both sides of the Atlantic appear to have heeded Buckner's call to action. The British World conferences have helped to refocus attention on the comparative histories of the so-called 'White Dominions'.[17] The Canadian experience figures prominently in a recent study of the development of the 'imperial press system' by Simon J. Potter, a historian based in Ireland.[18] David Cannadine considers Canada in his examination of British attempts to replicate parts of their class system in the settlement colonies.[19] Canada and the other self-governing colonies are emphasised in Andrew Thompson's study of the empire's impact on British society.[20] Bernard Porter has argued that ordinary Britons interacted mainly with the colonies of settlement and the United States, rather than with Britain's tropical empire. Porter thereby critiques the recent generation of British imperial historians who have focused on the tropical empire as the key to understanding the emergence of Britain's national identity.[21] He also targets postcolonialist historians such as Catherine Hall as particularly prone to exaggerate the importance of the non-white empire to the British.[22]

British imperial historians' re-engagement with Canada has been mirrored by developments within the Canadian historical community. Carman Miller's work on Canada and the Boer War has helped to revive interest in Canadian imperialism.[23] The evolution of Canada's honours system has also received attention from Christopher McCreery and others.[24] The older literature on Canadian imperialism ignored the topic of gender.[25] This lacuna has been remedied by

---

[17]   Buckner and Francis (eds.), *Canada and the British World*.

[18]   S.J. Potter, *News and the British World: the Emergence of an Imperial Press System, 1876–1922* (Oxford, 2003), p. 121.

[19]   D. Cannadine, *Ornamentalism: How the British saw their Empire* (Oxford, 2001).

[20]   A. Thompson, *The Empire Strikes Back: the Impact of Imperialism on Britain from the mid-Nineteenth Century* (London, 2005), p. 3.

[21]   B. Porter, *The Absent-Minded Imperialists: Empire, Society, and Culture in Britain* (Oxford, 2004), pp. 70–2.

[22]   C. Hall, K. McClelland and J. Rendall, *Defining the Victorian Nation: Class, Race, Gender and the British Reform Act of 1867* (Cambridge, 2000); C. Hall, *Civilising Subjects: Metropole and Colony in the English imagination, 1830–1867* (Cambridge, 2002); B. Ashcraft, G. Griffiths and H. Tiffin, *Post-Colonial Studies: the Key Concepts* (London, 2000).

[23]   Carman Miller, *Painting the Map Red: Canada and the South African War, 1899–1902* (Kingston, 1993).

[24]   C. McCreery, *The Canadian Honours System* (Toronto, 2005); J. Andrew Ross, 'All this Fuss and Feathers: Plutocrats, Politicians and Changing Canadian Attitudes to Titular Honours', in Colin Coates (ed.), *Majesty in Canada: Essays on the Role of Royalty* (Toronto, 2006), pp. 119–41.

[25]   C. Berger, *The Sense of Power: Studies in the Ideas of Canadian Imperialism, 1867–1914* (Toronto, 1970); H.B. Neatby, 'Laurier and Imperialism', in H. Blair Neatby (ed.), *Imperial Relations in the Age of Laurier* (Toronto, 1969), pp. 1–9.

Katie Pickles' study of the IODE[26] and Mark Moss's monograph on masculinity and militarism in pre-1914 Ontario.[27] Adele Perry has connected the culture of empire to another fundamental issue in Canadian history, namely, native-newcomer relations.[28] In the last decade or so, our understanding of the British impact on Canada has become much richer. As a result, we are now in a somewhat better position to assess whether the impact of the British Empire on Canada was largely positive or largely negative.

Problems with the Post-1993 British World Literature

The flurry of literature on the Anglo-Canadian relationship is both encouraging and frustrating. While it is encouraging that historians are again thinking about the relationship between Britain and Canada, the British world literature has some severe limitations. One of them is that the choice of topics by social historians has skewed our understanding of the British Empire's impact on Canada by over-emphasising its negative features. For instance, Mark Moss has shown that imperialism and militarism were linked to a particularly regressive conception of masculinity. Adele Perry has studied the decidedly negative impact of empire on natives. These studies are valuable. But there is another side to the story and so far no one has investigated whether British imperialism made Canadians more democratic or entrepreneurial than they would otherwise have been. Indeed, the post-1993 British world historiography has left political, economic and constitutional themes largely untouched. For instance, the place of Canada in British geopolitical strategy has been largely ignored by British world historians.[29] Just before the First World War, the influential British geographer Halford Mackinder declared that the economic centre of the British Empire would lie in Canada rather than in London in a generation.[30] The fact that such

---

[26] K. Pickles, *Female Imperialism and National Identity: Imperial Order Daughters of the Empire* (Manchester, 2002).

[27] M. Moss, *Manliness and Militarism: Educating Young Boys in Ontario for War* (Don Mills, 2001).

[28] A. Perry, *On the Edge of Empire: Gender, Race, and the Making of British Columbia, 1849–1871* (Toronto, 2001).

[29] The subject was, however, considered in the 1990s by J. Beeler, 'Steam, Strategy and Schurman: Imperial Defence in the Post-Crimean Era, 1856–1905', in Greg Kennedy and Keith Neilson (eds.), *Far-Flung-Lines: Essays on Imperial Defence in Honour of Donald Mackenzie Schurman* (London, 1996), pp. 27–54.

[30] H. Mackinder, 'Geographical Conditions Affecting the British Empire: I. The British Islands', *Geographical Journal* no. 33 (1909) pp. 462–76, 474.

predictions were made at the time is surely worthy of our consideration, as are the many economic bonds that linked Canada and Britain in this era. However, aside from Gregory Marchildon's brilliant study of Max Aitken's financial career,[31] the recent historiography has essentially ignored the economic aspects of the British world and has focused on the subjective identities of contemporaries. More attention could have been paid to how the 'imagined communities' of the past influenced and were influenced by flows of labour, capital and consumer goods.[32]

In addition, British world scholars have not really wrestled with the question of the extent to which the 'British world' included the United States. Thinking about this issue is crucial if we are to separate Britain's impact on North America as a whole from Britain's influence on Canada. The historical literature of the 1950s was marked by a tension between Donald Creighton's emphasis on Britain's rivalry with the United States and the more inclusive Atlanticism of Winston Churchill's 'English-speaking peoples'.[33] Historians of our generation need to think about whether the Canada-US border marked the boundary of the British world as an imagined community. Evidence both for and against this hypothesis can be found.

A more important difficulty with the recent literature is that historians of Canada are still failing to draw on interpretive frameworks that could add a comparative perspective and highlight the empire's beneficent aspects. Historians are right to be sceptical of grand theories of global history, but if we are to understand the impact of the British Empire on Canada, we should at least consider whether any of these frameworks is useful. However, deciding which paradigm is most suitable for Canadian historians is complicated because scholars of international renown have advanced several competing frameworks for understanding empire. In the next section of the chapter, I will sketch each framework or 'lens' and then suggest how it might be applied to the practical task of writing Canadian history. The scholars of chief importance include defenders of empire such as Deepak Lal and Niall Ferguson; the human rights scholar Michael Ignatieff; students of empire's relationship to race, class, and ethnicity; neo-classical economists who criticise empire; and scholars who discuss the

---

[31] G.P. Marchildon, *Profits and Politics: Beaverbrook and the Gilded Age of Canadian Finance* (Toronto, 1996).

[32] That identities influence economic behaviour is acknowledged in C. Tait, 'Brushes, Budgets, and Butter: Canadian Culture and Identity at the British Empire Exhibition, 1924–25', in Buckner and Francis (eds.), *Canada and the British World*, pp. 234–349.

[33] W. Churchill, *History of the English-Speaking Peoples* (Toronto, 1956–58). Churchill's emphasis on Anglo-Saxon fraternal unity has recently been revived by the popular historian A. Roberts, *A History of the English-Speaking Peoples since 1900* (London, 2006).

relationship between culture and economic performance. None of these lenses gives us a perfect view, but all have some merit. Moreover, all of these lenses allow us to see the positive aspects of the British Empire and suggest that Canadian historians should re-evaluate their generally negative views of British imperialism.

Lenses for Viewing the History of Empire

Thinking about the Anglo-Canadian relationship requires us to consider why Britain became the world's dominant power by 1815. This question in turn forces us to think about competing causal explanations for European global hegemony. Before we can begin to make moral or other evaluations about the British or European impact on Canada, we should understand the processes by which Europeans acquired global power. Some academics believe that the rise of the west was simply an accident of biology or global meteorology, a matter of microbes or climate change. In their eyes, had a few natural variables been different, other continents might have colonised Europe rather than vice versa.[34]

The theories that underscore the importance of natural forces are useful because they help to problematise what was once regarded as common sense, namely, that western dominance was the result of functionally superior economic and social institutions. The advantages of western institutions versus non-western institutions in a given epoch are matters that needs to be proven or disproved with evidence, not simply assumed, and Alfred Crosby and Jared Diamond are right to challenge ethnocentric notions of cultural superiority. But while many historians are willing to concede that fortuitous natural factors played a role in the global rise of Britain, few are willing to attribute everything to social exogenous variables, be they smallpox epidemics or England's large coal deposits. Even Marx's so-called materialist theory of history recognised that non-material factors such as ideologies and political structures played an important role in history.[35] The thesis that western dominance may have been partly due to superior institutions is certainly considered by Ernest Jones, the widely respected author of *The European Miracle: Environments, Economies, and Geopolitics in the History of Europe and Asia*. Jones tells the rags-to-riches tale of how a minor extension of the Eurasian continent was able to rise to global economic and

---

[34] A.W. Crosby, *Ecological Imperialism: the Biological Expansion of Europe, 900–1900* (Cambridge, 1986); J. Diamond, *Guns, Germs, and Steel: The Fates of Human Societies* (New York, 1997); G. Stokes, 'The Fates of Human Societies: A Review of Recent Macrohistories', *American Historical Review*, vol. 106, no. 2 (2001), pp. 508–25.

[35] G.A. Cohen, *Karl Marx's Theory of History: a Defense* (Princeton, 1978), pp. 364–88.

cultural dominance by 1900. Jones's argument incorporates socially exogenous factors such as climate change and epidemics, but he maintains that post-medieval Europe's political institutions were also part of the explanation.[36]

If Jones's argument that Europe's rise to global dominance was a function of superior political institutions is correct, it lends credence to the view advanced by other scholars that European imperialism benefited people living in overseas colonies by allowing for the diffusion of those institutions. Let us consider the arguments of those who stress the merits of European imperialisms (including the imperialism of the British Empire). Perhaps the strongest defender of empire is Deepak Lal. His main targets are Marxian scholars who argue that empire enriches the colonisers at the expense of the colonised and liberals who say that empire hurts both the imperialist country and the territories it governs. The account of empire provided by Marxian historians such as Immanuel Wallerstein will also be familiar to many readers. Wallerstein and his followers assert that colonialism was instrumental in the creation of a global economic system consisting of an exploiting core and periphery of commodity producing regions.[37] The liberal critique of empire has a long pedigree: as early as the middle of the eighteenth century, people in Britain were arguing that the acquisition of overseas colonies harmed Britain itself.[38] Lal maintains that both camps are wrong and that imperialism confers benefits all round, to the colonised as well as the colonisers. Lal argues not that the rulers of empires are more benevolent than the rulers of small states but that large polities are beneficent because they achieve political stability. They do so, according to him, by eliminating local conflicts, which, in turn, promotes security of the person, long-distance commerce, and durable property rights. Lal regards all empires as functional, but suggests that the empires established by western peoples offered their residents more benefits than non-western empires. Lal singles out the British and American Empires as particularly praiseworthy in this regard.[39]

Lal's interpretation suggests that British (and later American) imperialism has benefited people living in what is now Canada. There is certainly some plausibility to what Lal is saying about the advantages of large polities versus small

---

[36]   E. Jones, *The European Miracle: Environments, Economies, and Geopolitics in the History of Europe and Asia*, 3rd edition (Cambridge, 2003), pp. 104–26.

[37]   I. Wallerstein, *The Modern World-System: Capitalist Agriculture and the Origins of the European World-Economy in the Sixteenth Century* (New York, 1974); K. Pommeranz, *The Great Divergence: China, Europe, and the Making of the Modern World Economy* (Princeton, 2000); A. Gunder Frank, *Reorient: Global Economy in the Asian Age* (Berkeley, 1998).

[38]   E. Rothschild, 'Global Commerce and the Question of Sovereignty in the Eighteenth Century Provinces', *Modern Intellectual History*, vol. 1, no. 1 (Apr. 2004), pp. 3–25, 21.

[39]   D. Lal, *In Praise of Empires: Globalization and Order* (London, 2004).

ones. Canadian exporters, missionaries and travellers have been major beneficiaries of the two liberal empires Lal describes. Moreover, Canada is itself large enough to be considered a form of empire: the efforts of Sir John A. Macdonald and others to build a transcontinental Dominion that rivalled the United States produced a political unit that dwarfed both the pre-Contact Aboriginal polities and the separate colonies that joined Confederation. The imperial and sub-imperial projects pursued in the past confer benefits on ordinary people today. For instance, thanks to the ambitions of Macdonald and his contemporaries, it is now possible to travel across Canada without showing a passport or changing money. Most people would say that this mobility is a good thing.

Lal's analysis is, however, not wholly convincing because he glosses over the substantial differences between the many empires he surveys. Even the two English-speaking powers he considers exhibited major differences. The British Empire included vast territories that were formally British as well as extensive spheres of influence. The American reluctance to admit the reality of empire has made the United States unwilling to annex its overseas territories, even de facto colonies such as Guantanamo Bay.[40] Moreover, if we accept Lal's premise that bigger polities are better, then Britain's efforts to build up the Dominion of Canada as a rival to the United States appear somewhat retrogressive. If Lal's 'bigger is better' philosophy is correct, then Goldwin Smith's proposal for a single North American nation was more progressive than the nationalism of Sir John A. Macdonald. Another problem with Lal's analysis is that he fails to come to grips with the convincing argument that the existence of many small polities can be ultimately beneficial. For example, Ernest Jones has argued that Europe's political fragmentation contributed to its ability to catch up and eventually surpass China in the spheres of commerce, seafaring, and general technological prowess. Medieval Europe's failure to acquire a central ruling authority analogous to China's Emperor was crucial, he says, because the benefits of commercial and technical competition outweighed the costs of fragmentation (which included intermittent warfare and intra-European trade barriers).[41] Lal does not really consider the downsides of empires and if we are to arrive at a more balanced view of the British Empire's costs and benefits, we need to turn to other interpretative frameworks.

Niall Ferguson's more sophisticated defence of empire takes some of the possible rejoinders to Lal into account. The British Empire described by Ferguson combined vast scale with polyarchic diversity, with the colonial mini-Parliaments

---

[40] American and British imperialism are compared in C.S. Maier, *Among Empires: American Ascendancy and its Predecessors* (Cambridge, Mass., 2006) and B. Porter, *Empire and Super-Empire: Britain, America and the World* (New Haven, 2006), pp. 103–6. Porter's work is informed by J. Schumpeter, *Imperialism and Social Classes* (Oxford, 1951).

[41] Jones, *The European Miracle*, pp. 104–126.

ensuring a degree of local autonomy not seen in the far-flung dominions of Habsburg Spain. Ferguson's framework is more believable than that of Lal because he firmly distinguishes liberal empires (chiefly Victorian Britain and the twentieth-century United States) from the pre-liberal empires that characterised human history before 1800. Ferguson also separates the pre-1800 British Empire from the Second British Empire. He does not rehabilitate the former but does argue that the empire of the nineteenth and twentieth centuries enhanced the interests of the human race as a whole and increased total world product.[42]

Ferguson uses the history of abolitionism to make a general point about Britain's transition from an empire of oppression to an empire of liberalism: he shows that the British went from dealing in slaves to suppressing slavery within a few decades. In 1807, Parliament banned the shipment of new slaves across the Atlantic in British vessels. Abolitionist lobby groups won subsequent victories, forcing white colonists in the Caribbean to free their human property, sending the Royal Navy to interdict foreign slaving ships and eventually suppressing slavery in the interior of Africa.[43] Ferguson argues that liberty in a broader sense was also advanced by the British Empire after 1800, maintaining that important freedoms were implanted in both the neo-British societies of the Dominions and in the countries of the tropical empire. He links this shift in empire's outcomes to changes within the metropole, most notably gradual democratisation and the progressive extension of economic liberty.

By the Victorian period, Britain had a two-party system, an advanced capitalist economy, an active press and a vibrant civil society. These are features shared with the United States, the country that succeeded the British Empire as the global hegemon between 1914 and 1945.[44] Ferguson argues that the American Empire has promoted liberty in much the same way as the British Empire. In fact, he wants the United States to become even more imperialist and bemoans the American tendency to abandon imperial projects whenever costs escalate. Appealing to the Americans' sense of enlightened self-interest, Ferguson argues that the British Empire was a positive-sum game that benefited Britain and her colonies. Paul Kennedy argued in the 1980s that great powers decline when 'imperial over-stretch' overburdens their economies.[45] Ferguson replies that the

---

[42]   That is, the total size of the world economy. The growth of the world economy and the fluctuating shares of it enjoyed by different countries is discussed in A. Maddison, *Contours of the World Economy, 1–2030 AD: Essays in Macro-Economic History* (Oxford, 2007), pp. 379–82.

[43]   N. Ferguson, *Empire: the Rise and Demise of the British World Order and the Lessons for Global Power* (New York, 2003), pp. 177–8.

[44]   N. Ferguson, *Colossus: the Price of America's Empire* (New York, 2004), pp. 185–7, 279.

[45]   P. Kennedy, *The Rise and Fall of the Great Powers: Economic Change and Military Conflict from 1500 to 2000* (New York, 1987).

real problem with the American Empire is 'under-stretch,' with too much butter and not enough guns. He says that implanting liberal democracy overseas pays long-term dividends for both the imperialist power and the overseas colonies.

Ferguson's upbeat view of empire relies heavily on concepts taken from the New Institutional Economics (NIE), a school of thought that holds that a strong state willing to protect individual rights rather than simply *laissez-faire* is the prerequisite for capitalist industrial development. The NIE emerged in the 1970s in reaction to the limitations of the narrowly quantitative economic history that flourished in the 1960s.[46] Convinced that fortuitous natural endowments were of secondary importance in explaining national differences in per capita wealth, Douglass C. North and Mancur Olson asked economic historians to look at the political and legal institutions that were, in their eyes, the real foundations of development.[47] North and Olson argued that Europe, and particularly Britain, prospered because they were the first countries to evolve the type of institutions, particularly more secure property rights, that promoted faster technological progress and economic growth.[48]

Ferguson's institutional analysis is helpful in answering a major question of historical causation: why was the British Empire able to overtake the other European overseas empires between 1700 and 1815? Stuart England was a second-rate power and historians have long sought to explain how 'England's apprenticeship' in the seventeenth century gave way to the *Pax Britannica-* 'Workshop of the World' era of the nineteenth.[49] Moreover, Ferguson's emphasis on the liberalism of the Victorian Empire is consistent with Ian McKay's thesis that the Canadian project of building a transcontinental British Dominion was fundamentally about advancing the ideology of liberal individualism and private property.[50] Canadian historians who see McKay's 'liberal order' concept as a

---

[46]   D.C. North, 'Beyond the New Economic History', *Journal of Economic History*, vol. 34 no.1 (1974), pp. 1–7; D.C. North, *Institutions, Institutional Change and Economic Performance* (Cambridge, 1990); O.E. Williamson, 'The New Institutional Economics: Taking Stock, Looking Ahead', *Journal of Economic Literature*, vol. 38 no. 3 (2000), pp. 595–613.

[47]   M. Olson, *The Rise and Decline of Nations: Economic Growth, Stagflation and Social Rigidities* (New Haven, 1982); J. Bradford De Long, 'Overstrong Against Thyself: War, the State, and Growth in Europe on the Eve of the Industrial Revolution', in Mancur Olson and Satu Kahkonen (eds.), *A Not So Dismal Science: a Broader View of Economics and Societies* (Oxford, 2000), pp. 138–67.

[48]   D.C. North and B.R. Weingast, 'Constitutions and Commitment: The Evolution of Institutions Governing Public Choice in Seventeenth-Century England', *Journal of Economic History*, vol. 49, no. 4 (1989), pp. 803–32.

[49]   C. Wilson, *England's Apprenticeship, 1603–1763* (London, 1965).

[50]   I. McKay, 'The Liberal Order Framework: A Prospectus for a Reconnaissance of Canadian History', *Canadian Historical Review*, vol. 81, no. 3 (2000), pp. 617–45.

plausible interpretive framework for Canadian history will probably agree with Ferguson's description of the British Empire even if they reject his neo-liberal value assessments and normative statements.

Ferguson's interpretation has weaknesses as well as strengths. A major problem with his account of empire is that he discounts human rights abuses by the two liberal empires as regrettable but isolated incidences. Many First Nations historians would regard the very process of seizing territory as inherently immoral, regardless of the colonisers' behaviour on subordinate *ius in bello* issues such as the treatment of prisoners. Moreover, Ferguson's emphasis on the continuities and affinities between British and American imperialism will not ring true for many Canadians: did not British and American troops fight on Canadian soil? One can dismiss the war of 1812 as something that happened before Britain and the United States became fully liberal or fully democratic (if they ever did), but it nevertheless problematises Ferguson's notion of Anglo-American amity and the related concept of the liberal-democratic peace.[51]

Furthermore, a close examination of the historical record tends to falsify Ferguson's thesis that the British Empire promoted globalisation and freer markets. In reality, the British Empire promoted a form of regulated, semi-protectionist capitalism. It is certainly true that British imperialism opened parts of the non-western world to the global economy. Something similar happened in the early stages of Canadian history, but in post-Responsible Government Canada, as in Australasia, membership of the British Empire was eminently compatible with American-style tariffs. Protectionist tariffs are the antithesis of economic liberalism and globalisation. Indeed, the Canadians who complained the most about the end of British mercantilism in the 1840s were later among the strongest proponents of a national policy.[52] Sir John A. Macdonald's Anglophilia did not extend to the classical political economy of Ricardo and Mill.[53] The British preferential tariff Canada introduced in 1897 exacerbated Anglo-German tensions and contributed to the collapse of the liberal trade regime in pre-war Europe.[54] And in the interwar and post-1945 periods, imperialist sentiment in Canada reinforced the Commonwealth-wide tendency towards collectivism and

---

[51]   The democratic peace theory that clearly informs Ferguson's work has been the subject of a devastating critique by J. Gowa, *Ballots and Bullets: the Elusive Democratic Peace* (Princeton, NJ, 1999).

[52]   D. McCalla, entry for Isaac Buchanan in *Dictionary of Canadian Biography* (Toronto, 1966) vol. 11, pp.125–31.

[53]   C.D.W. Goodwin, *Canadian Economic Thought: The Political Economy of a Developing Nation, 1814–1914* (Durham, North Carolina, 1961), pp. 55–8, 64, 111, 126.

[54]   P. Kennedy, *The Rise of Anglo-German Antagonism, 1860–1914* (London, 1980), pp. 262–4, 291, 302, 319.

protectionism exemplified by the Ottawa Economic Conference.[55] The heyday of the British Commonwealth also saw the establishment of the (state-owned) Canadian Broadcasting Corporation[56] and Diefenbaker's *dirigiste* trade diversion strategy.[57] Perhaps 'liberal imperialism' is a true oxymoron, destined from the start to collapse under the weight of its inherent self-contradiction.[58]

The evidence that the British Empire encouraged Canadians to adopt statist-interventionist economic policies calls into question Ferguson's argument that British imperialism advanced the causes of economic liberalism and free markets. But liberalism is much more than an economic philosophy: it is a belief system with implications for a host of non-economic issues, such as the treatment of minorities and the rights of the accused in criminal matters. Perhaps the most plausible arguments in defence of the British Empire are those that revolve around non-economic matters. These arguments are the focus of the next section.

Empire and Human Rights

It is clear that Ferguson's interpretive framework has major flaws insofar as it attempts to describe the economic aspects of the British Empire. But a somewhat more plausible defence of liberal empire has been advanced by Michael Ignatieff. Ignatieff argues that societies lucky enough to have evolved advanced codes of human rights have a duty to spread liberal values such as security of the person, religious tolerance and gender equality. He argues that war and governance by outsiders are sometimes the only means of protecting the human rights of individuals living in other cultures. He suggests that if we are to avoid the pitfall of moral relativism, we must sometimes adopt a quasi-imperialist way of thinking. Ignatieff defines himself as a qualified admirer of the British Empire and argues that British imperialism sometimes advanced the cause of human rights.[59]

[55] F. McKenzie, *Redefining the Bonds of Commonwealth, 1939–1948: The Politics of Preference* (London, 2002).
[56] M. Vipond, 'The Canadian Radio Broadcasting Commission in the 1930s: how Canada's first public broadcaster negotiated "Britishness"', in Buckner and Francis (eds.), *Canada and the British World*, pp. 270–87.
[57] T. Rooth, 'Britain, Europe, and Diefenbaker's trade diversion proposals, 1957–58', in Phillip Buckner (ed.), *Canada and the End of Empire* (Vancouver, 2005), pp. 117–32.
[58] The idea that 'liberal imperialism' is oxymoronic is bolstered by the fact that libertarians (i.e., consistent classical liberals) such as those of the Cato Institute are among the most fierce critics of America's Empire.
[59] M. Ignatieff, *Empire Lite: Nation-building in Bosnia, Kosovo and Afghanistan* (London, 2003), pp. 4, 86–90, 114, 120, 122.

For Canadian historians, Ignatieff's 'values imperialism' raises a number of important theoretical questions. Until recently, Canadian policy towards Aboriginals was frankly assimilationist and aimed at the extinction of native languages. Although Tom Flanagan of the University of Calgary has recently attempted to extrapolate a justification for 'cultural imperialism' out of values imperialism,[60] this is certainly not Ignatieff's agenda. Ignatieff does not attempt to justify attempts to impose Christianity and the English language on Canada's First Nations. But Ignatieff's theory of universal human rights can be used to justify other British actions or policies in Canada. For instance, Barry Gough has shown that the heavy guns of the Royal Navy were crucial in suppressing slavery in the Aboriginal communities of British Columbia.[61] Ignatieff's framework suggests that, in this context, British naval power promoted human rights. Ian K. Steele's research on Iroquois treatment of prisoners during the Seven Years' War has shown that the contemporary European code of warfare was very much a cultural construct.[62] Eighteenth-century European ideas regarding the treatment of prisoners of war were much closer to the values embodied in modern international law than those of the First Nations of that period. Ignatieff's framework therefore suggests that the establishment of Euro-Canadian hegemony in eastern North America was a positive development from a human rights point of view.

Of course, one can share Ignatieff's belief that liberal values are of universal validity while rejecting his view that liberal empire is an efficient means of promoting human rights. Some critics of today's liberal imperialism use quantitative analysis to test whether liberal imperialism fulfils its humanitarian promises.[63] Canadian historians can borrow this approach. They should also consider where the ideas of pre-Contact Aboriginals were, in some spheres, more 'advanced' than those of the Europeans. Establishing a methodology for assessing the humanitarian costs and benefits of British colonialism in Canada is a topic far outside the remit of this chapter. However, a recent work by David Abernethy provides some guidelines for how this might be done without the debate degenerating into the competitive accumulation of anecdotal data.[64]

Ignatieff's belief that the British Empire may have advanced human rights in some instances raises the complex question of the connection between racism and imperialism. Many Canadian historians will incline to the view that Canada's

---

[60]   T. Flanagan, *First Nations? Second Thoughts* (Kingston, 2000), pp. 8–9, 197.

[61]   B.M. Gough, *Gunboat Frontier: British Maritime Authority and Northwest Coast Indians, 1846–90* (Vancouver, 1984), pp. 85–94.

[62]   I.K. Steele, *Betrayals: Fort William Henry and the Massacre* (Oxford, 1990), pp. 110–13.

[63]   B. Ibrahim Al-Rubeyi, 'Mortality Before and After the Invasion of Iraq in 2003', *The Lancet*, vol. 364, issue 9448 (2006), pp. 1834–5.

[64]   D.B. Abernethy, *The Dynamics of Global Dominance: European Overseas Empires, 1415–1980* (New Haven, 2000), pp. 363–408.

membership in the Empire-Commonwealth reinforced WASP (White Anglo-Saxon Protestant) supremacy within Canada. But we should consider whether countervailing tendencies were at work. Britain's concessions to French Catholics after 1760 enraged the rabid Protestants of New England and suggest that the arch-imperialists in London were more tolerant than the local Anglo-Saxons.[65] Slavery was abolished by legislation in the British Empire a generation before the Civil War in the United States. Although there were very few black slaves living in British North America in the 1830s, there is certainly something to be said in favour of an empire capable of and willing to extirpate an entrenched economic system. Moreover, London sometimes tried to restrain the greed of white settlers throughout its far-flung empire: the reaction of whites in the Thirteen Colonies to the Royal Proclamation of 1763 had parallels in Australia and southern Africa.[66] In addition, the Aboriginal rights acknowledged by the 1763 proclamation became entrenched in Canada's constitution precisely because Canada remained part of the empire after 1776.[67]

It is well known that Canada barred immigration by non-white British subjects at a time when it aggressively recruited immigrants in the British Isles.[68] But there is also evidence that the British government tried to discourage Canada and the empire's other dominions from passing racist immigration laws. At the 1897 Colonial Conference, Joseph Chamberlain declared that racial equality and colour-blindness were fundamental traditions of the British Empire. Today, Chamberlain is primarily remembered as a jingoistic imperialist and the architect of the Boer War. But his comments on the immigration laws of Canada and the other dominions have a remarkably modern ring. Speaking at a gathering of colonial premiers, Chamberlain said that colonies were right to make laws against the entry of paupers or those who were demonstrably immoral but that it was wrong to exclude just 'because a man is of a different colour than us'. He asked Wilfrid Laurier and the other delegates 'to bear in mind the traditions of the Empire which makes no distinction in favour of, or against, race or colour'. Chamberlain also said that to exclude by reason of their colour or race, 'all Her Majesty's Indian subjects ... would be an act so offensive to those peoples that it would be most painful, I am quite certain, to Her Majesty to have to sanction it.'[69]

[65]   F.D. Cogliano, *No King, no Popery: anti-Catholicism in Revolutionary New England* (Westport, Connecticut, 1995), pp. 41–58.

[66]   Weaver, *The Great Land Rush*, pp. 154–6, 353.

[67]   P.W. Hogg, *Constitutional Law of Canada* (Toronto, 2000, student edition), p. 574.

[68]   H. Johnston, *The Voyage of the Komagata Maru: the Sikh Challenge to Canada's Colour Bar* (Delhi, 1979).

[69]   *Proceedings of the Conference Between the Secretary of State for the Colonies and the Premiers of the Self-Governing Dominions at the Colonial Office, June and July 1897* (London: HMSO, 1897), Cmd. 8596, pp. 12–14.

In the decades after 1945, Canada became a much less racist country. Canada's ties with Britain also became less important in this period. Whether these two sets of phenomena were coincidental is an open question. One hypothesis worth testing is that the declining importance of the Empire-Commonwealth after 1945 and the concurrent worldwide decline in racism were two entirely unrelated phenomena. Because Canada is now home to several ethnic groups that were affected by these processes (natives, whites, not to mention many immigrants from the Indian subcontinent), Canadian historians are ideally placed to study this topic and make a major contribution to global history. The widespread assumption that racism and British imperialism were connected is one that deserves to be debated by Canadian historians rather than accepted uncritically.

The Dollars and Sense of Imperialism

Historians have other assumptions about empire that need to be re-examined. The prevailing view sees empire as a mechanism for transferring wealth from the colonies to the imperial power and suggests that the British Empire made the people of the colonies poorer than they would have been in the absence of empire. But the economics of empire were much more complex than the conventional wisdom allows. Canadian historians seeking to place their country's experience in a global context should pay attention to the debate over the costs and benefits of empire for Britain. The economic critique of imperialism can be traced back to the 1790s when Jeremy Bentham advocated that Britain abandon its remaining North American colonies on the grounds of national self-interest.[70] Some cliometricians now argue that possessing a colonial empire involved massive overseas expenditure that slowed Britain's economic growth at home. Other historians reject the thesis that the British Empire was a 'waste of money' and stress the commercial benefits of empire.[71] For those of us whose primary interest is the history of Canada, this academic debate is important. For one thing, the tangible evidence of British expenditure in Canada is still visible: a massive amount of British capital was tied up in works such as Halifax's imposing Citadel and Upper Canada's Rideau Canal. Although they did little to benefit taxpayers in Britain, these expenditures stimulated the local economy at an early stage in its development. In this sense, people in present-day Canada benefited from

---

[70]   D. Winch, 'Bentham on Colonies and Empire', *Utilitas*, vol. 9, no. 1 (1997), pp. 147—54.

[71]   L.E. Davis and R.A. Huttenback, *Mammon and the Pursuit of Empire: The Economics of British Imperialism* (Cambridge, 1988), pp. 262–79; cf. A. Offer, 'The British Empire, 1870–1914: A Waste of Money?', *Economic History Review*, vol. 46, no. 2 (1993), pp. 215–38.

being part of the British Empire in the same way people in Nunavut benefit from Canadian military expenditure in the region.

In addition to British government expenditure in present-day Canada, we also need to consider the sheer extent of British private investment in Canada. A great deal of capital flowed from Britain to Canada during the life of the empire. At least part of this inflow of money was due to Canada's political status. Until 1914, empire borrowers tended to receive better terms in British capital markets than fully sovereign debtors: Canada was like the Australasian Dominions and unlike the United States in that it financed its development through heavy borrowing in London.[72] In the eyes of some left nationalist historians, this reliance on London capitalists was plainly a bad thing.[73] My own viewpoint is that we need to gather more information before making *ceteris paribus* statements about whether Canada's remaining under the British flag after 1776 helped or harmed its long-term economic prospects: cheap credit can be beneficial or dangerous depending on the circumstances.

Imperial Legacies, Economic Culture and the Homo Economicus Model

Canada's membership of the British Empire facilitated the import of capital from Britain. But Britain did more than send money. It also implanted values that had a significant and positive impact on Canada's long-term economic performance. The concept of economic culture needs to be integrated into our understanding of the British legacy in Canada. In the 1990s, economists[74] and business historians[75] began to turn to culture to explain what neo-classical economic theory cannot. David Landes emphasises cultural differences in *The Wealth and Poverty of Nations: Why Some are So Rich and Some So Poor*, noting that the most prosperous nations in the world are either western or Sinitic in culture.[76] Gregory J.

---

[72] D.C.M. Platt, *Foreign Finance in Continental Europe and the United States, 1815–1870: Quantities, Origins, Functions, and Distributions* (London, 1984), p. 141; I. Stone, *The Global Export of Capital from Great Britain, 1865–1914: A Statistical Survey* (New York, 1999), Tables 1 and 2; L.E. Davis and R.J. Cull, *International Capital Markets and American Economic Growth, 1820–1914* (Cambridge, 1994), p. 1. P.J. Cain and A.G. Hopkins, *British Imperialism, 1688–2000*, 2nd ed., (London, 2002), pp. 135–50. See also Raymond E. Dumett (ed.), *Gentlemanly Capitalism and British Imperialism: The New Debate on Empire* (London, 1999).

[73] T. Naylor, *Canada in the European Age, 1453–1919* (Montreal, 2006).

[74] A. Sen, 'How Does Culture Matter?' in Vijayendra Rao and Michael Walton (eds.), *Culture and Public Action* (Stanford, 2004), pp.37–58.

[75] K. Lipartito, 'Culture and the Practice of Business History,' *Business and Economic History*, vol. 24, no.1 (1995), pp. 1–52.

[76] D.S. Landes, *The Wealth and Poverty of Nations: Why Some are so Rich and Some so Poor* (New York, 1998), pp. 174–9, 343–4.

Clark has advanced a similar argument by suggesting that it was something in eighteenth-century western workplace culture that allowed the west to escape the Malthusian trap that had ensnared all human societies for the previous 100,000 years.[77] Both writers reject the *homo economicus* assumption that human nature is a universal constant. If cultural differences do help to determine which countries are rich and which are poor, this forces us to re-examine our assessments of the historical processes by which western and, in particular, British culture, was implanted in Canada. After all, if the British Empire laid the cultural foundations of Canada's present-day affluence, there is something to be said for British imperialism.

The best-known proponent of the concept of economic culture is probably Samuel Huntington. Huntington has advanced the highly controversial thesis that the political and economic institutions of the United States are largely the product of the values that British Protestants brought with them to the Thirteen Colonies. He worries that the influx of Spanish-speakers will eventually convert parts of the United States into extensions of Latin America (i.e., violent, poor, and with an alleged Ibero-Catholic tendency towards dictatorships of either the extreme left or the extreme right).[78] One could argue that Huntington has brought all culturalist interpretations of economic performance into disrepute through his oversimplified and alarmist theories. But Canadian historians ought to consider the far more nuanced framework provided by Lawrence Harrison. Harrison displays a keen awareness of the national differences within the major cultural zones of the western hemisphere and acknowledges the possibility of rapid cultural evolution, using the transformation of Spain over the course of his own academic career as a case in point. But in the final analysis, his interpretation is similar to that of Huntington: North America has outperformed Latin America for cultural reasons.[79] If Harrison's thesis is right, it has important implications for how we study Canadian political and economic history.

Of course, culturalist or 'neo-Weberian' interpretations for national disparities in wealth are controversial. Proponents of the NIE insist that institutional differences, such as insecure land tenure, provide simpler and therefore better explanations for the gap between North and Latin America.[80] Stanley Engerman and Kenneth Sokoloff hold that non-cultural factors such as stronger democratic

---

[77]   G.J. Clark, *A Farewell to Alms: Brief Economic History of the World* (Princeton, 2007), p. 14.

[78]   S.P. Huntington, *Who are We? The Challenges to America's Identity* (New York, 2004), pp. 17–20, 59–62, 158–70.

[79]   L.E. Harrison, *The Pan-American Dream: Do Latin America's Cultural Values Discourage True Partnership with the United States and Canada?* (New York, 1997), pp. 12–14, 36–41, 150–53, 71–2.

[80]   H. de Soto, *The Mystery of Capital: Why Capitalism Triumphs in the West and Fails Elsewhere* (London, 2000), pp. 237–43.

institutions and the early development of mass schooling in North America drove the divergence in economic outcomes north and south of the Rio Grande.[81] Engerman and Sokoloff are very sceptical of cultural explanations, but their own findings point to the importance of political culture in understanding differences in income levels.[82] 'Legal origins theory' gives us yet another lens for examining the relationship between culture and economic growth. Canadian historians should consider the argument that common-law jurisdictions generally grow faster than civil-law ones because of differences in the values embedded in legal systems.[83]

Canadian historians seeking to assess Britain's impact on Canada's socio-economic evolution should consider all of these theories in charting their research agendas. One adopter of the culturalist approach to Canadian economic history is Marc Egnal. He argues that the gap in average living standards between New England, French Canada, and the slave-owning South that developed between 1750 and 1850 was partly a function of New England's superior cultural capacity for economic growth.[84] The great virtue of Egnal's research is that he manages to explore cultural differences without falling into the trap of seeing anglophones and francophones in North America as two monolithic groups. The culturalist approach to comparative economic history is intriguing and raises many questions for historians interested in Canada's relations with the Empire-Commonwealth. Although small in the grand scheme of human cultural diversity, the differences in economic and political culture between Britain and the United States were and remain quite real. These cultural differences influence everything from tort law to employment standards to the role of state in health care. Comparing Canada with the other two societies of what J.B. Brebner called

[81]   They also note the vast differences in average living standards between 'Latin American' countries. S. Engerman and K. Sokoloff, 'Factor Endowments, Institutions, and Differential Paths of Growth Among New World Economies: A View from Economic Historians of the United States', in Stephen Haber (ed.), *How Latin America Fell Behind: Essays on the Economic Histories of Brazil and Mexico, 1800–1914* (Stanford, 1997), pp. 260–304. In the terminology of Engerman and Sokoloff, the development of subsidised public schools in North America was a non-cultural factor that drove the continent's economic growth. However, one can quibble with this characterisation of educational systems as non-cultural, since attitudes to schooling are indeed rooted in culture, as are political norms.

[82]   Economic culture (i.e. values that influence individual choices over things like the income–leisure tradeoff) is distinct from political culture (which informs government decisions that indirectly influence the economy). Sen, 'How Does Culture Matter?', pp.37–58.

[83]   R. La Porta, F. Lopez-de-Silanes, A. Shleifer and R.W. Vishny, 'Law and Finance', *Journal of Political Economy*, vol. 106, no. 6 (1998), pp. 1113–55.

[84]   M. Egnal, *Divergent Paths: How Culture and Institutions Have Shaped North American Growth* (Oxford, 1996), p. vii, 53–4.

the North Atlantic Triangle[85] would seem to be a good way of investigating the evolution of the country's economic culture. We need to know far more about how membership in the Empire-Commonwealth influenced Canada's economic, political and business cultures in the days before America Inc. became overwhelmingly dominant and Great Britain plc disappeared over the horizon.

Of course, investigating the differences between Canadian and American politico-economic culture is complicated by the debris of yesterday's theories. In the 1960s, Gad Horowitz connected the relative strength of socialism in Canada to the British connection by tracing a genealogy of collectivist ideas back to the United Empire Loyalists. The many critics of Horowitz's thesis regarding the intellectual legacy of the Loyalists were probably right,[86] especially since the political culture of eighteenth- and nineteenth-century Britain was at least as committed to Dickensian *laissez-faire* as the United States.[87] But while Britain's drift to the (relative) left came only in the twentieth century, it occurred at a time when Britain still exerted a strong influence on Canadian political culture. As a recent collection of essays makes clear, the Commonwealth relationship was still a very important one for Canadians in the middle of the twentieth century,[88] the period in which the influence of socialist ideas in Britain was at its very peak. Canadian historians have only recently begun to investigate how the ideology of the Commonwealth influenced Canadian reactions to the rise of social democracy in Britain.[89]

One promising avenue of future archival research is the influence of British role models on the development of the Canadian welfare state. A possible topic related to this theme is the relationship between Tommy Douglas, the so-called 'father of medicare', and Aneurin Bevan, the architect of Britain's National Health Service.[90] Canadian discussions of British gun control and capital

---

[85]   J.B. Brebner, *North Atlantic Triangle: the Interplay of Canada, the United States and Great Britain* (New Haven, 1945).

[86]   G Horowitz, 'Conservatism, Liberalism and Socialism in Canada: An Interpretation', *Canadian Journal of Economics and Political Science*, vol. 32, no. 2 (1966), pp. 143–71; J. Ajzenstat and P.J. Smith, 'The "Tory Touch" Thesis: Bad History, Poor Political Science', in Mark Charlton and Paul Barker (ed.), *Crosscurrents, Contemporary Political Issues*, 3rd edition (Toronto, 1998), pp. 84–90.

[87]   E. Wallace, 'The Origin of the Social Welfare State in Canada, 1867–1900', *Canadian Journal of Economics and Political Science*, vol. 16, no. 3 (1950), pp. 383–93.

[88]   Buckner (ed.), *Canada and the End of Empire*.

[89]   But see J. Naylor, 'Canadian Labour politics and the British model, 1920–50', in Buckner and Francis, *Canada and the British World*, pp. 288–308. On the role of British role models in the construction of the Canadian welfare state, see D. Guest, *The Emergence of Social Security in Canada*, 3rd edition (Vancouver, 1997), pp. 42–4, 125; G. Gray, *Federalism and Health Policy: the Development of Health Systems in Canada and Australia* (Toronto, 1991), pp. 28, 40.

[90]   Lewis H. Thomas (ed.), *The Making of a Socialist: the Recollections of T.C. Douglas* (Edmonton, 1982), pp. 269–73.

punishment legislation are two other topics that might be studied. If Canada is indeed 'a Northern European welfare state in the worst sense of the term' (to quote Stephen Harper's speech to a gathering of American neo-conservatives in 1997),[91] this may be partly due to the very British connection he so loudly praised in July 2006. The British legacy in Canada does indeed include a culture generally receptive to free enterprise and some of our military traditions. But it also includes approaches to social policy and international law that set Canada apart from the United States.

One suspects that if historians had provided the reading public with a more complete view of the British impact on Canada, Mr Harper might have hesitated to make the statements quoted at the start of this essay. After all, certain features of Canadian society valued by people on the right can be traced to Britain, but so can institutions popular with those on the left. Extending from John Cabot to John Diefenbaker, the Anglo-Canadian special relationship laid down many sedimentary layers. Its sheer complexity requires Canadian historians to draw on multiple interpretive frameworks. The potential rewards for grappling with the comparative literature include the chance to escape from the parochialism inherent in 'national history'.

The existing British World literature provides a good starting point, but historians need to reconnect with socio-economic theory if we are to understand Britain's complex role in the making of Canada. Engaging with the theories surveyed in this chapter would have the incidental effect of increasing the relevance of Canadian historical writing to academics in other disciplines and to the reading public. As the comments by Mr Harper quoted above indicate, non-historians have not forgotten the importance of the British Empire in Canadian history. Although the British impact on Canada was not as positive as some neo-conservatives make out, it was probably much more beneficial than the recent historiography would suggest. I hope that the tentative conclusions provided in this chapter will generate future debate on the British Empire's contribution to the Canadian success story.

---

[91] CTV News, 'Full Text of Stephen Harper's 1997 Speech', 14 December 2005.

Chapter 5
After Inclusiveness: The Future of Canadian History

Christopher Dummitt

Of only one thing we may be certain: in time the new history will
experience the same fate as the old history, for Clio is an inspiring
muse but she has the alarming habit of devouring those who respond
to her charms.

Carl Berger, *The Writing of Canadian History*[1]

When I entered graduate school in the autumn of 1996, I was a man on a mission. I set out to study men and masculinity. The field was going to revolutionise
the way we looked at the past – or at least that's how I saw it. Like a great many
new fields since the 1960s, of which there have been many, masculinity studies
wrote itself into a historiographical tale of whiggish progress. The rate of evolution was steep, beginning with 'traditional' history that had ignored women and
gender altogether, moving on to women's history, then to gender history and
finally to masculinity. There were other ways you could tell the tale, other places
you could end up – with starring roles for issues of class, race and sex along the
way. At the heart of this story, though, lay one central feature: an ever-evolving
inclusiveness.[2]

The path of inclusiveness was a popular one. In the years between the 1960s
and 1990s, entirely new fields of historical inquiry opened up to professional

[1] C. Berger, *The Writing of Canadian History: Aspects of English-Canadian Historical Writing Since
1900*, 2nd edition (Toronto, 1986), p. 230.
[2] On gender history see J. Sangster 'Beyond Dichotomies: Re-assessing Gender History and
Women's History in Canada', *Left History*, vol. 3, no. 1 (1995), pp. 109–21; and the various
responses to that article in *Left History* vol. 3, no. 2 (1995). More generally see Berger, *The Writing
of Canadian History*.

scrutiny. A whole new generation of historians in Canada and elsewhere challenged the assumptions of their predecessors, taking up historical subjects previously considered unimportant, unworthy of study, or even taboo. The list of
new fields is now familiar and includes, amongst others, the history of class, race,
sexuality, gender, women, regionalism and the environment. Older subjects
were revamped and rewritten, most notably the study of native peoples, which
took a much greater interest in the perspectives of native peoples themselves.
Increasingly the historians who studied these topics came to their subjects with
a more radical array of theoretical perspectives including feminism, Marxism, literary theory and, more recently, postcolonial theory. The overall emphasis was
on getting away from top-down, elitist history associated with political history
of the nation-building kind.

It mattered that there was an enemy. This was not entirely clear at the time,
but it has become so since. The older and narrower brand of history, as well as
the historians who wrote it, were integral to how we thought of ourselves. So
too were the increasingly smaller numbers of historians who continued to write
on subjects like political and military history. Opening up a new subject of study
was about transgression − passing over borders and through bars. To truly transgress you need rules to break and people to enforce them. It was important that
there were those who disapproved, who said, 'that's not how it should be done',
or who, at the very least, had not bothered to do it that way when they had the
chance. These rule-setters were, after a fashion, our own version of historiographical 'others'.

This was the time of the History Wars. In Canada, one of the biggest campaigns was fought over the inclusiveness of Canadian history. It pitted those who
advocated a social history more open to all Canadians against those who fretted
that the turn away from political history would bring nasty consequences for
the Canadian nation.[3] This debate quickly became, and has since remained, a
mainstay in classes on methodology and historiography in universities. One of
the key actors in this debate was Michael Bliss. In his 1991 Creighton Centenary
Lecture at the University of Toronto, Bliss suggested that there were serious
consequences to 'the massive shift in historians' substantive interests, away
from political and constitutional history and towards the exploration of the

---

[3]   There was, of course, much more to the History Wars than this particular debate, including most
notably a debate over the 'cultural turn'. This latter debate did not break down upon the same lines,
but even those who disagreed could still unite in their support of a more inclusive history. The
debate over gender vs women's history referenced in note 2 was part of this. Also notable here was
the work of Bryan Palmer in *Descent into Discourse: The Reification of Language and the Writing of Social
History* (Philadelphia, 1990).

experiences of people in relationships flowing from such non-national connections as region, ethnicity, class, family and gender'.[4] That this shift had occurred could not be disputed. But what Bliss really wanted to note were the repercussions for the nation. It was not a coincidence, he argued, that the sense of community in Canada as a whole had withered at exactly the same time that Canadian historians had abandoned the nation as a unifying concept of analysis. Where Canadian history went, so went the nation.

Several years later, J.L. Granatstein was even more forceful in his condemnation of the way the turn to social history threatened to destroy what he saw as the essence of Canadian citizenship. In *Who Killed Canadian History?* Granatstein blamed a whole range of people – everyone from education officials to high school teachers to politicians – for turning their backs on the true story of Canadian history, which he associated with great men and military valour. Academic historians merited their own chapter of reprobation, in which Granatstein repeated Bliss's argument that the turn to private and social aspects of history threatened to devastate the future of Canadian citizenship.[5]

The lines in this battle were clearly drawn. 'Whose "national" history are we lamenting?' asked four prominent women's historians in response to Bliss's article. Certainly not the women who were left out of most traditional political history, nor the other socially marginalised groups who were equally ignored. '[T]hose of us teaching women's, labour, or native history', they argued, 'are teaching political issues. A definition of political, however, must include gender relations, native issues, class and regional differences if it is to mean anything in our country'. A.B. McKillop took a similar tack in his thoughtful critique of Granatstein's *Who Killed Canadian History?* He agreed that historians had a role to play in educating Canadians for citizenship. However, he suggested that Granatstein's definition of citizenship was sorely lacking. 'Citizenship is not simply a matter of acquiring a sense of past national accomplishment', he argued. 'It also involves acquisition of a sense of belonging to a larger whole through the formation of social identity'.[7] In acquiring this larger personal and social identity, the nation walked hand in hand with such things as sexuality, ethnicity and community. McKillop and other critics said much more than this, of course;

---

[4]   M. Bliss, 'Privatizing the Mind: The Sundering of Canadian History, the Sundering of Canada', *Journal of Canadian Studies*, vol. 26, no. 4 (1991), p. 6.

[5]   J.L. Granatstein, *Who Killed Canadian History?* (Toronto, 1998).

[6]   L. Kealey, R. Pierson, J. Sangster and V. Strong-Boag, 'Teaching Canadian History in the 1990s: Whose "National" History Are we Lamenting?' *Journal of Canadian Studies*, vol. 27, no. 2 (1992), p. 130.

[7]   A.B. McKillop, 'Who Killed Canadian History? A View from the Trenches', *Canadian Historical Review*, vol. 80, no. 2 (1999), p. 272.

but the main critique of Bliss and Granatstein focused on the restrictive and unequal nationalism that the latter seemed to want to foist upon Canadian history. Much of Canadian history written during and since has been about decentring, disrupting or fragmenting the kind of national history that Bliss and Granatstein wanted historians to celebrate.[8]

A funny thing happened on my way through graduate school. The Blisses and Granatsteins of Canadian history started to disappear. Starting in the mid-1990s and continuing until today, Canadian universities saw the largest wave of retirements in their history. The scale of the retirements matched the scale of hiring that took place in the 1960s when Canadian universities expanded at an unprecedented rate. These retirements elicited a number of concerns. Some worried about whether the professors would be replaced and in what disciplines. Others fretted over the loss of expertise and knowledge. Still others, and I was certainly in this category, were not concerned at all, seeing this as a great opportunity to finally get a job.

What seems to have gone by almost entirely unnoticed is that the repercussions of their departure were as much intellectual as logistical. We have all pretty much carried on as if things were still the same, as if the old resistance to an ever more inclusive history is as strong as ever. Of course, it is not as if nothing changed. As all the older professors went out the door, the new young doctors were welcomed right in. There were dinners, handshakes and plenty of grants and junior research chairs to make us all feel welcome, at least the ones who got the jobs anyway. But something fundamentally important has not changed. We are still acting as if the old guys are still here. We spend all our time talking to them. When we get into the lecture theatre, we call them to account. When we write our reviews, our essays, our books – especially the introductions to our books – we are still talking to them. The retired, the recently gone, the no longer with us – they are so important to who we are, to how we define ourselves. We may not have given them the best retirement parties but we still seem to love them, to need them, to keep on invoking their thoughts and our responses, replaying the old debates again and again, seminar after seminar, introduction after preface after foreword.[9]

---

[8] For a sceptical view, see B. Palmer, 'Of Silences and Trenches: A Dissident View of Granatstein's Meaning', *Canadian Historical Review*, vol. 80, no. 4 (1999), p. 678.

[9] The main textbook of the more inclusive history, Conrad and Finkel's *Canada: A National History* still sets itself up as representing a project and perspective under attack: 'Social history ... has its critics,' the authors note. '[These critics] argue that it focuses the energy of historians into narrow topics, that it yields interesting but ultimately insignificant findings, and that it destroys the unifying national focus that earlier political studies offered. In response to such charges, we argue that the new

Yet, although we do not seem willing to recognise it, the battle has been won. With a few grumpy exceptions, the university professoriate has been won over to a more inclusive history. A study published in the January 2007 issue of the American Historical Association's magazine *Perspectives* clearly outlines the changes to the profession in the United States, and these are likely similar to (if not less dramatic than) those in Canada. It showed that by far the largest general fields that historians now claim to be affiliated with are those generally associated with the inclusive history: social; women's and gender; and cultural. In fact, after social history, women's and gender history is the second most popular field of specialisation amongst American historians.[10] Steven High's contribution to this volume, his call for historians to share authority with those they study, is, it seems to me, premised on exactly this transformation. It assumes a largely progressive history and group of historians, practitioners of history from below, keen to open up the historical project to those traditionally excluded. High's argument makes sense precisely within a profession that is already largely committed to inclusiveness in general, even if it has not followed through on the specifics he suggests. This transformation in the historical profession needs to be acknowledged. It is time to stop acting as if we are still in the trenches. The History Wars have been won, not only by the glory of intellectual debate but by the more sure method: attrition through retirement.

The consequences for Canadian history are dramatic. The most important innovations of the last thirty years arose out of the struggle to create a more inclusive history. The main dividing line in the profession has been between those advocating a more bottom-up social history and those calling for a return to narrowly defined political history. In the future this will no longer be true. The professoriate is already committed to a programme of exposing the prejudices of the past. The battle between social and political history has lost any of the intensity it once possessed. Although there will undoubtedly continue to be new books on previously prohibited subjects, these will not shake the

---

social history offers a more comprehensive view of what happened in the past. We also maintain that there cannot be and never was an official version of Canada's history.' M. Conrad and A. Finkel, *Canada: A National History* (Toronto, 2003), p. xxi. The same kind of rhetoric appears in other general works. In native history, the authors trumpet the fact that until recently such history was written from the European perspective, looking westward across the continent, not eastward towards the oncoming settlement. See O.P. Dickason, *Canada's First Nations: A History of Founding Peoples from Earliest Times*, 3rd edition (Toronto, 2002), pp. x–xi. My aim here is to point out that such injunctions that have sparked off useful intellectual questions in the past are now more often rhetorical than intellectual; instead of offering new insights, they reaffirm belief.

10   R. Townsend, 'What's in a Label? Changing Patterns of Faculty Specialization Since 1975', *Perspectives*, vol. 45, no. 1 (January 2007).

foundations of the way we think. They will be additions, not re-evaluations. A bottom-up, inclusive 'Peoples" history of Canada is now the standard version of history in Canadian universities.[11] What now?

Canadian History at the Crossroads

What is abundantly clear is that the majority of the public is not with the professors. A trip to the Canadian history section in any bookstore is confirmation of that. And that is if you can even find a section devoted to the nation's history; Canadian history is usually stuffed in under the vague heading 'Canadiana', a term which encompasses everything from the latest Céline Dion biography to coffee table books adorned with pictures of misty lakes and lonely moose. If you search very hard you might find a few books by academics, usually shelved with their narrow spine hidden between advice manuals on *How to be a Canadian* and the collected works of Pierre Berton. The one thing that no one criticised in J.L. Granatstein's *Who Killed Canadian History?* was his assessment of the sales records and print runs of the average Canadian academic history book. The numbers have risen somewhat in the intervening years. The university presses who publish them usually start – and end – with runs in the neighbourhood of 800 to 1,000 copies. Many of these are bought by libraries and other institutions. The rest are largely taken up by fellow academics and graduate students. Hardly any will end up in a bookshop outside a university. Even fewer will show up in the hands of a Canadian who is not already a historian or related to one.[12]

This helps to explain the incredible gap between what the public thinks of Canadian history, and the kind of history actually practised by historians. It is a not altogether uncommon occurrence for those who practise the more inclusive history – whether covering such subjects as gender, sexuality or race – to be faced with the question: 'But isn't that sociology?' or worse yet, just deadened silence mixed with a perplexed look and a quick change of subject. If academic historians have radically altered their perspective about what counts as history, the same

---

[11]   This was notably the theme taken by the CBC when they opted to do a major television, web and book project on Canadian history. Although I speak in this chapter primarily with reference to the main textbook series of the inclusive history, Alvin Finkel and Margaret Conrad's various books on the *History of the Canadian Peoples*, it is worth noting that one of their competitors also takes up a similar title, though admittedly with not quite the same historical agenda: see the various versions of J.M. Bumsted's survey *The Peoples of Canada*.

[12]   One avenue that has had some success in taking the inclusive history to a more public audience is the publishing of works with Toronto's Between the Lines Press. See, for example, C. Heron: *Booze: A Distilled History* (Toronto, 2003) and M. Dawson, *The Mountie: From Dime Novel to Disney* (Toronto, 1998).

cannot be said, at least not to the same extent, for the general public. By far the most shelf-space in any history section in a Canadian bookstore is devoted to military history, followed by politics and local history – with the best option being some combination of the three. The same is true on television, where channels like History Television seem to play continuous runs of documentaries on the Second World War. There has been, of course, a move to greatly expand the kind of history shown on these channels. On the day I wrote this paragraph, History Television ran a programme on the Great London Smog of 1952 – a neat blend of social and environmental history. But it was sandwiched in between episodes of *JAG* (an American drama about military justice) and several episodes of *Sea Hunters*, a programme of underwater discovery which on this occasion was looking at the wartime wrecks around the D-Day landing sites and the HMS Doterel, a nineteenth-century British warship. If you were having trouble sleeping, you could catch *Tour of Duty* at 2 a.m. and *V for Vendetta* at 3 a.m.

It is tempting to blame the problem on imagination-challenged television producers with short-term profits on the brain or on bookstores that would rather sell coffee than books. But it might also be worth thinking through how academic history contributes to this problem. What do we do as academic historians, and as practitioners of a more inclusive history, that widens the gap between public and professional conceptions of history? For although there has been an explosion in the number of Canadian history titles since the 1970s, volume has not necessarily translated into vitality. Discussion on the internet listserv H-Canada gives some sense of the malaise. In the summers of 2005 and 2006 the questions that most excited Canadian historians were 'Why is Canadian history boring?' and 'Why are Canadian history textbooks boring?'[13] Opinions varied, but the existence of the conversation itself was not a good sign.

Just as significant as the malaise in the public sphere of Canadian history is the lack of genuine intellectual debate in the profession itself. Although Canadian historians disagree on minor points of interpretation, they are a relatively homogeneous bunch compared to Canadian society at large. Attacks on Granatstein and Bliss have been the most exciting highlights of recent years. Yet the profession could by and large unite against such a narrow nationalist position, which meant that these debates united more than they divided. Such disputes behind them, Canadian historians could settle comfortably into their work, occasionally pointing out the inadequacies of an older national history that went out of date at least ten years ago.

[13]   The discussion in 2005 was sparked by a very interesting article by Allan Greer, published in the 20 August 2005 edition of the *Ottawa Citizen* and then posted to H-Canada on 29 August 2005. For the discussion see the H-Canada discussion logs for August and September 2005 at www.h-net.org/~canada/.

Instead of being pushed by genuine debate, the inclusive history has marked its progress by pointing to moments when subjects previously ignored by other historians were incorporated into the fold. At each point, there may have been clashes of personality, but the intellectual and ideological conflict is more assumed than real. My own field of women's and gender history is a good example. The evolution of this field that I noted earlier is frequently reiterated in articles and books – so much so that it has become something of a mantra.[14] Women's historians challenged the older national and political historians to consider the experiences of women. Then women of colour pointed out the Eurocentric bias of the first generation of women's history. Then the historians of sexuality suggested that homosexuality had been ignored. Gender historians chimed in with the argument that gender is relational – including both men and women – and so the history of masculinity needed to be written. Although at each step on the ladder there was some shoving and manoeuvring for position, none of these developments (except for the first) was actually a radical challenge to what had come before. Perhaps the clearest indication of a lack of genuine conflict is that the personnel did not change. It was often the same historians, and their graduate students, who moved from one area to the next. Joan Sangster, for example, went from doing important early work on women, work and the left to studies of Aboriginal women and the law. Another early women's historian, Veronica Strong-Boag, made the same transition.[15] While some of the individuals may have disagreed on matters of methodology, this group of historians largely shared a homogeneous view of how history should work.[16]

---

[14] Joan Sangster criticised the emergence of this kind of disciplinary narrative in 'Beyond Dichotomies'. But the general trend is still evident in N. Forestell, K. McPherson and C. Morgan (eds.), *Gendered Pasts: Historical Essays in Masculinity and Femininity* (Toronto, 2003) and V. Strong-Boag, M. Gleason and A. Perry, *Rethinking Canada: The Promise of Women's History* (Toronto, 2002).

[15] Strong-Boag was the author of, amongst other things, *The New Day Recalled: The Lives of Girls and Women in English Canada, 1919–1939* (Toronto, 1988) but then went on to edit the critical collection *Painting the Maple: Essays on Race, Gender and the Construction of Canada* (Vancouver, 1998) and write a biography of a mixed race poet, *Paddling Her Own Canoe: The Times and Texts of E. Pauline Johnson* (Toronto, 2000). Similarly Sangster was the author of important early work in women's history including *Dreams of Equality: Women on the Canadian Left, 1920–1950* (Toronto, 1989) and has subsequently focused a great deal of attention on aboriginal women. See Sangster, 'She is Hostile to Our Ways: First Nations Girls Sentenced to the Ontario Training School for Girls, 1933–1960,' *Law and History Review*, vol. 20, no. 1 (2002), pp. 59–96; 'Criminalizing the Colonized: Ontario Native Women Confront the Criminal Justice System, 1920–60', *Canadian Historical Review*, vol. 80, no. 1 (1999), pp. 32–60.

[16] This is, I recognise, to overlook distinctions that some see as significant – those between socialist feminists and postmodern feminists or liberal feminists, for example. But the larger point strikes me as most important: these are frequently differences between individuals who, in the larger

A glance through the Canadian textbook most closely associated with the more inclusive history, Margaret Conrad and Alvin Finkel's *Canada: A National History*, shows the problem clearly. The text has sections specially set out as historiographical debates. They are meant to show students how history changes over time as a result of differences of opinion based on both contradictory perspectives and different types of evidence. The concept itself is incredibly useful; it just is not clear whether there are enough current debates to fill the pages. Almost all of the debates in *A National History* come from the years between the 1960s and the 1980s. In only two instances do writers from after 1990 make any significant contribution. And there were no contributions by those in the first few years of this new millennium before the text was published in 2003. Although some of these debates feature well-articulated and distinct positions – the divisions between Fernand Ouellet and Allan Greer over the causes of the Rebellions of 1837–8 being a good example – most of these debates are over relatively small issues of interpretation. In covering the more recent period, it was necessary to look outside the historical profession – to economics and political science – to even find dissenting voices.[17]

Bryan Palmer aptly diagnosed the problem in 1999. 'In our current historiographical moment', he pointed out, '... all is presented as advance and accomplished sophistication, albeit unwhiggish in its ostensible break from all past conventionalities... . There is no contention here. *None!* The "other" has silenced differentiation. This is not so much the trenches as an overly crowded honeymoon suite'.[18] Palmer implied that the solution was to have more historians writing from a Marxist or historical materialist perspective. Yet the more dramatic change would come from the other end of the political spectrum. One does not have to share their beliefs to acknowledge the fact that recruiting more conservatives and (capital L) Liberals to the profession would make for much more significant debate. Instead of splitting hairs between those standing from the NDP leftward, we might actually see debates about our history that all Canadians could recognise and engage with. And it is from that starting point that we could hope to spread the insights of the more inclusive history to a broader constituency.

---

context, are politically close-knit – they are all feminists. When I teach gender history classes to groups of students in which usually only a tiny minority admit to being feminist and in which a sizable majority profess outright hostility towards feminism, I can't but think that to make denominational differences the major focus of discussion is to lose sight of the bigger picture.

[17]   See Conrad and Finkel, *Canada: A National History*, various pages.

[18]   Palmer, 'Of Silences and Trenches', p. 681.

This is certainly the case in native history, where the stakes are high and the field has been more wide open. Two scholars, Gerhard Ens and the political scientist (and Stephen Harper adviser) Thomas Flanagan, have acted the role of fox in the academic chicken coop. Both have gone against the academic grain by widely criticising other historians for being too sympathetic with native peoples and allowing this to cloud their representations of the past. One of the main areas of debate has centred on how to depict Louis Riel and the causes of the 1885 Métis rebellion. Ens and Flanagan have both suggested that the federal government was not to blame, as other historians have claimed, for the displacement of the Métis and their resentment against the federal government. The debate has more than intellectual consequences. The same types of arguments have been taken up in the courts in cases dealing with native land claims and treaty rights, with historians appearing as witnesses on both sides.[19] One could be small-minded and berate the very existence of opinions which may seem unsavoury. Yet the fact is that Ens and Flanagan represent the ideological viewpoint of a huge number of Canadians. The absence of these kinds of voices, so long as the attitudes they represent are widespread, would diminish academic debate. And it would also mean that the arguments of those who disagree with Ens and Flanagan would be given much less public voice. The kind of debate that they have brought to native history is exactly what the profession needs more of: radically divergent opinions that force an intense scrutiny of sources and arguments. For the most part, however, these kinds of debates are the exception not the rule.

This lack of significant debate should give us reason to pause. This is especially so when it occurs alongside some of the other developments I have been discussing: that the public is largely oblivious to the kind of history we write and to changes in the profession; that we have not acknowledged the significant intellectual challenge that follows from the recent wave of retirements; nor have we really appreciated that, far from being the new kid on the block, the inclusive history is now the leader of the gang. I am not concerned that all of these developments will mean the end of the Canadian nation. Nor do I want to lament all of the changes that have overcome the profession or castigate what has become an ever more inclusive history. Rather, what I want to suggest is that

---

[19] Flanagan's most controversial salvo was perhaps his *First Nations, Second Thoughts* (Montreal and Kingston, 2000) but see also *Riel and the Rebellion: 1885 Reconsidered*, 2nd edition (Toronto, 2000). For Ens see G. Ens, *From Homeland to Hinterland: The Changing Worlds of the Red River Métis in the Nineteenth Century* (Toronto, 1996). And for alternative views see D.N. Sprague, *Canada and the Métis, 1869–1885* (Waterloo, 1988); 'Dispossession vs. Accommodation in Plaintiff vs. Defendant Accounts of Métis Dispersal from Manitoba, 1870–1881', *Prairie Forum*, vol. 16, no. 2 (Fall 1991), pp. 137–56. For a review of several key works, see R.L. Barsh, 'Boxing the Four Corners of Aboriginal Self-Government', *Acadiensis*, vol. 34, no. 1 (Autumn 2004), pp. 116–44.

now is a good time to sit up and take stock. With the older political and social history debates largely behind us, we have a genuine opportunity for fresh ideas and new directions. The difficult – but in my view necessary – task is to come to grips with the limits of the kind of history that now predominates in the profession. For all the benefits that it has brought, the inclusive history is not perfect. We have not reached some kind of Fukuyama-esque 'End of History' where everything from here on in will simply be an elaboration of the basic principles as laid down in 1970. Coming out from under the rubble of the History Wars, it is time to check for cracks in the foundation.

The Prejudice of Inclusiveness

The foundations of our current orthodoxy are firmly entrenched in the new left soil of the 1960s. Carl Berger's description of what he called 20 years ago 'the new history' is an apt characterisation of the inclusive history. 'In so far as it possessed a consistency of feeling', Berger observed:

> the new left was hostile to hierarchy and authority (including
> interpretations of history that seemed to justify the flawed present).
> Those who shared its sentiments were disillusioned with electoral
> politics, instinctively sympathized with the rebels of the past –
> William Lyon Mackenzie, Louis Riel, and Norman Bethune – and
> identified, despite their own predominantly middle-class
> backgrounds, with the victimized and dispossessed – blacks,
> immigrants, workers, women, and native peoples. In some respects
> the new left was profoundly anti-historical and showed little
> appreciation for evolution and continuity ... . The new history ...
> owed not a little of its critical spirit to contemporary reform
> movements that were questioning institutions and practices. For
> some, history became a force for remedial action and moral criticism,
> a weapon for attacking the abuses of the present by exposing their
> sources and pointing to better alternatives not taken in the past.[20]

Any connoisseur of Canadian history should recognise the description. The distrust of authority, the belief that history should be a form of politics, the emphasis on using history to expose past prejudice, the dislike of narrative history and any emphasis on continuity – these sentiments define much of what

---

[20]   Berger, *The Writing of Canadian History*, 2nd edition, pp. 264–5.

used to be called the new social history. The last 20 years have seen these sentiments spread throughout most areas of the historical profession to become its
new common sense.

The history that rests on top of these new left foundations has been renovated
several times over the years without altering the basic structure. In particular, the
concerns of identity politics and the postmodern cultural turn of the 1980s and
1990s added new perspectives. Other contributions to this volume continue the
tradition, most notably that of Adele Perry. Perry suggests that inclusiveness itself
was never actually the goal of truly radical historians. Rather, the task was, and
is, to rethink the past through such categories as race, class and colonisation – to
reorient the historical project itself. Yet this project of rethinking and remaking
is essentially one branch – the most radical – of the inclusive history. It operates
within the same basic assumptions: the idea that history is a form of politics, that
its goal is to decentre and disrupt contemporary forms of power. Whether one's
project is the more limited attempt to simply recover the past experiences of previously marginalised peoples or the seemingly more radical project of reconfiguring historical practice, many of the general principles are still the same. And,
by and large, this somewhat diverse base now makes up the core of what we can
think of as the inclusive history. One of this history's creation tales is that it came
into existence to overcome the political blind spots of previous generations. This
adds to the current historiography a feeling of righteousness – a sense that history is now more complete or cutting-edge because of our open-mindedness.[21]

The unfortunate irony of this situation is that while we are attuned to the
prejudices of the past in a way like never before, contemporary historians are
almost wholly deaf to our own prejudices. And prejudices there are, however
awkward this term might seem and however discomfiting this might be to admit.
Every generation of historians is shaped indelibly by its social context, this generation no less than the previous.[22] Perhaps more than any previous generation,

---

[21] One example of this is the introduction to a recent work on the history of immigrant women
in Canada. The authors chastise earlier histories of immigrant women for failing to give a great deal
of attention to non-European women immigrants. Yet the number of such women in Canada before
the 1970s was minuscule and the historiography being criticised is made up mostly of works that
were written in the 1970s and 1980s, works unlikely to deal with the most recent period (when the
numbers of non-European women did increase significantly) as history. See M. Epp, F. Iacovetta and
F. Swyripa (eds.), *Sisters or Strangers: Immigrant, Ethnic and Racialized Women in Canadian History*
(Toronto, 2004).

[22] It is worth keeping in mind Carl Berger's comments, drawing on the English historian
Herbert Butterfield: '... there are hidden and unsuspected factors behind any national tradition of
historical writing, and these need to be raised as far as possible to the level of consciousness so that
they can be neutralized and brought under control'. See Berger, *The Writing of Canadian History*, 2nd
edition., p. ix.

the historians of inclusiveness have been aware of these kinds of limitations in those who preceded them. But the silences and distortions in the current historiography are very different from those of a generation ago. They arise directly out of the great project of creating a more inclusive history. It is the prejudice of inclusiveness itself – the attempt to overcome earlier narrow-mindedness, social hierarchies and injustice – that is now the problem.

The inclusive history has left us with four major dilemmas (though no doubt others could come up with a different list). First, the inclusive history has not actually been inclusive. Some historical subjects – notably high politics and religion, though there are others – have been deliberately shunted aside and not explored as fully as their historical significance warrants. Second, while the commitment of inclusive historians to certain kinds of analytical categories, especially class, race and gender, initially helped to open our vision to new historical realities, this is no longer the case. Indeed, an over-reliance on searching out inequalities along these lines has often gone hand in hand with a type of analytical disdain for subjects and people who do not fit these priorities. Third, the inclusive history has largely abandoned narrative and synthetic histories that try to answer big questions and tell large stories in a way that the public might find compelling. Finally, the inclusive history's emphasis on breaking down social reality into various analytical parts has not been matched by a recognition that these parts need to be put back together again in order to make history accessible to the general public and to reflect lived reality. Many of these developments made sense when the inclusive history set itself up as a challenge to other ways of telling Canadian history. Now that the inclusive history is itself the dominant perspective in the discipline the situation has changed. The strategies of opposition are, after all, not the tactics of government

Let's start with the omissions. That they exist should not be in dispute. The absences in the older national and economic histories were ones of ignorance or accident. The silences of inclusive history are altogether different. They were not accidental; they were deliberate. Fed up with a national history that would explore the slightest nose twitch of allegedly great men while ignoring whole social classes with a shrug, many of the new social historians understandably turned their backs on the interests of their predecessors. Even J.M.S. Careless, no spring chicken in 1969, admitted the errors of the earlier historians. Contrary to what you might expect from the history books at the time, he pointed out, most Canadians' lives did not 'greatly focus on Ottawa and the deeds of hero federal politicians, or on the meagre symbols of some all-Canadian way of life.'[23] He suggested instead that the true meaning of a Canadian past might be found in

---

[23]   Careless, 'Limited Identities', p. 3.

'limited identities' – of class, region, ethnicity or otherwise – which the slender rope of the Canadian nation only barely secured. If Careless rather tentatively pushed historians to open up their embrace, others were much less shy. The idea that categories like class or race were in any way limited, certainly in relation to the nation, was cast aside rather quickly. A new generation of historians rushed to the archives to order from what must have seemed a suddenly and miraculously expanded new menu of historical subjects. Michael Cross and Gregory Kealey, editors of a series of social history texts written in the early 1980s, described the project in the broadest terms: 'Where once social history was seen as what was left over after political and economic history was written, social history now is a "global" discipline, which can embrace politics and economics as well as the history of social groups or charitable institutions. The ideal of social history is to write the history of society and to create social change'.[24]

Although the Cross and Kealey volume on pre-industrial Canada contained an artfully written piece by Cross on the 1837 Rebellion in Upper Canada showing how social and political history could be combined, the general trend was away from political history and anything that smacked of the 'colony to nation' story.[25] To continue to work in a field like political or military history suggested that one was not with the times. Work did continue to be done, but it was done by a group of Canadian historians who were – sometimes by volition, sometimes not – increasingly isolated from each other and from the moving thrust of the profession. Some indication of the trend can be found by glancing over the winners of the Canadian Historical Association's John A. Macdonald Prize since the late 1970s. The award is given annually to the book selected as the best work in Canadian history published that year. Over the last several decades the award has been given almost exclusively to works of social history. The only work of strictly political history to have won the prize in over three decades was the first volume of John English's biography of Lester Pearson, and that as far back as 1990.[26] This is as clear a sign as any of changing disciplinary priorities and values.

The inclusive history, then, has been deliberately less inclusive in some respects. The treatment of military history in Alvin Finkel and Margaret Conrad's

---

[24] M.S. Cross and G.S. Kealey, *Pre-Industrial Canada, 1720–1849: Readings in Canadian Social History, Volume 2* (Toronto, 1982), p. 5.

[25] M. Cross, '1837: The Necessary Failure', in Cross and Kealey, *Pre-Industrial Canada*, pp. 141–158.

[26] A couple of other works – H.V. Nelles *The Art of Nation-Building* (1999) and Jonathan Vance's *Death So Noble* (1990) – might be said to awkwardly fit into the category of more old-style political or military history. Yet both are more aptly seen as blending genres in a style more akin to cultural history.

Canada: A National History, is indicative. It deals only vaguely with Canada's armed forces in both the great wars of the twentieth century. In a 20-page chapter on the Great War only two pages are devoted to the experience of those in combat. The Second World War receives slightly better treatment, but over-all, the focus of the text is less on the military experience of war and much more on its domestic and social implications.[27] One does not have to be a rabid nation-alist or avid military history buff to think that something here is askew. It is not so much that the text is wrong in pointing to the many domestic repercussions of war. Rather it is that this emphasis on the domestic is so radically contrary to what people at the time thought was important. It is worth remembering that the conscription crisis of the Second World War was not only about French-English relations, it was also directly tied to the horrific toll of the European campaign which had followed on from the D-Day landings in 1944.

The same types of absences mark the inclusive history's treatment of religion. As with military history, a small group of specialists have continued to write the history of Canada's various denominations. But when religion is incorporated into more mainstream accounts, it comes as a representative of something else rather than of its own accord. Again, Finkel and Conrad's *Canada: A National History* is instructive. The index has listings for religion in connection with a variety of subjects including religion in Europe, class and ethnicity, culture, imperialism, religious holidays, its role in schools, the separation of church and state, the social function of church and social welfare.[28] There is nothing on belief, theology or faith. Even following entries which are simply listed as 'religion' to their places in the text leads not to discussions about religion itself but rather to questions of class and social belonging. All of these issues are important, but they are not balanced by an appreciation of the role of religion as such in the lives of Canadians who believed that faith meant much more than just strawberry socials. One senses that for many contemporary Canadian historians, most of whom are secular, faith and religiosity are matters of only secondary concern. Such subjects do not fit the remit of a more inclusive history. Middle-class piety is not the kind of thing to stir the hearts of anyone whose primary loyalties are to the downtrodden and dispossessed. But by largely ignoring these subjects, the end result is a history which is just as skewed, albeit in a different fashion, as the older nationalist literature. So although some contemporary historians continue to claim that the omissions of Canadian history fall into the old categories – of race or class or gender – the reality is something else altogether. [29]

---

[27]   Conrad and Finkel, *Canada: A National History*, pp. 358–77, 421–40.

[28]   *Ibid.*, pp. 189–90, 492–3, 540–41.

[29]   For an example of a recent reference to these kinds of omissions which in fact are no longer omissions, see Epp, Iacovetta and Swyripa (eds.), *Sisters or Strangers?*

If the inclusive history now leaves us with a new set of omissions, it also bequeaths an equally troublesome legacy of distortion. This is the second major dilemma. The inclusive history is predominantly a study of categories – of race, class and gender most notably, but also of analytical categories in principle. These are both the tools and the language of history in contemporary Canada. When used judiciously they allow for incredible new insights onto the past. Yet even as such categories shape how we see the past: they can also distort our vision. This happens in a number of ways but the one which is perhaps most disturbing is that which occurs when the categories stand in for history itself. This is the clumsy mismatch that results when it is too readily assumed that one's categories of analysis represent the essence of any single historical issue, so a history of morality, for instance (which I will touch on later) becomes a history of the categories used to understand it. In most recent years, this has meant histories of class, race and gender. Replace morality with any other historical subject and the same distortion repeats itself: the most important feature of such histories becomes issues of class, race and gender. The category becomes the history.

Any kind of historical writing distorts the past in its selection process. History is not merely recounting the facts; our claim to expertise rests on our ability to weigh and judge what should be considered important. For an earlier generation of historians, the concepts of objectivity and truth served as beacons in the dark, noble dreams to crawl toward in the hazy inbetween world of memory and history. But such concepts have largely fallen into disrepute in recent years, especially among North American historians (though not to the same extent in the United Kingdom).[30] Even if most historians have not bought into the more radical postmodern rejection of truth and fact, most remain unwilling to either champion the old noble dream or to offer any new justifying concept. The result is an empty space at the foundation of the profession, not the rejection of older principles *tout court* but neither the embrace of any identifiable system of belief that gives justification for what we do. In the end, the de facto justification seems to be based on the ongoing project of inclusiveness. If history is no longer about discovering truth in the past, it is now about making history more socially just.

However valuable this project has been, it has also meant that categories and issues of interest to the historian in carrying it out have taken a greater and greater hold on what could threaten to become a downward spiral of well-intentioned solipsism. Historians, of course, need categories. But these also need to be faithful to the language and context of the period and peoples under

---

[30]   These kinds of questions are so commonly known as to perhaps negate the need for a footnote, but an entry point could be J. Tosh, *The Pursuit of History: Aims, Methods and New Directions in the Study of Modern History*, 3rd edition (London, 2002); K. Jenkins, *Refiguring History: New Thoughts on an Old Discipline* (London, 2003) and R. Evans, *In Defence of History* (London, 2000).

scrutiny. At the very least we need to be aware of the limitations of our categories, of the way life is lived in between and beyond whatever concepts we have of identifying its contours.[31]

The history of morality provides a good example of how the process can go wrong. The field is wide-ranging and includes everything from the history of alcohol, drugs and sexuality to the moral ideology behind the development of compulsory state education. What unites the field is a commitment to a set of analytical categories and approaches. The inclusive history has dealt with these subjects mostly through the prism of regulation. Quite broadly, this is an approach which seeks to expose the class, race, gender (and other) prejudices of attempts to regulate behaviour in the past. Moral regulation is itself a slight variation on an earlier 'social control' approach. The difference is that the moral-regulation approach sees power as working in less of a top-down fashion. Much of the history of modern Canada from the mid nineteenth through to the late twentieth century is now told from a perspective which takes for granted this moral regulation approach.[32] The overarching emphasis is on the rise of a bourgeois culture that repressed various groups in exerting its own class, race and gender interests. And the alternating current here is how much, if any, agency was exercised by those responding to this bourgeois agenda.

As one perspective on a few select developments in modern Canadian history this approach was valuable. As the 'new normal', however, it wildly distorts the past. Most importantly, it implicitly overlooks the major development in the history of morality over the twentieth century: the transformation in the very bourgeois culture it seeks to critique. The twentieth century witnessed a sea change in attitudes toward morality. These changes are more than obvious to the most casual observer of the last century: attitudes towards everything from sex and drugs to the way one should walk down the street were revolutionised. Yet a student interested in this subject would have a hard time finding a book written by a Canadian historian which explains what happened, because the trajectory does not fit the priorities of the inclusive history.[33] Most historians

---

[31] Even E.H. Carr, that great critic of the individual in history, argued for a greater balance between the social and the individual, not the abandonment of particularity and accident altogether. And he wrote in a very different time, when the Great Man view of history predominated. And even Carr could see an important role for the individual, especially in his own field of Soviet history where the differences between Stalin and Lenin demanded that such issues be raised. See E.H. Carr, *What is History?*, 2nd edition (London, 1987 [1961]), pp. 166–170.

[32] Much of this work is usefully synthesised in T. Loo and C. Strange, *Making Good: Law and Moral Regulation in Canada, 1867–1939* (Toronto, 1997).

[33] There are a few exceptions, though even here the emphasis tends to be on the continuance of regulation. See A. McLaren and A. Tigar McLaren, *The Bedroom and the State: The Changing Politics*

repeatedly look at the regulation which continued, or new types of regulation which sprang up, either ignoring or at the very least downplaying the profound changes that occurred.

Part of the problem is that the moral regulation approach, much like the inclusive history more generally, is based in a set of 1960s political beliefs which are not themselves historicised. This approach tends to assume that our contemporary state of moral relativism is the natural, good and proper starting point for any historical analysis of morality. From this vantage point, one assumes that any kind of moral regulation is intrinsically problematic. The historical project then becomes a process of showing the many ways in which moral regulation has continued to operate. The awkward fact that such regulation both diminished considerably and changed qualitatively in the twentieth century is either overlooked or explained away because it does not fit within the parameters.[34] What is significant to point out here is the way in which a commitment to a certain kind of political project and especially certain analytical tools manages to distort a significant portion of modern Canadian history.

Ironically, this focus on the continued existence of regulation throughout the twentieth century has ultimately failed to explain how and why the inclusive history's own position of moral relativism has come to occupy such a dominant (though certainly not unchallenged) position in contemporary Canada.[35] It is the very changes of the twentieth century, the questioning of moral authority and the increased acceptance of moral relativism, that have allowed the inclusive historians to be so sceptical of any attempts to regulate behaviour in the past. Yet the intense focus on certain kinds of categories and questions has meant that this

---

and *Practices of Abortion and Contraception in Canada, 1880–1997*, 2nd edition (Toronto, 1997); Heron, *Booze: A Distilled History*.

[34] For example, the only book to yet give a history of drug use in Canada during the 1960s deals only superficially with the growth in the use of marijuana and other drugs and instead focuses on the continued illegality of the drug. See M. Martel, *Not this Time: Canadians, Public Policy and the Marijuana Question, 1961–1975* (Toronto, 2006). See also my review of recent works in drug history, C. Dummitt, 'Mackenzie King was not a Libertarian: Drug History and the Forgotten Sixties,' *BC Studies*, no. 153 (Spring 2007), pp. 107–115.

[35] For example, in *The Trouble With Normal: Postwar Youth and the Making of Heterosexuality* (Toronto, 1997) Mary Louise Adams tells us that the postwar years saw the emergence of a concept of heterosexuality which was about reinforcing sexual standards and allowing some liberalisation within very narrow boundaries by excluding a whole range of other behaviours as abnormal. It is not that this view is entirely incorrect. But its insistence on the continuance of regulation means that it misses a whole range of experience in the fifties (including the significance of Elvis Presley and his hips!) that those at the time experienced as profoundly important. Tellingly, the 2005 movie biopic about Johnny Cash, *Walk the Line*, is much better at getting at more of the changes in sexual culture of the 1950s and early 1960s, including the continuance of regulation.

fact is not acknowledged. The inclusive historians are the midwives of historical changes they refuse to take seriously.[36]

It may be that the wide-ranging history of morality over the course of the twentieth century is simply too large a story to be told in the current intellectual climate. This relates to the third dilemma the inclusive history has created: the abandonment of the big story. One of the other main features of recent historical writing has been its distaste for narrative, or any kind of history that offers overarching explanations across wide stretches of time and space. The sources for this lack of faith are many: a desire to challenge the exclusionary narratives of the older national history; a postmodern scepticism about any kind of rational or universalist project; a commitment to the local and the small; an unwillingness to suffer a type of history which, by its very nature, would not be wholly inclusive; and a feeling that general texts are intrinsically boring because they are written at too general a level of abstraction.[37]

This scepticism towards big stories is often sold as a radical challenge to previously dominant paradigms – as a decentring or disrupting of the powerful. Yet the trend away from synthesis and narrative in history has mirrored changes in the broader society. Since the 1970s it has become commonplace to question everything from expertise and objectivity to rational knowledge itself. The big modern story, like the big modern mega-project, is out of fashion. The postmodern condition in which we find ourselves celebrates uncertainty, multiplicity, non-linear thinking and pastiche in everything from television to architecture to the internet.[38] This kind of thinking now pervades the historical profession in Canada: we seem to continually trumpet concepts like hybridity and multiplicity. One can even see this trend in other chapters in this book – a confidence in the inherent value of things like marginality, uncertainty and especially transnationalism. While there is no doubt value in studying the past always with an open mind as to when national borders did and did not matter, it would be strange, and lacking in intellectual rigour, to trumpet transnationalism and similar concepts in principle. When events and processes, people and ideas are best understood this way, then

---

[36] I make the same point more extensively in Dummitt, 'Mackenzie King was not a Libertarian'. The other side of this debate (non-existent in Canadian academia) can be equally frustrating in its conservative bewailing of social change. See J. Burnham, *Bad Habits: Smoking, Taking Drugs, Gambling, Sexual Misbehavior and Swearing in American History* (New York, 1993).

[37] For a discussion of the dilemmas faced by those who do try to write large synthetic works – and especially the criticism directed at them – see Joceylyn Létourneau's and H.V. Nelles's reviews of each other's work in *Revue d'Histoire de l'Amérique Française*, vol. 59, no. 4 (printemps 2006).

[38] See D. Harvey, *The Condition of Postmodernity: An Enquiry into the Origins of Cultural Change* (Oxford, 1989); J.D. Hoeveler, Jr., *The Postmodern Turn: American Thought and Cultura in the 1970s* (New York, 1996).

they ought to be interpreted through such a lens. But there seems to be a danger that these concepts could become our new common sense, accepted without question. Do we risk creating a new orthodoxy in which everything uncertain and indeterminate is good, is to be studied and even celebrated? What is wrong with certainty and borders, with uniformity and clarity? The ironic danger is that we might all become uniform and pure in our celebration of hybridity.

Seen in this context, the turn away from synthesis and narrative is much less of a radical move than it is often presented as. Indeed, it is far more in line with contemporary culture than many of its adherents might like to admit. In assuming that coherence and narrative are inherently problematic we are no different from previous historians who assumed the opposite, or who assumed that the nation was the ultimate starting and ending point in Canadian history.

The result of this abandonment of the big story has been the almost total absence of coherent attempts to explain the Canadian past, either as a whole or even in substantial chunks.[39] We revel in a continual state of correction. Any range of concepts, from the nation to history in general, are continuously fragmented, decentred and deconstructed. The emphasis is on showing how seemingly common sense ideas about Canadian history are incorrect. The recent CBC history project Canada: A People's History demonstrated the deficiencies of this approach. This was a major effort to put academic history into the mainstream, with the hefty promotional arm of the CBC pushing it into the open. Yet its treatment of post-1945 Canadian history was a series of unrelated stories of popular culture, politics and people. The only link was chronology – all of these events, people and processes belonged to postwar Canada. Any move towards collective explanation and analysis was entirely absent.

A truly original task would be to fashion an overarching explanation for key periods in Canadian history – and, indeed, to make a convincing case for what such periods would be. Where is the great Canadian book on the emergence of multicultural Canada? Such a book could include everything from the rise of non-European immigration alongside the decline of 'British' Canada and the development of French Canadian nationalism. Where is the Canadian history of morality – a book that would show Canadian historians had the imaginative scope to match that of our greatest philosopher, Charles Taylor?[40] And where,

---

[39] There have been a couple of recent attempts to offer syntheses of Canadian history but these have not, by and large, attempted to work into that synthesis much of the new work on the social and cultural history of recent years. See H.V. Nelles's very readable A Little History of Canada and R. Bothwell, The Penguin History of Canada (Toronto, 2006).

[40] The incredible intellectual and historical scope, for example, of his Sources of the Self: The Making of Modern Identity could be an example and something of a model for Canadian historians to tackle in their own disciplinary fashion.

perhaps most of all, is the history of democracy in Canada – a book (or books) that could inform the heated rhetoric of democracy that so pervades our contemporary culture? There are many others that are needed, but this should at least provide a flavour. That these books would be broad, controversial and difficult to write, there can be little doubt. They would also be ambitious and original. In his critique of Granatstein's *Who Killed Canadian History?*, A.B. McKillop admitted that Canadian historians had not yet 'managed to forge an appropriate new synthesis of Canadian history, but this would require a fundamental rethinking of the meaning and shape of the very idea of nation at a time when, throughout the world, nations and their identities are in flux. It is doubtful if any contemporary historian of any country has accomplished this in a way that adequately addresses problems of collective identity at the end of the second millennium'.[41] McKillop may very well be right, but this should be an invitation, not an excuse. Several years into the beginning of the third millennium, this is exactly the task that lies ahead.

There are signs that things are changing. Recently Ian McKay has offered an original, and seemingly well-received, prospectus for understanding Canadian history writ large. McKay challenges the traditional account which holds up the United States as the sole symbol of New-World liberalism, and instead suggests that Canada should also occupy this ground.[42] For McKay, liberalism was the uniting ideology in Canada, so much so that Canada should itself be understood as a liberal project of rule.[43] McKay defines this liberalism in a very particular way – one which originates in his own political project and rigorously respects the ideological confines of the inclusive history. Yet his ambition and creativity are novel. McKay is meticulously careful to insist he is not attempting a synthesis of Canadian history; instead he argues that what is needed is a 'reconnaissance'. Yet McKay's work is extremely attractive because it brings the past together in a way which makes sense on a large scale. Synthesis may be a bad word, yet it is exactly McKay's ability to do something that looks an awful lot like synthesis which is so exciting.

The stumbling block for any new synthesis, McKay's or others', is the writing. How can one best blend analysis and prose? This leads to the fourth and final dilemma the inclusive history has left us: the abandonment of storytelling methods that are both analytical and entertaining. The building blocks of inclusive

---

[41]   McKillop, 'Who Killed Canadian History?' p. 298.

[42]   Though of course in rather a different way than that suggested by classic works in this vein, for example, Louis Hartz and S.M. Lipsitz.

[43]   I. McKay, 'The Liberal Order Framework: A Prospectus for a Reconnaissance of Canadian History', *Canadian Historical Review*, vol. 81, no. 4 (2000), pp. 620–621. See also McKay, *Rebels, Reds, Radicals: Rethinking Canada's Left History* (Toronto, 2005).

history are social classes, groups and peoples. Inclusive history is about analysing the social, economic or political patterns that underpin everyday existence and which can often go unnoticed or certainly unexamined. In order to make these social processes and categories visible, inclusive historians are constantly engaged in a process of breaking down the everyday into small and finite categories like race or sexuality. As much as the inclusive history is about expanding our idea of what counts as history, it is also simultaneously about breaking that history down into smaller and smaller pieces. It is a destructive history, not necessarily in the sense of being negative, but insofar as it insists that the past must be torn up into analytical categories in order to be understood.

The effect of this on the writing of history has not been altogether benign. Carl Berger was a prescient early witness to these changes:

> Academic scholars have increasingly occupied themselves with anonymous social patterns, with groups and classes rather than with individuals; they prize analysis over narrative and description; their most original books do not tell a story but answer questions; and they frequently take as their points of departure evaluations of the corpus of existing literature and its shortcomings. All this tended to make access to the past difficult for the general reader; it was almost as though the historian had interposed himself or herself between the reader and history.[44]

With a few notable exceptions, this summary has only become more true in the intervening years. When Margaret MacMillan, the author of the bestselling *Paris 1919: Six Months that Changed the World*, addressed an audience of over 150 at Canada House, England, in March 2007, she opened by saying that historians like two things: to tell good stories, and to tell them about fascinating people. That she has done this is true. And that such a type of history is incredibly popular is also true. Yet MacMillan was certainly not describing the priorities of the inclusive history. The inclusive history has been distrustful of narrative history and tales of individual character or personality. Its focus has been more on specialised debates and a style of writing that closes off access to the uninitiated.

The effect on the openness of historical writing is the opposite of what is intended. Even while history becomes more open to marginalised people and to the workings of social power, the writing of history itself has become ever more aloof and inaccessible. It is often suggested that inclusive historians are more democratic than those of previous generations who thought of themselves as

[44] Berger, *The Writing of Canadian History*, pp. 268-9.

national sages. Yet really one kind of expertise has simply replaced another. The centrepiece of this analytically preoccupied history is the historian him/herself. It is the historian's analysis which is needed to guide the reader through all of the various categories and historiographical problems. Although the intent is quite different, this kind of history establishes strong professional barriers that make the historian's knowledge that much more prized. Expertise is not something to be embarrassed about. Professionalism is not an intrinsic evil. The bigger question is how effectively historians convey this expertise to the public. On this issue, the inclusive history has less to be proud of.[45]

In analysing the past with our various categories (whether race, class or gender – although these could equally be anything from age to political ideology) the inclusive history has taken the past apart piece by piece so that all the details can be seen up close. The attempt is to rob ideas and structures of their seeming naturalness, to show that they are historically constructed, that they can be examined outside a single logic. Like nineteenth-century botanists, the inclusive historians have dissected these historic animals and labelled them, pinning them to computer screens and the pages of academic monographs. This is a natural impulse and somewhat necessary; it is simply what historians do. The problem is that instead of putting the past back together again, the inclusive history has simply left it there like some natural history specimen, grouped with thousands of others like it – visible but dead.

What we need is a catch and release policy. We are killing the past in order to understand it, but what we instead need to do is to get it into our sights, shoot it with the tranquilliser dart, bring it in for examination, and then let it out again to be read or discarded as the public deems fit. This is all about balance. Yes, analytical history is needed, but analysis is much more meaningful when it is accompanied by great stories and the examination of timeless human dramas. History's greatest strength has always been its naturalness, its closeness to life and the beating pulse of a culture. This is what distinguishes history from the social sciences. One of the great dilemmas that has followed from the dominance of the inclusive history has been the disrepute into which this type of historical writing has fallen. Along with the deliberate abandonment of some subjects, the analytical disdain for others, and the abandonment of synthesis, this is a major dilemma for the historical profession today. It is also an opportunity. Surely a truly inclusive history would want this inclusiveness to apply not only to history's subject matter but also to its writing. Ultimately this means relearning a

---

[45]   Donald Wright points out how the move towards professionalism in Canadian history had unanticipated consequences in the first half of the last century. See Wright, *The Professionalization of History in English Canada* (Toronto, 2005).

primary lesson: history is not only a tool of social criticism and abstract thought, it is also a craft and an art.

Looking Forward

Disciplines need stories. As historians we tell ourselves stories about our origins, our present and even our future. My contention in this chapter has been that Canadian historians need new stories. An earlier version of the chapter had the rather Augustinian title, 'Confessions of a Cultural Historian'. I had thought that the best way to point out the inadequacy of the inclusive history's story would be to show how my own work exhibited these problems. On reflection this seemed unwise; but it is worth pointing out that this essay is not only a critique, it is also a self-critique, a confession. Over the last few years, in my own work, and especially in my teaching, I found myself telling the story of the inclusive history with an ever greater sense of unreality. Even as I witnessed the growing authority of the inclusive history within Canadian academia I kept talking of the inclusive history as an outsider, a challenger, a marginalised voice. The next breakthroughs in Canadian history were all to be about breaking through the prejudices of some nebulous concept of normality. It slowly became apparent that this very story of marginalisation had become the new status quo. The inclusive history is itself the new orthodoxy but with a difference – it depends on this fact not being recognised.

At the same time, part of the inclusive history's story is true. Many of the new perspectives that it has developed over the last 30 years have not made the leap over to Canadian society at large. If the inclusive history is dominant within the profession, it is not nearly so successful outside academe. For someone trained within the inclusive history, this has often proved frustrating. When I listen to public debate about the place of boys and men in contemporary Canada, for example, I can't help but be amazed at how little the insights of my own field, gender history, are taken into account. The media presents deeply ahistorical and problematic notions of masculinity and gender and simply assumes these to be universally true. If they had read but a fraction of the works in gender history produced over the last couple of decades, journalists might ask different questions. Or would they?

Why are so many of the key insights developed in the inclusive history restricted to academe? Part of the answer, certainly, is that the inclusive history tells stories that are uncomfortable to hear. It truly has exposed the limits of conventionalities, past and present. But a closer look at the profession itself offers other answers too. It shows the deliberate omission of some key areas of human experience, and the politically and analytically motivated distortion of others. It reveals a profession ill at ease with telling big stories that can explain key questions about Canada's national past. And perhaps most significantly, it exposes a profession that has lost touch with a previously cherished ability to tell stories. That I am painting with broad strokes in making this assessment is undoubtedly true. That there are important exceptions is also true, luckily. But the inclusive history has created new dilemmas for the historical profession. And facing up to these dilemmas means telling new stories about the discipline, not as it was but as it currently exists.

The challenge for an ambitious young graduate student or scholar today could be quite different from when I entered the profession only just over a decade ago. Such a scholar could choose to write a broad-ranging and engaging work, one that addresses both town and gown. They could see that the most important and original historical tasks today are writing back into Canadian history the fields which were thrust to the side over the last 30 years. The great challenge is, indeed, to blend these various strands of history into ever more complex and compelling narratives. Canadian historians do not always have to be part of the wrecking crew; they can also be architects. It is possible to create a history which builds even as it tears down, which dreams even as it remembers.

Chapter 6
Nation, Empire and the Writing of History in Canada in English

Adele Perry

Historians have been yoked to the nation since the discipline professionalised in the closing days of the nineteenth century. This is as true for historians of Canada writing in English as it is for others. In the first decades of the twentieth century they tended to emphasise Canada as a component of the British Empire. Sometime in the heady years following the Second World War, historians of Canada writing in English traded in the rubric of the empire for that of the nation. Here, I would like to address the limitations of both when read through two areas of recent scholarship from which historians of Canada have been notably absent: transnational and postcolonial perspectives on history and critical analyses of race, gender and the Canadian nation. Rethinking the nation's role in historical scholarship in these ways has the potential to produce different narratives about northern North America and Canada, ones rooted in new standards of what is considered a relevant topic, a feasible question and a reliable archive.

The argument made here joins those in Michel Ducharme and Katie Pickles' chapters in trying to nudge Canadian history in a more global direction. It also aims to push it in a more postcolonial one. 'Postcolonial' is a slippery term that can cloak a rigidly progressive view of history, one that is perhaps especially ill-suited to use in reference to settler colonies in general and Canada in particular – places where decolonisation per se is unlikely to occur.[1] Adding a final stop of post-colony to the linear, progressive trajectory of colony-to-nation compounds rather than addresses the problem.[2] If postcolonial cannot describe a current state of political being, it can signal a methodology, one designed to provoke, as

---

[1] On this point see E. Furniss, *The Burdens of History: Colonialism and the Frontier Myth in a Rural Canadian Community* (Vancouver, 1999), pp. 13–14.

[2] See N. Besner, 'What resides in the Question, "Is Canada Postcolonial?"' in L. Moss (ed.), *Is Canada Postcolonial? Unsettling Canadian Literature* (Waterloo, 2003).

Diana Brydon explains, 'a process of radical questioning toward an unknown and destabilized future'.[3]

Like a number of chapters in this volume, including Steve High's call to rethink the relationship between communities and their historians, this one owes much to a linked range of radical interventions into historical scholarship made over the last three decades.[4] The demands that history make room for women, the working class, migrants, Aboriginal people or queers were never simply requests for inclusion, if they were that at all. The point that history remains incomplete without adequate recognition of one group or another does have undeniable purchase in liberal pluralist political climates. It also has rhetorical clout in a discipline where the lure of total history remains strong. It also has genuine political meaning in contexts where exclusion functions as a powerful symbol of social alterity. But to see these interventions as simply recuperative misses the point. Historians arguing for gender history, the history of sexuality or the history of race did not claim that men, heterosexuals or white people had been excluded from history: they argued that all history needed to be reconceptualised through these analytics.[5] We cannot be, as Christopher Dummitt's essay here phrases it, 'beyond inclusion'. The case that inclusion has been achieved has not been conclusively made, and, more profoundly, it was never the goal of revisionist historiography in the first place. That goal was to rethink the past through the categories of race, ethnicity, class, gender, region, sexuality and colonisation. I want to propose here that it is time we began to do so through a postcolonial, transnational and critical reading of the nation.

To present the insertion of Canada within narratives and understandings of global history as somehow radical or revisionist would probably seem ironic to most students of history in the first decades of the twentieth century. In these years Canadian history written in English placed Canada firmly within wider frames and more particularly imperial ones that sought to confirm and explicate Canada's place within the British empire. I agree with Magda Fahrni that historians writing

---

[3] D. Brydon, 'Canada and Postcolonial Questions, Inventories, and Futures,' in Moss (ed.), *Is Canada Postcolonial?*, p. 49.

[4] See R. Hann, G.S. Kealey, L. Kealey and P. Warren (compilers), *Primary Sources in Canadian Working Class History* (Kitchener, 1973); V. Strong-Boag, 'Raising Clio's Consciousness: Women's History and Archives in Canada', *Archivaria* 6 (Summer 1978), pp. 70–82; S. Maynard, 'In search of "Sodom North": the writing of lesbian and gay history in English Canada, 1970–1990', *Canadian Review of Comparative Literature*, no. 21 (Spring 1994), pp. 117–132. Despite relatively vigorous demands for the need for readings of the past that are anchored in Aboriginal, migrant, and racialised peoples' experiences, an anti-racist perspective on Canadian history has not been articulated in a programmatic fashion. The closest example is probably T. Stanley, 'Why I killed Canadian history: Towards an anti-racist history of Canada', *Histoire Sociale/Social History*, vol. 33, no. 65 (2000), pp. 79–103.

[5] See J. Parr, 'Gender History and Historical Practice', *Canadian Historical Review*, vol. 76, no. 3 (September 1995), pp. 354–76; M.L. Adams, *The Trouble with Normal: Postwar Youth and the Making*

in English presume the difference between Canadian and Quebec history too easily and too often. In doing so historians foreclose more productive sets of comparisons and connections. Yet the politics of nation and empire have worked themselves out in Canadian history written in French and in English in very different ways, ones that merit attenuated and specific analyses.[6]

As Barry Ferguson explains, the '"imperial question" was, arguably, the political and economic touchstone of turn-of-the-century Canada'.[7] It certainly was for George Wrong, chair of the history department of the University of Toronto and a central figure in the process of professionalisation that Donald Wright has convincingly linked to masculinisation and a self-conscious Anglicisation.[8] In a series of scantily documented essays written in a passionate first-person voice and published between 1909 and 1926 Wrong explained Canada's relationship to the British Empire to an audience of American scholars. He argued that Canada's ties with Britain were ones of history but, more importantly, ones of ongoing and shared sentiment and mutual interests. During the heat of the Great War he would take pains to clarify that the link between Canada and Britain was not a racial one. It was instead a bond rooted in 'the solid reality of education as that on which the best life of the nations must be established – education in judgement, responsibility, and self-control.'[9] Wrong explained that Canada had been self-governing in domestic affairs 'from the first' and laboured to reconcile this argument with a history that he knew included long swathes of military rule and law officials unilaterally sent out from London.

George F. Stanley also put Canadian history in an imperial frame, but one that looked very different to Wrong's. Stanley was an Alberta farm boy who earned a doctorate from Oxford in 1935 and taught history at Mount Allison University. He famously interpreted the Red River Resistance of 1869 and the Northwest Rebellion of 1885 as archetypal struggles of advanced and primitive. 'Both the Manitoba insurrection and the Saskatchewan rebellion were the manifestation in Western Canada of the problem of the frontier, namely the clash between primitive and civilized peoples.' This, he calmly asserted, was a local example of a worldwide phenomenon. 'In all parts of the

---

[6] *of Heterosexuality* (Toronto, 1997); A. Perry, *On the Edge of Empire: Gender, Race, and the Making of British Columbia, 1849–1871* (Toronto, 2001).

[6] S. Gagnon, *Quebec and its Historians: 1840 to 1920*, trans. Y. Brunelle, (Montreal, 1982), Chapter 4.

[7] B. Ferguson, *Remaking Liberalism: The Intellectual Legacy of Adam Shortt, O.D. Skelton, W.C. Clark, and W.A. MacIntosh, 1890–1940* (Montreal and Kingston, 1993), p. 66.

[8] D. Wright, *The Professionalization of History in English Canada* (Toronto, 2005), Chapter 2. Also see C. Berger, *The Writing of Canadian History: Aspects of English-Canadian Historical Writing since 1900*, 2nd edition (Toronto, 1984).

[9] G. M. Wrong, 'The Growth of Nationalism and the British Empire', *The American Historical Review*, vol. 22, no. 1 (October 1916), p. 51.

world', continued Stanley, 'in South Africa, New Zealand, and North America, the penetration of white settlement into territories inhabited by native peoples has led to friction and wars'. The Canadian northwest was no exception. Like the Maori of New Zealand or the Tswana of Southern Africa, the Métis and Cree were primitive peoples who were no match for the inevitable and onward march of civilisation.[10]

Stanley's work inserted Canada into a global analysis of empire that found continuities between North America, the Antipodes and Africa, and assumed that indigenous peoples and conflict were central to this story. Wrong, on the other hand, offered a vision of empire that put the experience of settlers and self-governing dominions at the core and argued for their increased power and authority within a reimagined and decentralised empire. To him Canada, Australia and New Zealand were exemplary stand-outs in what was otherwise a 'conquered Empire'.[11] As such, Wrong hoped that Canada could share more fully in Britain's responsibility for governing what he elsewhere called the 'dependent empire'. In 1909 he argued that Britain ruled 'some 350,000,000 alien people, unable as yet to govern themselves.' Wrong was cheered at the thought that Canada might soon bear 'her share of Britain's burden'.[12]

Wrong's interpretation of empire and Canada's place in it was in no small part a politics of race. Where Stanley saw civilised and primitive peoples, Wrong saw eastern and western ones. 'The British Empire', he explained, 'links East and West and the West hopes to pass on to the East its own education and freedom and thus to bridge the chasm between the two sections of mankind'.[13] In arguing that Canada should have increased powers within the empire and, later, the Commonwealth, Wrong was not critiquing imperialism as much as he was calling for a refashioning of it on the grounds that settler colonies deserved to be acknowledged as a disseminator of civilisation rather than a recipient of it. 'My hope', he wrote in 1909, 'for the future is that a Britain, brought daily into closer touch with the vital needs of the masses of her people, and a Canada, sobered and chastened by a grave sense of responsibility as member of a world-wide empire, may work together in pursuit of a high Christian civilisation.' Wrong's dream was for a 'league of states, Great Britain, Canada, Australia, New Zealand,

[10]   G F.G. Stanley, *The Birth of Western Canada: A History of the Riel Rebellions* (Toronto, 1992 [1936]), p. xxv.

[11]   G. M. Wrong, 'Nationalism in Canada', *Journal of the Royal Institute of International Affairs*, vol 5, no. 4 (July 1926), p. 181. Tellingly, South Africa drifted in and out of his argument over the course of the early twentieth century.

[12]   G.M. Wrong, 'Canadian Nationalism and the Imperial Tie', *Proceedings of the American Political Science Association*, vol. 6, no. 6 (1909), p. 107.

[13]   Wrong, 'The Growth of Nationalism', p. 54.

and South Africa, girdling the world'.[14] This vision of a consensual empire had wide appeal. It offered a way for liberal scholars like O.D. Skelton and Adam Shortt to reconcile their belief in Canada's place in the British Empire with a mistrust of British power heightened by the recent Boer War.[15] This enthusiastic vision of an egalitarian empire appealed to scholars compelled to reconcile the at times conflicting pulls of local experience and imperial ties. Wrong was compelled to explain his vision of Canada and the British Empire in the context of growing American influence. Wrong published in American journals for an audience he assumed to be both unknowing and incredulous. He tried to reconcile Canada's subject position within the British Empire with her nationhood and, especially in the wake of the Great War and the Balfour Declaration, her increasing ability to regulate relationships with other nations.

These balancing acts were accomplished by ample recourse to racial and gendered thinking. Wrong worked to present Canada as both a colony and a nation by employing familial and masculinist language. Here, young nations were children, metropoles mothers, and nations states of 'full manhood'.[16] It was only in metaphor that women were present; Wrong's vision of Canada and history was emphatically male. It was also emphatically white. Historians of Canada in the early twentieth century were part of what Australian historian Marilyn Lake has identified as the transnational quest for a 'white man's country'. Asian exclusion was critical to this, as it was for Wrong and many others for whom the gap between metropolitan and settler identities hardened around the issue of race and migration policy.[17] Wrong argued that the restriction of immigration was a critical feature that distinguished Canada from Britain.[18] A few years after 'Chinese' immigration to Canada was outlawed in its totality by 1923's Chinese Immigration Act, Wrong defined Canada as 'the one large state in America with a population almost wholly European'.[19] In Wrong's essays Canada's history as a French colony and the continued presence and cultural strength of French

[14] Wrong, 'Canadian Nationalism and the Imperial Tie', p. 109.

[15] Ferguson, *Rethinking Liberalism*, p. 89. Also see N. Hillmer, 'The Anglo-Canadian Neurosis: The Case of O.D. Skelton', in Peter Lyon (ed.), *Britain and Canada: Survey of a Changing Relationship* (London, 1976), pp. 61–84.

[16] Wrong, 'Nationalism in Canada', p. 193.

[17] See R. V. Mongia, 'Race, Nationality, Mobility: A History of the Passport,' in Antoinette Burton (ed.), *After the Imperial Turn: Thinking With and Through the Nation* (Durham and London, 2003); E. Dua, 'Racializing Imperial Canada: Indian Women and the Making of Ethnic Communities', in Antoinette Burton (ed.), *Gender, Sexuality, and Colonial Modernities* (London, 1999).

[18] Wrong, 'The Growth of Nationalism', p. 54.

[19] Wrong, 'Nationalism in Canada', p. 193. See Chinese Immigration Act, 1923, 13–14 George V., c. 38 accessed at www.asian.ca/law/cia1885.htm.

Canadians were figured as interesting but politically inconsequential. Indigenous history was effaced with an ease and a totality that is striking even within its historical context. This was a vision of Canada rooted in the experience of Ontario and Quebec and defined as white and male.

The curious and highly particular combination of imperial, racial and national positions through which early twentieth-century historians read the past and present also shaped the development of the history that was taught in schools. Timothy J. Stanley and Ken Montgomery have explored how ideas of empire and race – and more particularly white supremacy – were encoded in school curricula in twentieth-century English Canada. Sometimes the linking of empire, race and history was painfully overt, the kind of shopworn jingoism that prompted feminist and pacificist Frances Beynon to despair at the prospect of 'being asked to harangue a company of poor defenceless school children on Empire Day on the subject of loyalty'.[20] At other times the Canadian past was read in a manner that Montgomery helpfully identifies as banal racism, where the core contention that 'humanity is naturally divided into a finite set of discrete types' is 'banally inscribed' into historical narratives.[21]

As the twentieth century wore on the politics of nation and empire would increasingly be evoked in tandem in school histories, just as they were in scholarly ones. The junior high social studies curriculum adopted in the province of British Columbia in 1928 listed eleven 'right ideals and attitudes to be developed' by the study of a unified course in geography, history, and citizenship. Number one was 'love for the other nations of the British Empire and for our constitutional monarchy'.[22] The senior curriculum adopted there in 1936 argued that history should not valorise war but teach students 'to be tolerant of the views, rights, and privileges of others', 'be free of national arrogance' and 'cultivate good will toward the people of other lands'. An unalloyed faith in Canada's

---

[20]   F.M. Beynon, 'Loyalty and Political Corruption', *Grain Growers' Guide*, 3 June 1914. Thanks to Kurt Korneski for this reference. Also see his 'Britishness, Canadianness, Class and Race: Winnipeg and the British World, 1880s–1910s', *Journal of Canadian Studies*, vol. 41, no. 3 (Spring 2007), pp. 161–84.

[21]   K. Montgomery, 'Banal Race-thinking: Ties of Blood, Canadian History Textbooks and Ethnic Nationalism', *Paedagogica Historica*, vol. 41, no. 3 (June 2005), pp. 317–8. See also T.J. Stanley, 'White Supremacy and the Rhetoric of Educational Indoctrination: A Canadian Case Study', in Jean Barman, Neil Sutherland, and J. Donald Wilson (eds.), *Children, Teachers, and Schools in the History of British Columbia* (Calgary, 1995). Sherene Razack's work is also helpful for registering and unpacking the presence of banal racisms. See in particular her *Looking White People in the Eye: Gender, Race, and Culture in Courtrooms and Classrooms* (Toronto, 1998).

[22]   British Columbia, Department of Education, *Programme of Studies for Junior High Schools of British Columbia, 1927–1928*, p. 6. Available online at www.mala.bc.ca.homeroom/Content/Topics/Programs/2001/JNRHI/Socstud.htm.

place within the British Empire was invoked alongside this soft pluralism. 'We are a British people', the guide explained further. 'It is to be expected, therefore, that we should trace the story of man up to the early period of British history, continue with the progress in Britain up to the discovery of America, and then view the development of the Canadian people up to the present.'[23]

Here imperialism emerges as fluid, polyglot ideology, compatible even with antiwar sentiments and a vague internationalism. Yet such flexibility fell away when specific topics for study were specified. What remained was a vision of Canadian history that minimised indigenous histories, truncated the history of France and French-speaking settlers in Canada, and effaced non-white settlement. Canada's history proceeded as follows for grade eleven students, each subject studied in three- to five-week chunks: 'The Age of Discovery', 'Champlain and the Colony of New France', 'The English Colonies on the Atlantic Coast', 'The Advance to the West', 'Over the Mountains', 'Pacific Coast', 'The Coming of British Settlers to Canada', 'Pioneering on the Plains', 'The Colony of B.C.' and, finally, 'The Growth of Canada's Transportation and Communication Facilities'.[24]

After the Second World War, Canadian historians writing in English began to reject, sometimes overtly and sometimes by intellectual default, the core connections that underlay these popular and scholarly histories: that Canadian history was best understood as part of the British Empire. This rejection was part of what José Igartua has rightly identified as the 'other quiet revolution' that fundamentally reframed questions of Canadian identity between 1945 and 1971. English Canadians increasingly rejected the framing of Canada as British in exchange for a new national language that framed Canada as a distinct, independent and bicultural nation.[25] Historians writing in English increasingly took their job as an implicitly or explicitly nationalist one. They called for an ambitious new history of Canada, written for and by Canadians. In the 1960s and 1970s their vision would motivate and inform a critical growth in the institutional authority and production of Canadian history. In this new, increasingly voluble and sophisticated history Canada was reimagined; its indigenous and imperial past were downplayed and in its place emerged a bilingual, bicultural and North American history that befitted the vague English Canadian cultural nationalism of the day.

---

[23] 'History and Citizenship Curriculum, 1936', British Columbia, Department of Education, *Programme of Studies*, accessed at www.mala.bc.ca/homsroom/Content/Topics/Programs/2001/ss36.index.htm, 1, 2, 8.

[24] 'History and Citizenship Curriculum, 1936', p. 8.

[25] J.E. Igartua, *The Other Quiet Revolution: National Identities in English Canada, 1945–1971* (Vancouver, 2005).

This shift can be registered in a number of ways. R. Douglas Francis has traced it in the intellectual biographies of historians Frank Underhill and Arthur Lower, who leveraged their wartime experience to develop a new, nationalist politics of Canadian history predicated on a disavowal of the British Empire and Canada's role in it.[26] Marlene Shore argues in the flagship *Canadian Historical Review* that sometime after the Second World War historians writing in its pages began to suggest that 'Canada's North American heritage was of prime importance in understanding her past.'[27]

The new vision of the Canadian past was concerned with asserting Canada's distinct identity and explaining imperial ties and patterns not as insignificant as much as a precursor to what was, in fact, our real history. The oft-quoted title of Arthur Lower's 1947 book, *From Colony to Nation*, summed up the presumed trajectory well enough. This view acknowledged Canada's imperial past, both French and English, but saw it as essentially a prelude to Canada's true history as an independent, bicultural and resolutely North American nation. Ramsay Cook, Jack Saywell and John Richer evaluated the relevance of Canada's imperial past in 1971. Canada's status as a French and then British colony was once, they argued 'a theme of great urgency – perhaps even the dominant theme – in Canadian historical writing.' It was no longer, they explained, because 'the Commonwealth association, for all its historical significance', was now tenuous and, for many, irrelevant.[28] Here was whig history at its best: the past transformed into a progressive, inevitable march, each step better than the last, leading from the colonial past to the national present.

This newly nationalist English Canadian history was fuelled by a sense of underdog justice honed around the historic association of capital H history with the supposed old-world and the very real institutional politics that sustained them. English Canada shared much of the Australian experience analysed by Ann Curthoys: a small network of post-secondary education and a middle-class anxiety that Canada lacked 'a worthy intellectual national culture and was merely a second-rate derivation of Britain'.[29] In a context where an Oxford undergraduate degree was a virtual precondition to a permanent post at the University of

---

[26] R. D. Francis, 'Historical Perspectives on Britain: The Ideas of Canadian Historians Frank H. Underhill and Arthur R.M. Lowe', in Phillip Buckner and R. Douglas Francis (eds.), *Canada and the British World: Culture, Migration, and Identity* (Vancouver, 2006).

[27] M. Shore, '"Remember the Future": The *Canadian Historical Review* and the Discipline of History', *Canadian Historical Review*, vol. 76, no. 3 (September 1995), p. 426.

[28] R. Cook with J. Richer and J. Saywell, *Canada: A Modern Study* (Toronto, 1971), Introduction, np.

[29] A. Curthoys, 'We've Just Started Making National Histories and You Want us to Stop Already?', in Burton (ed.), *After the Imperial Turn*, p. 70.

Toronto's history department and where the legitimacy of Canadian history as a field remained in doubt well into the 1960s, writing, thinking and teaching about Canada in Canada had an undeniable revolutionary cachet. This context gave renewed power to the nineteenth-century idea that historians are at best custodians of the nation, a tenet that was articulated with new vigour and different emphasis. In his 1967 presidential address to the Canadian Historical Association, Richard Saunders argued that 'It is a duty that the discipline and profession of history to which they belong and which they likewise serve owes to the nation, to Canada.'[30]

With such imperatives imperialism slipped from view. Sometimes it reappeared only to be explained as nationalism. In his influential 1970 work *The Sense of Power: Studies in the Ideas of Canadian Imperialism, 1867-1914*, Carl Berger argued in conclusion that 'Imperialism was one form of Canadian nationalism.'[31] This argument is salutary in the way it prompts us to think of imperialism and nationalism as non-sequential. We might read this as a canny foreshadowing of the argument that would emerge in the 1990s from critical histories of nation and empire: as Antoinette Burton puts it, 'that the nation is not only *not* antecedent to empire, but that as both a symbolic and material site the nation ... has no fixity outside of the various discourses of which it is itself an effect.'[32] But Berger takes something very different away from the simultaneity of nation and empire in English Canadian men's thought. This recognition does not prompt a rethinking of the relationship between imperialism and settler nationalism as much as a reaffirmation of the latter. Berger's argument is not remarkable in many respects, but the fact that this work remains the standard reference for studies of English Canada and imperialism surely is.

If anything, indigenous peoples receded farther from view as the nation came into sharper focus. First Nations peoples and history had occupied a position, if a relatively small one, in the Canadian history written in the first decades of the twentieth century by scholars like Stanley and Harold Innis. By the mid twentieth century, they and their chroniclers had for all intents and purposes disappeared.[33] These new histories of Canada were rooted in a quest for an authentic settler experience of North America. That the fractures within that settler identity were considered central is made clear by the acknowledgements, variously

[30] 'The Historian and the Nation', presidential address read before the Canadian Historical Association, June 1967, accessed at www.cha-shc.ca/english/publ/jcha-rshc/addr_alloc/, p. 2.

[31] C. Berger, *The Sense of Power: Studies in the Ideas of Canadian Imperialism, 1867–1914* (Toronto, 1970), p. 259.

[32] A. Burton, 'Who Needs the Nation? Interrogating "British" History', [1997] reprinted in Catherine Hall (ed.), *Cultures of Empire: A Reader* (London, 2000), p. 141.

[33] Shore, 'Remember the Future', p. 430.

phrased, that Canada's was a history of both French and English. Indigenous peoples or issues find little place in Berger's study beyond the vague role assigned to the Red River resistance as an originary point of Canadian nationalism.

The most serious challenge to the new national histories of Canada would come from a diverse and at times fractious group of historians writing under the broad rubric of social history. In the 1970s and 1980s these historians of labour, women, Aboriginal peoples and migration would draw attention to the fact that so much Canadian history was the top-down political history of one elite or another. The arrival of these scholars and arguments on the historical scene reflected a massive expansion of post-secondary education in the 1960s and 1970s and, perhaps more fundamentally, an interrelated shift in who wrote history and what was considered a legitimate topic thereof.[34]

Yet for all the changes it brought, this new social history of English Canada laboured largely within the same national conventions as the conservative, political history that it criticised. Social history, as Phillip Buckner has argued, 'inevitably involved a comparative, transnational perspective and so rescued Canadian historiography from some of its parochialism'.[35] But with some notable exceptions, like Bruno Ramirez's comparative study of Italian and Quebec migration,[36] the nation remained as the underlying frame of reference, if no longer the primary analytic. What scholars saw as constituting Canadian history changed, but the framing of it within the confines of nation rarely did.

The residual centrality of the nation to Canadian history written in English became clearer in the sharp debates that occurred in the 1980s and 1990s. Ink was spilled arguing whether cheerful stories of national triumph or critical histories of race, gender and class better served the nation, but nobody really questioned that ours was, at heart, a project of nation. Even Jack Granatstein's over-engaged and intemperate attack on this new social history could not fault historians with abandoning their mission to the nation. Instead, it made the blander argument that

---

[34]   On these changes in Britain, see C. Hall, 'Feminism and Feminist History', in *White, Male, and Middle Class: Explorations in Feminism and History* (London and New York, 1992) and in the United States, see J.W. Scott, 'Feminism's History', *Journal of Women's History*, vol. 16, no. 2 (2004), pp. 10–29. In Canada, see V. Strong-Boag, 'Contested Space: The Politics of Canadian Memory', presidential address read before the Canadian Historical Association, June 1994, accessed at www.cha-shc.ca/english/publ/jcha-rshc/addr_alloc/.

[35]   P. Buckner, 'Whatever Happened to the British Empire?', presidential address read before the Canadian Historical Association, June 1993, accessed at www.cha-shc.ca/english/publ/jcha-rshc/addr_alloc/, p. 7.

[36]   B. Ramirez, *On the Move: French-Canadian and Italian Migrants in the North Atlantic Economy, 1860–1914* (Toronto, 1991).

social historians' work failed to serve the nation *well*.[37] As Franca Iacovetta has recently pointed out, the avalanche of critical responses to Granatstein's argument rarely took explicit issue with his contention that history was a project of the nation and should be so.[38] This mirrored the Australian context, where heated conflicts between women's and Aboriginal historians and political historians were underwritten by a common belief in the national aims of historical scholarship. As Marilyn Lake explains, history was 'a contested terrain, but in these confrontations the terrain in question has remained that of the nation-state'.[39]

But the fiction of the nation is always taxing to maintain, especially so in contexts where the radical unevenness of colonial and national developments constantly chip away at the nation's claims to totality and coherence. Canada is an excellent example of this, and we need not resort to David Cannadine's flippant march through Canadian history to make this point.[40] It is undeniably difficult to locate what in 1960 W.L. Morton called approvingly the 'one narrative line in Canadian history'[41] when that line must be made to stretch through culturally and politically diverse indigenous peoples, French colonies, British colonies, a national entity called Canada created in 1867 but limited in geographical scope until 1949, deeply ensconced in a British Empire, articulated differently in

[37]   J.L. Granatstein, *Who Killed Canadian History?* (Toronto, 1998). Notable responses were M. Bliss, 'Privatizing the Mind: The Sundering of Canadian History, The Sundering of Canada', *Journal of Canadian Studies*, vol. 26, no. 4, Winter 1991–1992, pp. 5–17; G.C. Brandt, 'National Unity and the Politics of Personal History', *Journal of the Canadian Historical Association* (1992), vol. 3, no. 11; G. Carr, 'Review Essay: Harsh Sentences: Appealing the Strange Verdict of Who Killed Canadian History?', *The American Review of Canadian Studies* (Spring and Summer 1998), pp. 167–176; G.S. Kealey, 'Class in English-Canadian History Writing: Neither Privatizing, Nor Sundering', *Journal of Canadian Studies*, vol. 27, no. 2, Summer 1992, pp. 123–9; L. Kealey, R. Pierson, J. Sangster and V. Strong-Boag, 'Teaching Canadian History in the 1990s: Whose "National" History Are We Lamenting?', *Journal of Canadian Studies*, vol. 27, no. 2, Summer 1992, pp. 129–31; A.B. McKillop, 'Who Killed Canadian History? A View From the Trenches', *Canadian Historical Review*, vol. 80, no. 2 (June 1999), pp. 269–99; B.D. Palmer, 'Of Silences and Trenches: A Dissident View of Granatstein's Meaning', *Canadian Historical Review*, vol. 80, no. 4 (December 1999) pp. 676–86; Stanley, 'Why I killed Canadian History'.

[38]   F. Iacovetta, 'Gendering Trans/National Historiographies: Feminists Rewriting Canadian History', *Journal of Women's History*, vol. 19, no. 1 (2007) pp. 210–1.

[39]   M. Lake, 'White Man's Country: The Trans-National History of a National Project', *Australian Historical Studies*, vol. 34, no. 122 (October 2003), p. 347. Also see her 'Nationalist Historiography, Feminist Scholarship, and the Promise and Problems of New Transnational Histories: The Australian Case', *Journal of Women's History*, vol. 19, no. 1 (2007), pp. 180–6.

[40]   D. Cannadine, 'Imperial Canada: Old History, New Problems', in Colin M. Coates (ed.), *Imperial Canada, 1867–1917* (Edinburgh, 1997), pp. 1–19.

[41]   W.L. Morton, 'The Relevance of Canadian History', presidential address given to the Canadian Historical Association, June 1960, accessed at www.cha-shc.ca/english/publ/jcha-rshc/addr_alloc/, p. 1.

French and in English, bifurcated by province, and always in the context of the larger and more powerful settler society directly to its south.

This narrative line is forever wandering across time, space and communication. Anyone who teaches Canadian history is familiar with the jurisdictional quandaries. Which parts of British and French North America that were later territorialised as the United States should be included? We are accustomed to constituting northern North America before European contact and the northern colonies of France and Britain as 'pre-Confederation Canada'. Yet, to state the obvious, we know that there was no Canada per se until Confederation. Lumping the divergent histories of indigenous northern North America, northern French America, and (some of) British North America only makes sense if we take contemporary territorial divisions as durable and appropriate goalposts. Given this ahistoricism, it is not surprising that these goalposts shift depending on the context in which the material is being taught or studied. Thus seventeenth- and eighteenth-century and, to a much smaller extent, nineteenth-century histories of New France and British North America appear in works on 'American' history as well.[42] The particular quandaries change as we move through the nineteenth century, but they do not go away. Do we exclude books or ideas that were not written or published in Canada from our purview even if they were of enormous significance to its history? How do we deal with Newfoundland before it swapped its role as a British colony for that of a Canadian province in 1949?

It can be hard work maintaining the fiction that the nation state is a discrete and reliable container, but historians remain remarkably committed to doing so. Elizabeth Vibert's conclusion – that, as a scholar 'trained by Africanists, intrigued by India, writing a doctoral dissertation on British representations of Indigenous peoples in a little studied region of the trans-border Pacific Northwest', she was better understood as a 'colonial historian' than a Canadianist – remains unusual.[43] Most of us speak confidently of ourselves as 'Canadianists' and mount courses, advertise jobs and organise expertise along those lines. This is not simply institutional. Critical discussion of the Canadian nation and those inside and outside it has come largely not from historians but from proponents of critical race theory working on the margins of the discipline.[44] Ian McKay's far-thinking argument

---

[42]   See, for a recent example, M.J. Schueller and E. Watts (eds.), *Messy Beginnings: Postcoloniality and Early American Studies* (Rutgers, NJ, 2002).

[43]   E. Vibert, 'Border Crossings: A Review Essay', *BC Studies*, no. 119 (Autumn 1998), p. 97.

[44]   Iacovetta makes this point in 'Gendering Trans/National Histories'. This literature is now substantial. See, for instance, S. Thobani, *Exhalted Subjects: Studies in the Making of Race and Nation in Canada* (Toronto, 2007); S. Razack, *Dark Threats and White Knights: The Somalia Affair, Peacekeeping and the New Imperialism* (Toronto, 2004); E. Dua and A. Robertson (eds.), *Scratching the Surface:*

for a 'liberal order framework' asks us to think of 'Canada-as-project',[45] but takes his questioning of the nation not much further. In 2005 Allen Greer issued a call to reject Canadian history 'bathed in an atmosphere of national piety' in favour of globally and continentally framed analyses. This argument didn't pick up much intellectual traction beyond Granatstein's reiteration of his contention that Canadian history is often taught as 'one of oppression and shame', and a short burst of discussion on the history listserv H-Canada.[46]

This putative commitment to national histories is belied and challenged by scholarly practice that crosses borders with increasing regularity. Our research is becoming more transnational in practice if not in theory. That the chapters by Katie Pickles, Michel Ducharme and myself in this volume all argue for one form of internationalism or another makes that point, as do the spate of recent histories that chart new trajectories between and across national lines. Histories of women like Mary McGeechy and Margaret Wrong remind us that for some people internationalism was a conscious choice and a politics.[47] Steve High and Karen Dubinsky show us that it is possible and fruitful to write histories of the postwar era, whether the deindustrialisation that shook central North America from the 1960s to the 1980s or honeymooning and tourism in Niagara Falls, without waging a continual and failing battle to locate the border in phenomena that stretched unevenly across central North America.[48]

Histories of migration are necessarily transnational to a lesser or greater extent, and it is through them that historians of Canada are taking their place in wider discussions of gender and migration.[49] Recent histories of Mennonites have been

Canadian Anti-Racist Feminist Thought (Toronto, 1999); S. Razack (ed.) *Race, Space and the Law: Unmapping a White Settler Society* (Toronto, 2002); R. Walcott, *Rude: Contemporary Black Canadian Cultural Criticism* (Toronto, 2000); *Atlantis: A Women's Studies Journal*, special issue on 'Whose Canada Is It? Immigrant Women, Women of Colour, Citizenship and Multiculturalism', vol. 24, no. 2 (Winter 2000), H. Bannerji, *On the Dark Side of the Nation: Essays on Multiculturalism and Gender* (Toronto, 2000).

[45]   I. McKay, 'The Liberal Order Framework: A Prospectus for a Reconnaissance of Canadian History', *Canadian Historical Review*, vol. 81, no. 4 (December 2000), p. 621.

[46]   A. Greer, 'Canadian History is so Boring', *National Post*, 20 August 2005; J. Granatstein, 'Getting History Right', *Ottawa Citizen*, 27 August 2005; www.h-net.org/~canada/ (and search for 'Greer Granatstein').

[47]   M. Kinnear, *Woman of the World: Mary McGeachy and International Co-operation* (Toronto: 2004); R.C. Brouwer, *Modern Women Modernizing Men: The Changing Missions of Three Professional Women in Asia and Africa, 1902–69* (Vancouver, 2003).

[48]   K. Dubinsky, *The Second Greatest Disappointment: Honeymooners, Heterosexuality, and the Tourist Industry at Niagara Falls* (Newark, NJ, 1999); S. High, *Industrial Sunset: The Making of North America's Rust-Belt, 1969–1984* (Toronto, 2003).

[49]   See F. Iacovetta and D. Gabbacia (eds.), *Women, Gender and Transnational Lives: Italian Workers of the World* (Toronto, 2002).

especially effective at breaking with the tradition of beginning in one national space and ending in another. In taking us between Russia, Germany, Canada, Panama, Mexico and the United States, Marlene Epp and Roy Loewen offer us histories of multiple national, linguistic and geographical spaces simultaneously and, in doing so, provide us with remarkable examples of what a transnational history that includes Canada might look like.[50] Dubinsky's new work on the politics of international and transracial adoption in the twentieth century suggests some of the ways that historians might map new and productive connections between places where we are certainly not taught to find them.[51] So, in a very different way, does John Weaver's history of 'the great land rush' and global modernity.[52]

The rediscovery of imperial frames of reference also is providing another route by which Canadian history is finding more global frames of reference. In the past few years three volumes zeroing in on Canada's connection to the British, and to a much lesser extent French, empires have been published.[53] By any reckoning, this is something of a watershed in a historiographical context where scholarly production remains patchy and episodic. That these volumes are collections of essays makes clear that this growing new scholarship on Canada and imperialism is of recent vintage, and will likely mature and grow as articles become monographs and, eventually, paraphrases in textbooks. This work is buttressed by a small spate of monographs that find Canada's place in the new social history of the British Empire.[54] In doing so, these histories illuminate the connective tissue that tied Canada to the metropole and, in cases like the female migration efforts studied by Lisa Chilton, to other colonial spaces like Australia.[55]

Historians of what is apocryphally referred to as pre-Confederation Canada and regions on the margins of Canada's geographical and cultural scope find

---

[50]   M. Epp, *Women Without Men: Mennonite Refugees of the Second World War* (Toronto, 2000); R. Loewen, *Diaspora in the Countryside: Two Mennonite Communities and Mid-Twentieth-Century Rural Disjuncture* (Winnipeg, 2006).

[51]   K. Dubinsky, 'Babies Without Borders: Rescue, Kidnap and the Symbolic Child', *Journal of Women's History*, vol. 19, no. 1 (Spring 2007), pp. 248–53.

[52]   J. Weaver, *The Great Land Rush and the Making of the Modern World, 1650–1900* (Montreal and Kingston, 2002).

[53]   P. Buckner and R. D. Francis (eds.), *Canada and the British World*; P. Buckner (ed.), *Canada and the End of Empire* (Vancouver, 2005); C. Coates (ed.), *Majesty in Canada: Essays on the Role of Royalty* (Dundurn, Ontario, 2005).

[54]   K. Pickles, *Female Imperialism and National Identity: Imperial Order Daughters of the Empire*, (New York, 2002); I. Radforth, *Royal Spectacle: The 1860 Prince of Wales Visit to Canada and the United States* (Toronto, 2005).

[55]   L. Chilton, *Agents of Empire: British Female Migration to Canada and Australia, 1860s–1930* (Toronto, 2007).

themselves particularly ill-served by the national organisation of Canadian history. It is for this reason that scholars of Canada's west, north, and the seventeenth, eighteenth and nineteenth centuries have been most willing to move from a practice of transnational history to an explicit argument for it. All national borders can be porous, and the ones of marginal, colonised and formerly colonised places have been particularly ill-equipped to sustain the fantasy of nations as territorially bounded, discrete and finite entities. It is from the multiple margins of west and indigenous that the fictions of the modern nation are less sustainable and less appealing. Historians of the northwest like Ted Binnema and Sheila McManus have argued convincingly that the territories to the east of the Rocky Mountains be thought of as one analytic unit, the late arriving border fixed at the 49th parallel notwithstanding.[56] On the other side of the Rockies the administrative and social history of the Hudson's Bay Company has prompted scholars to produce work that chips away at presumed distinctions between American and Canadian history and between British and American versions of colonialism.[57] It is the lived histories of shared geographical space that the authors call the Pacific Northwest rather than the unstable political containers of British Columbia, Washington and Alaska that provide the frameworks for recent work by Paige Raibmon and Carol Williams.[58]

Borders are also being crossed in less literal ways. Studies grounded in particular geographical spaces cross borders when they resist the desire to treat those places as simple manifestations of the local or the national. Thus when historians like Sarah Carter and Myra Rutherdale conceptualise their studies of cultural imagery in the late nineteenth-century prairie west and missionaries in the north in a wider international scholarship on gender and colonialism they find new ways of seeing those rooted histories.[59] Likewise Cole Harris and Dan Clayton's insightful histories of west-coast colonialism roam widely and draw insights and comparisons wherever they find them while returning to the particular spaces of

---

[56] T. Binnema, *Common and Contested Ground: A Human and Environmental History of the Northwest Plains* (Norman, OK, 2001); S. McManus, *The Line Which Separates: Race, Gender, and the Making of the Alberta–Montana Borderlands* (Edmonton, 2005).

[57] E. Vibert, *Traders' Tales: Narratives of Cultural Encounters in the Columbia Plateau, 1807–1846* (Norman, OK, 1997); R.S. Mackie, *Trading Beyond the Mountains: The British Fur Trade on the Pacific, 1793–1843* (Vancouver, 1997).

[58] P. Raibmon, *Authentic Indians: Episodes of Encounter from the Late-Nineteenth-Century Northwest Coast* (Durham and London, 2005); C.J. Williams, *Framing the West: Race, Gender, and the Photographic Frontier in the Pacific Northwest* (New York, 2003).

[59] M. Rutherdale, *Women and the White Man's God: Gender and Race in the Canadian Mission Field* (Vancouver: UBC Press, 2002).

Vancouver Island and British Columbia.[60] By firmly locating North America within the affective and political logics of empire these works both support and, to some extent, prefigure Ann Laura Stoler's influential call to situate North America within global understandings of imperialism.[61] That so many of these works focus on the geographical spaces west of the Great Lakes and on the analytic categories of gender, race and empire does not suggest that these are the only useful terrains of thinking outside national histories as much as it makes clear where, exactly, the fictions of nation are most likely to fray and unravel.

My point in cataloguing the various ways that historians writing in English are breaching and reaching beyond categories of nation is to argue that, in effect, we are closer to a transnational or postcolonial history of Canada than we might think. Given the extent to which current scholarship is moving in imperial, transborder, and transnational directions, why do we continue to cleave to the assumption that the nation of Canada can somehow contain and guide our work? It is in part because the labours of this kind of historical work are so unevenly borne. As Lake argues, the extent to which the histories of colonial societies are now acknowledged as worthy of meaningful historical discussion seems predicated on the extent to which they may be seen as contributing to the knowledge of metropolitan places.[62] For all the recent work on the United States-Canada borderlands, what is mobilised as 'the' borderland in the American academy is overwhelmingly the one on its southern flank.[63] That so many of the winners of the Albert B. Corey prize for the best book on the history of American-Canadian relations or on the history of both countries were affiliated to Canadian universities makes clear which partner in this relationship is most willing to register its existence.[64] In different ways, Canada remains an unacknowledged and insignificant other of French imperial, British imperial and North American historiography. Tying the binds between nation and history

---

[60] C. Harris, *The Resettlement of British Columbia: Essays on Colonialism and Geographical Change* (Vancouver, 1997); C. Harris, *Making Native Space: Colonialism, Resistance, and Reserves in British Columbia* (Vancouver, 2003); D.W. Clayton, *Islands of Truth: The Imperial Fashioning of Vancouver Island* (Vancouver, 2000).

[61] A.L. Stoler, 'Tense and Tender Ties: The Politics of Comparison in North American History and (Post) Colonial Studies', [2002], reprinted in Ann Laura Stoler (ed.), *Haunted by Empire: Geographies of Intimacy in North American History* (Durham and London, 2006).

[62] Lake, 'White Man's Country'.

[63] See, for instance, J. Adelman and S. Aron, 'From Borderlands to Borders: Empires, Nation-States, and the Peoples in Between in North American History', *American Historical Review*, vol. 4, no. 3 (June 1999), pp. 814–41. For a discussion of the other borderlands, see E. Jameson, 'Dancing on the Rim, Tiptoeing through Minefields: Challenges and Promises of Borderlands', *Pacific Historical Review*, vol. 75, no. 1 (2006), pp. 1–24.

[64] www.historians.org/prizes/AWARDED/CoreyWinner.htm.

even closer is an understandable if ultimately unsatisfying response to our con-tinued marginalisation as one of the inconsequential 'others' of North American history.

Thinking transnationally does not mean rejecting the state as an object of inquiry or an analytic category. It means not assuming the *a priori* salience of the nation and instead accessing particular regimes of state rule as they do or do not present themselves. To import a phrase from a different historiographical con-text, thinking transnationally asks us to not presuppose the object of our inquiry, but to track and explore its makings and un-makings.[65] Often we will conclude that the state and the nation did matter very much. Elizabeth Jameson and Jeremy Mouat begin their discussion of the west in Canadian and American his-toriography with the argument that the nation is not fixed or absolute but con-clude that it has profoundly shaped how scholars have seen the west and its peoples.[66] While the media is much enamoured with the rhetoric of a global world with falling borders, we also live in an era where borders and control of them are assuming increasing, and at times plainly ominous, authority over our lives. There can be no doubt that the nation does matter, most of all to the many people who find themselves outside its purview and unable to claim its rights. Contemporary activists in groups like No One Is Illegal are drawing increasing attention to the relationship between states, nations and nationalisms, borders, race and colonisation.[67] In questioning the state's right to exclude and crimi-nalise, No One Is Illegal is doing anything but denying the impact of the nation and the state on human lives. My argument here is not to reject the nation as a category of analysis or experience, but to strip it of the ontological primacy and, in doing so, better see its real power at work. Historians of Canada need to begin to write histories that reject what sociologist Nandita Sharma calls the 'artificial homeyness' of the nation and instead think long and hard about what the nation means for peoples and communities.[68]

In the early years of the twentieth century historians tended to emphasise Canada as a part of the British Empire, if a complicated one. Around the mid-dle of the century historians began to explicitly reject this frame in favour of one that emphasised Canada as a distinct and North American nation. For all the

[65] M. Valverde, 'Poststructuralist Gender Historians: Are We Those Names?', *Labour/Le Travail*, no. 25 (Spring 1990), p. 228.

[66] J. Mouat and E. Jameson, 'Telling Differences: The Forty-Ninth Parallel and Historiographies of the West and the Nation', *Pacific Historical Review*, vol. 75, no. 2 (May 2006), pp. 183–230.

[67] See, for instance, http://nooneisillegal-montreal.blogspot.com; http://toronto.nooneisillegal.org; www.vipirg.ca/campaigns/noii/index.html; http://noii-halifax.blogspot.com.

[68] N. Sharma, *Home Economics: Nationalism and the Making of 'Migrant Workers' in Canada* (Toronto, 2006), p. 30.

changes that social historians brought to the intellectual table in the 1970s and 1980s, the nation has remained the critical and largely unquestioned under-girding to Canadian history written in English. Three recent developments – the creation of a rich international scholarship arguing for transnational and post-colonial perspectives on the past, the growth of critical feminist scholarship on the nation in Canada, and the increasingly transnational scholarship of practising historians – all prompt us to question the meaning, impact, and limits of the nation as an experience and a tool of analysis. Doing so will help us craft more critical and compelling histories of what lay on both the inside and the outside of the nation.

Acknowledgements

I would like to acknowledge conversations with and assistance from Barry Ferguson, Gerry Friesen, Kurt Korneski, Tamara Myers, Steve Penfold and Ryan Eyford. Christopher Dummitt and Michael Dawson deserve thanks for pulling this project together. The support of the Canada Research Chairs Programme is also gratefully acknowledged.

Chapter 7
Transnational Intentions and Cultural Cringe: History Beyond National Boundaries

Katie Pickles

This chapter draws upon my personal experience working across the boundaries of Canadian history, New Zealand history and, in seeking transnational understanding, Australian and British history. Taking conference sessions, job advertisements, new books and book series titles as indicators, at the beginning of the twenty-first century there has emerged a trend for transnational and cross-cultural approaches to history.[1] This is a change of focus from the historiographies that dominate research and teaching in Canadian, New Zealand and Australian universities: products of the 1970s' questioning of previous hegemonic imperial narratives and their replacement with historiographies imbued in cultural nationalism.[2] With gender, race and class as categories of analysis the then new social and cultural histories focused on recovering history marginalised by previous grand narratives. The parameters for research were drawn from

---

[1] Some examples of books are: A. Burton (ed.), *After the Imperial Turn: Thinking With and Through the Nation* (New Haven, 2003); A. Curthoys and M. Lake (eds.), *Connected Worlds: History in Transnational Perspective* (Canberra, 2006); K. Grant, P. Levine and F. Trentmann (eds.), *Beyond Sovereignty: Britain, Empire and Transnationalism, c. 1880–1950* (Basingstoke and New York, 2007); K. Pickles, *Transnational Outrage: The Death and Commemoration of Edith Cavell* (Basingstoke and New York, 2007); I. Tyrrell, *Transnational Nation: United States History in Global Perspective since 1789* (Basingstoke and New York, 2007). For the call to pay attention to 'the world's place in New Zealand' see P. Gibbons, 'The Far Side of the Search for Identity: Reconsidering New Zealand History', *New Zealand Journal of History*, vol. 37, no. 1 (2003), pp. 38–47.

[2] Examples here are Canada: J.A. Lower, *Canada: An Outline History* (Toronto, 1971, 1991); D. Morton, *A Short History of Canada*, 6th edition (Toronto, 2006); R.C. Brown and R. Cook, *Canada, 1896–1921: A Nation Transformed* (Toronto, 1974). New Zealand: W.H. Oliver with B.R. Williams (eds.), *The Oxford History of New Zealand* (Auckland, 1981), and G.W. Rice (ed.), *The Oxford History of New Zealand*, 2nd edition (Auckland, 1992); K. Sinclair, *A History of New Zealand* (Harmondsworth, 1959), with revised editions through to 2000; K. Sinclair, *A Destiny Apart: New Zealand's Search for National Identity* (Wellington, 1986).

national boundaries. In countries obsessed with moving on from a British impe-rial past to construct national identities, emphasising uniqueness was politically astute and the machinery of the state encouraged national-focused research by citizens and/or those working at national institutions through nationally funded research grants. Such a climate made it possible for the postcolonial promise of abandoning restrictive histories to be hijacked by nation-building projects that are easily critiqued for insecurity and self-doubt: the very same two qualities that those writing from their respective nations hoped to escape.[3]

But now that nation-bound approaches are being questioned, are scholars prepared to address the identity politics that underpin them? In the recent 'his-tory wars', and the resurgence of studies of a British world, there has been some discussion of the politics of who can write for whom.[4] The debate has seen two familiar sides line up: those of the 'old left' who, critiquing the colonial project, write histories of difference, diversity and the marginalised, versus those of the 'old centre right' and 'old right' who rail against 'political correctness' and post-structural, postmodern and postcolonial ways of doing history and instead seek a return to what they consider to be traditional history.

To take the discussion off in a more productive direction, one might ask whether it should matter any more for those researching and writing history what their citizenship or ethnicity is, or where they are based. My experiences suggest it does matter, and that nation-based mindsets and inferiority complexes are alive and well in the historical professions of Canada, New Zealand and Australia. Specifically, there is the perpetuation of a 'cultural cringe', including the 'cringe inverted' – involving the parochial construction of insiders and outsiders – that needs to be addressed if transnational history is to be pursued. Furthermore, dri-ven by identity politics of gender and race, gaps between doing the history of Anglo-Canada and New Zealand reveal the importance of local politics and confirm not only that the historiographies of 'white settler societies' are volatile and insecure but also that addressing the sore points and picking at the scabs are

---

[3]   L.J. Hume, 'Another Look at the Cultural Cringe', *Revivalist*, Winter 2003. First published in the Political Theory Newsletter in 1991 and reprinted as a pamphlet by the Centre for Independent Studies. Hume wrote that 'communities that are truly sure of their place in the world do not embrace nationalistic postures or feel a need to assert their independence. The nationalists protest too much'.
[4]   For Canada see J.L. Granatstein, *Who Killed Canadian History?* (Toronto, 1998, 2007). For Australia see S. Macintyre and A. Clark (eds.), *The History Wars* (Melbourne, 2003); K. Windschuttle, *The Fabrication of Aboriginal History, Volume One: Van Diemen's Land 1803–1847*, (Sydney, 2002); K. Windschuttle, *The Killing of History: How a Discipline is being Murdered by Literary Critics and Social Theorists* (Sydney, 1994). For New Zealand see P. Munz, 'Te Papa and the Problem of Historical Truth', *History Now*, vol. 6, no. 1 (2000), pp. 13–16; K. Howe, 'Can you Find a Nation's Soul in its National Museum?', *History Now*, vol. 7, no. 3 (2001), p. 8.

useful places to focus research. Finally, I consider how neither Canada nor New Zealand prioritises teaching about the other – a reflection of nation-based disciplines that is a serious stumbling block to transnational knowledge when a 'teaching/research nexus' guides the overall direction of scholarship.

Persistent Cringing

Parochial identity politics underpins the writing of much history about Anglo-Canada and New Zealand. In both places history as a discipline has contributed to the development of the nation state and the construction of national identity.[5] Similarities are evident, especially in imperial legacies, and in examining western notions of gender, race and labour relations. The major differences in historiographies, in Canada the importance of French Canada and the United States, and in New Zealand, Maori and bicultural history, are all implicated in national formation. Both places have spent the past 40 years building largely self-contained parochial historiographies that remain eerily engulfed under a veil of cultural cringe. An indicator of the restricted appeal of such introversion is that the vast majority of Canadian and New Zealand historians are based within the country that they research. It would be a sign of maturity for Canadian and New Zealand history to be taken seriously outside their respective national boundaries. Ironically, an age of 'trans' and 'posts' that dismantles the nation as an entry point for inquiry risks rendering nation-based scholarship even more parochial.

Despite well-developed national historiographies, Canadian and New Zealand history both still suffer from a dose of cultural cringe. This emanates from the legacy of imperial feeling that Canada and New Zealand do not have their 'own' histories, and subsequently the ones being written are somehow inferior. Hence they are variously regarded as 'easy', 'common knowledge' and 'boring'.[6] The best term for describing the inferiority complex of Canadian and New Zealand

---

[5]   Despite the inadequacy of national frameworks, Lake has recently drawn attention to the on-going power of the nation-state in historiography and activism. M. Lake, 'Nationalist Historiography and Feminist Scholarship: The Promise and Problems of New Transnational History. The Australian Case, *Journal of Women's History*, vol. 19, no. 1 (2007), pp. 180–186.

[6]   In 2005 similar debates occurred on H-Net lists in Canada, New Zealand and Australia. In Canada the catalyst for discussion was A. Greer, 'Canadian History is Boring ...', *Ottawa Citizen*, 20 August 2005. Greer blames problems in Canadian historiography on 'patriotic sermonizing', writing that 'Around the world, it has been standard practice since the 19th century to force history into national moulds to serve nationalist purposes. In some countries, the history served up to school children is blatantly jingoistic; in others, such as Canada, a kindlier form of national celebration prevails. But whether belligerent or liberal, orthodoxies designed to shape young minds are bound to have a stultifying effect'.

historiography comes from the other former White Dominion, Australia.[7] In 1950 A.A. Phillips published an essay titled 'The Cultural Cringe' and coined a term that has taken on multiple meanings that extend beyond the confines of its direct applicability to Australian literature. The cringe is applicable to a wide range of studies, and Phillips' essay became a foundation piece for postcolonial scholarship in Australia and around the British world. In his essay Phillips dissected an ingrained inferiority complex. He argued that, first, the cringe appeared in 'a tendency to make needless comparisons', with the Australian reader asking 'Yes, but what would a cultivated Englishman think of this?' He named the problem of British knowledge and Britishness being considered the constant superior point of comparison for Australian achievement. He wrote that 'We cannot shelter from invidious comparisons behind the barrier of a separate language; we have no long-established or interestingly different cultural tradition to give security and distinction to its interpreters; and the centrifugal pull of the great cultural metropolises works against us. Above our writers – and other artists – looms the intimidating mass of Anglo-Saxon achievement'.[8] Australia being largely 'of Britain', forming a derivative culture that mimicked Britain as the 'mother country', had produced Australian cultural cringe with two major characteristics: first the 'cringe direct', of constantly looking up to Britain and down upon Australian scholarship. An important second characteristic was the 'cringe inverted', as Phillips put it, manifest 'in the attitude of the Blatant Blatherskite, the God's-Own-country-and-I'm-a-better-man-than-you-are Australian Bore'. Out of a sense of inferiority arose a reactionary parochialism.

Phillips considered that a second effect of the cringe was intellectual insecurity, the 'estrangement of the Australian intellectual'. He wrote that the Australian 'cultural crust' felt 'thin', and that there was 'a certain type of Australian intellectual who is forever sidling up to the cultivated Englishman, insinuating "I, of course, am not like these other crude Australians. I understand how you must feel about them; I should be more at home in Oxford or Bloomsbury" (the use of Bloomsbury as a symbol of intellectuality is badly out of date; but then, so as a rule is the Australian Cringer)'.[9]

Phillips wrote of 'the Englishman' as 'so quietly convincing about his superiority. The beautiful sheen of his self-assurance exercises an hypnotic influence

---

[7]   At the same time in Canada there was discussion of a parallel inferiority complex. See D. Merrill, 'That Inferiority Complex', *The Empire Club of Canada Speeches 1948–1949* (Toronto, 1949), pp. 254–67.

[8]   A.A. Phillips, *On The Cultural Cringe* (Melbourne, 2006), p. 2. Essay first published in *Meanjin*, no. 4, 1950.

[9]   How fitting that the Rethinking Canadian History conference was held in Bloomsbury.

on its victims'.[10] The cringe combined a dose of insecurity with a measure of parochialism that still strikes a chord in Canada, New Zealand and Australia at the beginning of the twenty-first century.

Personal Cringing

My undergraduate education in the 1980s was a process of awakening to the presence of the cringe. My degree at the University of Canterbury was in a double major in Australian, New Zealand and Commonwealth history, and human geography. I was a student in a history department that had emerged from the sole teaching of British history, firmly ensconced in an imperial framework, to offer New Zealand history and then to emphasise the Commonwealth connections of a 'British world'; the sort of ties that have received a recent resurgence. In my undergraduate training the imperial past was not downplayed, and at the same time national historiography emphasised colonial nationalism and New Zealand's part in the Commonwealth. Taught in the context of New Zealand's claim as the most British of colonies, and Christchurch the most English of cities, my lecturers were scholars trained in imperial history who had come to teach nation-based as well as comparative courses. Through a combination of residual cultural cringe and an awareness of the small scale of New Zealand's history, there was more awareness of the history of the other White Dominions than in Canada at the same time. The influence of individual lecturers was vital here, in particular Chris Connolly, David McIntyre, Luke Trainor and Len Richardson, but the general atmosphere and emphasis was indicative of history departments around New Zealand at the time. In such an environment, the construction of colonial identity became an academic interest. And if personal experience plays a part in our interests, I was born in the United Kingdom, and moved to New Zealand at the age of seven. Immigration is a constant theme in my work.[11]

It was historical geography that took me to Canada to the University of British Columbia (UBC) to work with Graeme Wynn, a scholar of multiple citizenships who has taught, researched and written about Canada, New Zealand and the British world.[12] It was 1989 and my enthusiasm for the settlement of Europeans

---

[10]   Phillips, *On the Cultural Cringe*, pp. 3–4.

[11]   See in particular L. Fraser and K. Pickles (eds), *Shifting Centres: Women and Migration in New Zealand History* (Dunedin, 2002).

[12]   In 1981 Wynn wrote 'But to step back, to accept that basic structural relationships may underlie particular events, to see New Zealand as one of several "settler societies", and to seek broad interpretive themes in the hubbub of their various pasts is to move towards a comparative perspective that

overseas, combined with the life-cycle approach to women's history, constructions of patriarchy, and exploring women's everyday experiences, meant that understanding was sought on a transnational and local scale, and only incidentally nationally. It was at UBC that I was introduced to the crisis of representation taking place in western universities. I became influenced by and contributed to a branch of scholarship focused on critiquing historical geography's complicity in the imperial enterprise, and on a scale that again necessarily ranged across national boundaries. I did not question who I was to write about Canadian subjects – my subjects were, after all, like myself, women and British subjects – this is how I justified it. This is how I came to be an 'outsider' studying Canadian history.[13] Looking back, historical geography's emphasis on regional immersion also spurred me on as an outsider researching Canada. When research for an MA on the lives of girls and women in mid nineteenth century Pictou County, Nova Scotia took me to Halifax in the summer of 1990 I was fortunate that Suzanne Morton, then completing a PhD at Dalhousie University, enthusiastically shared with me her extensive knowledge of Canadian women's history.[14]

Arriving from New Zealand meant that I, more than other Canadian graduate students in the 1990s, had the history of the British world as a central concern. I read Anglo-Canadian and New Zealand historiographies as counterparts because of their shared part in the British imperial past. To historians of Canada and New Zealand it is obvious that the countries have common historical economic, social and cultural characteristics. It is how, and if, the British past should be addressed that is controversial. Political currents have affected the development of national historiographies. For example, in considering the historiographies of New Zealand and Anglo-Canada there is a gap between whether the British world has remained important: in New Zealand history departments since the 1970s there has been a general acknowledgement of the ubiquitous presence and importance of the British Empire in New Zealand's history, and this has become the basis of some historians' critical research. This has been the case in studies of law and immigration, and especially in Maori history

broaches a wider discourse about the nature of society while offering new insights into the particular case.' G. Wynn, 'Reflections on the Writing of New Zealand History', *New Zealand Journal of History*, vol. 18, no. 2 (1984), pp. 104–16, p. 108.

[13]   Because my grandfather was born in Edmonton in 1914 (his parents were part of the pre-Great War wave of Welsh migration to Canada) combined with the Canadian government's ongoing twentieth-century preference for 'British stock', I am a Canadian citizen.

[14]   See K. Pickles, 'Locating Widows in Mid-Nineteenth Century Pictou County, Nova Scotia', *Journal of Historical Geography*, vol. 30, no. 1 (2004), pp. 70–86.

through the living history of the relationship between Maori and the crown, most symbolically through the signing of the Treaty of Waitangi, and the presence of the Waitangi Tribunal that is attempting to redress the past. There was no need to ask 'whatever happened to the British Empire?' in New Zealand.[15] Likewise, in Australia, with the grievous convict past playing an important part in national historiography, and the construction of 'White Australia' being a popular topic, emphasising British immigration, combined with ongoing calls for and debate over whether Australia should become a republic, there is no need to ask 'whatever happened to the British Empire?' In contrast, in Canada the relative lack of political importance of Britain to Canada, especially in the face of the importance of the United States, has made the study of empire marginal. Combined with calls for Quebec's sovereignty, Canada has had clear competing national identities, perceived by some as threats. Hence the development of interventionist and protectionist measures in constructing national identity (more than in New Zealand) that have had flow-on effects on Canadian history. Examples here are federal and provincial government educational funding initiatives of research grants and publication subsidies that reify national boundaries, Immigration Canada's 'Canadians first' hiring policy, and the end result of indeed wondering 'whatever happened to the British Empire?'

In Canada I continued my interest in postcolonial approaches to the past – that is, knowledge that offers a critique of how imperial power operated in the past. I was influenced by a rapidly growing interdisciplinary literature from around the former British Empire. Reacting to cultural cringe underpinned the development of these postcolonial approaches.[16] The influential idea of 'mimicry' in postcolonial thought owes much to the cringe.[17] In his critique of the cringe, Leonard Hume asserted that the cringe has particularly been the domain of those for whom 'cultural hegemony' forms a starting point for their thinking. Indeed,

---

[15] See P. Buckner, 'Whatever Happened to the British Empire?', *Journal of the Canadian Historical Association*, 4 (1994), pp. 2–32.

[16] For example, B. Ashcroft, G. Griffiths and H. Tiffin, *The Empire Writes Back: Theory and Practice in Post-colonial Literature* (London and New York, 1989); H.K. Bhabha (ed.), *Nation and Narration* (London and New York, 1990), especially Sneja Gunew's chapter 'Denaturalizing Cultural Nationalisms' and her discussion of the cringe on p. 103. For Canada see L. Hutcheon's work, in particular *Splitting Images: Contemporary Canadian Ironies* (Don Mills, 1991) and L. Hutcheon, *The Canadian Postmodern: A Study of Contemporary English-Canadian Fiction* (Don Mills, 1988).

[17] See H.K. Bhabha, *The Location of Culture* (London and New York: Routledge, 1994); D. Chakrabarty, *Habitations of Modernity: Essays in the Wake of Subaltern Studies* (Chicago, 2002); D. Chakrabarty, *Provincializing Europe: Postcolonial Thought and Historical Difference* (Princeton, NJ, and Oxford, 2000).

my work on Britishness has often used the language of 'hegemonic identity'.[18] I was interested in those applying postcolonial critiques to what Stephen Sleemon has termed the 'second world', another name for the White Dominions where, unlike the 'third world', settlers from the 'first world' were in control of nation-building that modelled itself on Britain.[19]

With my interest in feminism and postcolonialism I saw the British past in Canada as an important area for inquiry. Pursuing the construction of colonial identity in Canada was my PhD topic that led to the monograph *Female Imperialism and National Identity: Imperial Order Daughters of the Empire*. With echoes of the cringe, I was happy to reveal that the largest women's patriotic organisation in the Empire was Canadian-centred, not British. I argued that the IODE had more of an influence in promoting an Anglo-Celtic Canada than any other Canadian organisation. Moving beyond the cringe and signalling the international relevance of Canadian history, my study was published outside Canada, as part of the Manchester University Press Studies in Imperialism Series and I was particularly pleased that in his general editor's introduction John MacKenzie wrote that the IODE had 'a significance far beyond the very considerable boundaries of Canada' and, highlighting my transnational concerns, that 'its history reflects important issues of national identity in respect of the all-too-adjacent United States, Britain, and other dominions and imperial territories'.[20]

The area I work in has continued to allow plenty of freedom to transgress national boundaries. It is the feminist and postcolonial examination of Britishness that has made up the central focus of my research interests, variably across and in Canada and New Zealand, and also involving Australia and Britain. Building upon my work on the IODE, in another project I have argued that the first academic women in Anglo-Canada, New Zealand and Australia were 'colonial counterparts', whose experiences were shaped by colonial settings that were infused with powerful gender-, race- and class-specific codes concerning

---

[18]   Strongly disagreeing with such language, Hume wrote in 1991 that 'The grip of this theoretical approach on latter-day Left intellectuals therefore explains their apparently slack treatment of evidence, their neglect of a large body of evidence that seems to contradict their assertions, and their summoning of further evidence that turns out to be either spurious or to point towards quite different conclusions'. Hume, 'Another Look', p. 30. Hume attempts to mirror Phillips' powerful ending in his critique, concluding that 'The best way to sum up the whole campaign may be to paraphrase Voltaire's famous aphorism about the existence of God. The cultural cringe — that pervasive, unthinking, admiration for British and foreign things — did not exist, but it was needed, and so it was invented' (p. 32).

[19]   S. Sleemon, 'Unsettling the Empire: Resistance Theory for the Second World', in P. Mongia (ed.), *Postcolonial Theory: A Reader* (London and New York, 1996), pp. 72–83.

[20]   K. Pickles, *Female Imperialism and National Identity: Imperial Order Daughters of the Empire* (Manchester and New York, 2002), pp. ix, viii.

knowledge and the university. If the small number of academic women in the early years of the twentieth century walked the corridors of their respective institutions virtually alone, there were other women at the same time, scattered throughout Anglo-Canada, New Zealand and Australia, following glaringly similar life courses in eerily similar institutions. These women were aware of one another through international networks. As an outsider I have viewed Canada as a site of colonisation. My work on the IODE in the Canadian north revealed them as 'forgotten colonisers'. The idea of Canada as a site of colonisation led to the co-edited collection with Myra Rutherdale, *Contact Zones: Aboriginal and Settler Woman in Canada's Colonial Past.*[21] Our original idea in collaborating was to edit a book of transnational essays, yet the Canadian publishing industry plays to the Canadian market, and it is believed that there is not a large market for Canadian history outside Canada – more evidence of the cringe.

Through working in both places I am aware that a strong feature of the historiography in Canada and New Zealand is that they have often developed in parallel. Parallel historiographies developed in the subfields of the new social and cultural histories: labour and women's history in particular. There have been cross-fertilisations and borrowings, both of ideas and scholars, most explicitly through scholars who have researched and taught in both countries such as Andrée Lévesque and Bettina Bradbury. But if there has been interaction of ideas and themes, research has carried on within national boundaries. To take the example of writing women into history in Anglo-Canada and New Zealand, the 1970s saw the emergence of women's history in both countries as part of second-wave feminism. Metropolitan concepts of liberal, radical and Marxist feminisms influenced the early themes of exploration in women's history in both countries. The image of the strong and capable Anglo-Celtic pioneer, and the complicity of women's history in developing national legends at the expense of diverse identities appeared in both places. Common themes emerged in the historiography of both countries, in particular work, education, health, politics, the vote, religion, war, biography, crime and law. There was the parallel development of women's history textbooks and resources.[22] Women's historians in

---

[21] K. Pickles, 'Colonial Counterparts: The First Academic Women in Anglo-Canada, New Zealand and Australia', *Women's History Review*, vol. 10, no. 2 (2001), pp. 273–97. K. Pickles and M. Rutherdale (eds.), *Contact Zones: Aboriginal and Settler Women in Colonial Canada* (Vancouver, 2005).

[22] Examples of parallel publications are: for New Zealand, B. Brookes, C. Macdonald and M. Tennant (eds.), *Women in History: Essays on European Women in New Zealand* (Wellington, 1986); B. Brookes, C. Macdonald and M. Tennant (eds.), *Women in History 2* (Wellington, 1992); C. Daley and D. Montgomerie (eds.), *The Gendered Kiwi* (Auckland, 1999). For Canada: A. Prentice and S. Mann Trofimenkoff (eds.), *The Neglected Majority: Essays in Canadian Women's History*, vols. 1 and 2 (Toronto, 1985); K. McPherson, C. Morgan and N. Forestell (eds.), *Gendered Pasts: Historical Essays on Femininity and Masculinity in Canada* (Don Mills, 1999).

both countries have carved out similar careers: Margaret Conrad, Alison Prentice, Joan Sangster and Veronica Strong-Boag in Canada, Sandra Coney, Barbara Brookes, Charlotte Macdonald and Margaret Tennant in New Zealand. There have been transnational gatherings for women's historians for many years, but 'comparative' work has been comparatively rare.

Nation-based historiographies have not made working across boundaries easy. If Canadian history is largely nation-based, it has by both accident and design had connections with New Zealand. Canadian historiography has informed work on New Zealand and vice versa. I am testament to these connections, as well as an active creator of them. During my graduate study in Canada I applied the historiography and background knowledge of women's history and Britishness in New Zealand to Canada. I was interested in Pictou County because of a transnational connection: I had read about Norman McLeod and his followers who left Nova Scotia for Waipu, New Zealand.[23] Despite all of my graduate work being on Canadian topics, because the postcolonial and feminist themes were applicable to New Zealand I was appointed to a lectureship in New Zealand history. Coming full circle, I was influenced by Canadian historiography in writing my lectures about New Zealand and framing New Zealand research questions. An example here is my study of single British women migrants to New Zealand as a part of the 1922 Empire Settlement Act. Drawing upon work about those women who went to Canada by Marilyn Barber, Jan Gothard and Paula Hamilton's work on those who went to Australia, and Cecillie Swaisland's work on those who went to South Africa, I was able to contribute the New Zealand story.[24] Likewise Julia Bush and Eliza Reidi's work on the Victoria League in Britain has informed my work on the League in New Zealand.[25] And visiting Montreal's Oratoire St Joseph and reading Leonard Cohen on Catherine Tekakwitha led me to research colonial sainthood in Australasia.[26]

---

[23]   See F. Kidman, *The Book of Secrets* (Auckland, 1994, 1987) and M. Molloy, *Those Who Speak to the Heart: the Nova Scotian Scots at Waipu, 1854–1920* (Palmerston North, 1991).

[24]   K. Pickles, 'Single British Women as New Zealand Domestic Servants During the 1920s', *The New Zealand Journal of History*, vol. 35, no. 1 (2001), pp. 22–44.

[25]   K. Pickles, 'A Link in "The Great Chain of Empire Friendship": The Victoria League in New Zealand,' *Journal of Imperial and Commonwealth History*, vol. 33, no. 1 (2005), pp. 29–50.

[26]   K. Pickles, 'Colonial Sainthood in Australasia', *National Identities*, vol. 7, no. 4 (2005), pp. 389–408; A. Greer, *Mohawk Saint: Catherine Tekakwitha and the Jesuits* (Oxford and New York, 2005); L. Cohen, *Beautiful Losers* (Toronto, 1966, 1991).

Cringing Historiographies

If there is a case that parallel historiographies enable transnational projects, the cringing is a real barrier. Elements of the cringe from 1950 are alive in the twenty-first century, with features of the cringe bedded down in the historiographies of Anglo-Canada and New Zealand, for example the cringe inverted, which has gained momentum through nation-based historiographies. Centring Canadian experiences written by Canadian scholars has had a number of effects. First, with a small national pool of historians engaging with each other's work, research has become clustered in specialised areas. This is reflected by the current collection of historians studying Aboriginal history, as evidenced by the large number of papers in that area at the 2007 CHA conference. This is not to agree with the political right of the history wars that there has been a takeover and that there is too much scholarship in left-leaning areas, in particular compensatory guilt-driven history. Rather, it is to point out that by adhering to national boundaries the cringe underlies and limits the parameters of historiography.

Second, the style of Canadian history, as evidenced in who is referenced by Canadian scholars, has echoes of both elements of cringing. Publications in sub-fields often reference the same names of academics within their disciplinary boundary. Select referencing is not of course, unique to Canada, but I think it is particularly acute there. And I think it represents gatekeeping by those dedicated to a national historiography written by and for insiders. For example, in the introduction to my book *Contact Zones, Aboriginal and Settler Women in Colonial Canada*, a reference to New Zealand Maori scholar Linda Tuhiwai Smith was deleted after a peer reviewer suggested that they hadn't heard of her. Smith's work on decolonising methodologies in researching indigenous peoples is held in high regard internationally. Was questioning who she was a way of saying that her work doesn't count?[27]

Third, evocative of the inferiority complex side of the cringe, in supposedly postcolonial times when Canada has its own scholarship written by insiders, there is the frequent name-dropping of cherry-picked big names from elsewhere – a cringeful, servile bowing to the scholarship of elsewhere that implies that the work of Canadians is not good enough. Over the last decade material in scholarly monographs and journal articles that was formerly relegated to footnotes has increasingly appeared prominently in the text. I myself am guilty of this 'according to' and 'borrowing from' syndrome. I think our generation has been somehow forced into academic name-dropping, and flagging intellectual

---

[27] L. Tuhiwai Smith, *Decolonizing Methodologies: Research and Indigenous Peoples*, 2nd edition (Dunedin and London, 1999).

colours. Interesting here is that those referenced have often never studied Canada in any depth, but a theoretical point, often made by them some years ago, is connected to Canada's cutting-edge scholarship. Such referencing is a feature of the move from empirical to theory-based approaches, and it is effectively those attempting to write postcolonial history who end up committing cultural cringe. At a time when scholarship is standing on shoulders of ever bigger giants it is a paradox that individuals are being singled out and deified. Furthermore, those cited are often from other disciplines, as if it is fine to mention distant influences on work, while those responsible for the empirical slog from within Canadian history will not be personally highlighted.

New Zealand history is more empirically based and suspicious of theory, hence 'cringe referencing' is less pronounced. Another difference is that in New Zealand history, a result of its being a smaller community, it is common to reference the work of honours papers and MA theses, while the larger body of Canadian historical work makes this practice rare. New Zealand history is, however, subject to increasing cultural cringe from within the discipline and outside it. For example, 'international' scholars are being considered for the *New Zealand Journal of History* editorial board, my own department is prioritising hiring in the area of European and American history (not New Zealand) and a state Performance Based Research Fund (PBRF) based on the British Research Assessment Exercise considers New Zealand history local, and therefore inferior to history being produced internationally.

A fourth issue that must be addressed if transnational history is to be pursued is to ask who really can write for whom. Again the cringe surfaces: on the one hand Canadians, New Zealanders and Australians are possessive about 'their own' history and suspicious of outsiders who write it. Yet, on the other hand, they ask why, for example, Germans or Americans would be interested in their history. In all three places, influenced by the politics of the past 40 years that has emphasised 'the personal is political', there is a strong sense of writing one's own history that does not apply to those working in the same institutions who instead choose to write about the history of Europe and other regions of the world. The writing of Pakeha (broadly defined as 'non-Maori') history by 'outsiders', even those who have spent time studying and researching in New Zealand, is treated separately from those writing parochially. For example, in his review of American-based Michele Dominy's *Calling the Station Home: Place and Identity in New Zealand's High Country* by Tom Brooking it matters that Dominy's 'most worthwhile contribution to our historical literature' is made as an outsider.[28]

---

[28]   T. Brooking, review of M. Dominy, *Calling the Station Home: Place and Identity in New Zealand's High Country* (Lanham, MD, 2001), in *New Zealand Journal of History*, vol. 35, no. 1 (2001), pp. 113–4.

Overseas academics who apply their knowledge to New Zealand can be treated as a novelty, or with suspicion. Most importantly, it clearly matters who has written 'our history'.[29] The aforementioned surprise that anybody outside New Zealand would want to write New Zealand history combines with parochial protection. Meanwhile, the annual publication *Books on Canada* includes only Canadian presses, implying that no publisher outside Canada would publish Canadian content. Furthermore, Canada has built a federal protective industry to facilitate the research and publication of Canadiana. This includes the Social Sciences and Humanities Research Council of Canada (SSHRC) and the Aid to Scholarly Publications Programme (ASPP), where Canadian presses dependent upon funding from the ASPP send manuscripts for an additional Canadian-focused round of peer review.

It does not necessarily follow that a high degree of institutionalised parochialism in the historical profession leads to insecurity. On the contrary, it can be argued that because it has robust parochial historiography with a supportive state infrastructure, Canada finds the outsiders who do want to research and write Canadian history less threatening than outsiders are found in funding-strapped New Zealand. And proudly distinct historiographies, as in the case of French-Canadian history, are confident enough to welcome research by outsiders.

If transnational history necessitates opening up 'our history' to outsiders, then a fifth important point is to ask if Canadians who write Canadian history and New Zealanders who write New Zealand history are prepared for the challenges of opening up to more outsiders, especially academic tourists who publish work that might be strong on theoretical insights, but lack culturally specific nuances. Canada, New Zealand and Australia all make claims to be nations that welcome immigrants, but is the writing of history in the hands of an establishment? It appears that there is a scale of acceptability in the topics that outsiders can work on. In both Canada and New Zealand the safest ground for those encroaching upon topics for which they have no identity claim is to concentrate on transgressing borders. Examples here are the Montreal History Group's location between French and English Canada, while in New Zealand those considering intermarriage and race relations are on the safest ground.

---

[29]   L. Sargisson and L. Tower Sargent, *Living in Utopia: New Zealand's Intentional Communities* (Aldershot and Burlington, 2004).

Gaps

While there are many parallels in the development of Canadian and New Zealand historiography, there are also many significant gaps. The cringe also informs the areas of difference, specifically through the parochial politics of who can write for whom. The big gaps, if clichéd, concern Canada's colonisation by not one, but two empires (the French and the British), as Magda Fahrni states in her chapter, and the importance of the neighbouring empire (the United States). New Zealand does have a history of Americanisation but it is vastly different from that of the Canadian experience, and the French colonisation of New Zealand was brief and confined to the small town of Akaroa on Banks Peninsula.[30] There is also a gap between the politics of writing indigenous history in Canada and New Zealand. In Canada predominantly non-Aboriginal Canadians are writing Aboriginal history and connections to 'living history' outside the academy are not a priority. In contrast, New Zealand Maori history is considered to belong to Maori. Pakeha historians writing Maori history do so as 'honorary Maori' after immersing themselves in the Maori world for years, gaining the *mana* (or respect) of Maori. Scholars without these credentials risk being openly challenged. All research with Maori content needs the approval of the local tribe to be eligible for government funding. As with the parochial politics of writing about settlers, undertaking postgraduate study or a post-doctoral fellowship, doing one's time can lead to credibility. Do the gaps between the Canadian and New Zealand historiographies offer insights and future directions for scholarship? Allan Greer has suggested that places in Canada can be 'a site to examine basic issues about clashing empires and relations between colonisers and natives'.[31] Could each place benefit from learning from the other's mistakes and successes?

The cringe was strongly tangled up in the identity politics of those writing social and cultural history that became important in the 1980s. Here the identity politics of who can write for whom was central. The area where I work, feminist and postcolonial history, experienced crises of representation. The reaction was to withdraw to writing about 'ourselves', or to shift to seeing all as representation, effectively killing off the subject. Internationally, by the end of the 1980s a crisis of representation and accompanying accusations of white,

---

[30]   There is currently debate concerning the relative influences of Britain, Australia and the United States on New Zealand culture. For a summary of the debate see P. Mein Smith and P. Hempenstall, 'Introduction' to special issue 'Empires, Islands, Edges: New Zealand's Worlds', *Thesis Eleven*, no. 92 (2008), pp. 5–10.

[31]   Greer, 'Canadian history is so boring ...'.

middle-class, heterosexist bias led to the fragmentation of the woman subject herself. Those who had been involved in writing women's and gender histories changed tack and, along with a new generation of scholars, set new trajectories for the 1990s that included the history of colonisation and the history of sexuality. Often, the focus shifted from women's bodies to the construction of masculinity. In New Zealand, the inclusion of Maori women from the 1970s meant that a crisis of representation was not as strongly felt as in Canada. In addition, essentialism remains strong, and it is considered preferable for Maori women, or those who have been immersed in the community, to write their own history. Cultural history, including leisure, consumption and fashion is a new comfortable area for Pakeha gender historians. Alternatively, in Canada, a cluster of gender historians have turned to writing Aboriginal history and histories of cultural encounter. There is a gap in that Canadian non-Aboriginal gender historians are studying Aboriginal history that their counterparts in New Zealand shy away from.

The 1990s saw both countries face the effects of the end of second-wave feminism. Through the 1990s there was similar research being conducted in both countries, as well as areas of divergence. In New Zealand the centenary of women's suffrage in 1993 sustained an essentialist approach to women's history. Meanwhile, in Canada there were accusations that women's history had come to dominate Canadian history.[32] The larger number of Canadian historians has allowed for a more diverse number of topics to be researched than in New Zealand, where the number of feminist historical scholarly monographs published remains low. More than Canada, New Zealand has a commitment to writing bicultural (Maori and Pakeha) history. The history of other ethnic groups is a more recent and much smaller component of the historiography than in Canada. New Zealand's immigration history was more homogeneous than Canada's, but there is plenty of room to examine other ethnicities – something that my Canadian studies led me to emphasise in *Shifting Centres*.

Finding Better Pathways

In the twenty-first century, while Phillips' 1950 identification of the cringe is still useful, his way of overcoming it is unsatisfactory. Viewing the cringe as 'a worse enemy to our cultural development than our isolation', Phillips suggested

---

[32]   See Granatstein, *Who Killed Canadian History?* See also F. Iacovetta, 'Gendering Trans/National Historiographies: Feminists Rewriting Canadian History', *Journal of Women's History*, vol. 19, no. 1 (2007), pp. 206–213.

that the way beyond cringing was to develop national historiographies. Yet, with hindsight, as I have argued in this chapter, his way of moving beyond the cringe, through advocating the development of national historiographies, has served to reinforce it. It is pertinent that Phillips argued that that 'the opposite of the Cringe is not the Strut, but a relaxed erectness of carriage.' Here I think that he was advocating a humble confidence; the middle ground that Phillip Buckner has sought in the British World conferences. Buckner is one of a number of scholars who have argued that Canada has developed its own historiographical tradition out of a sense of cultural nationalism that has ironically downplayed previously dominant British imperial influences. He is a longtime crusader for advocating the British influence on both Canada's history and historiography as a central concern. The implication of Buckner's project is to eventually move beyond nationalist histories, and to seek transnational comparisons with other parts of the British world. Buckner has facilitated a series of conferences that bridge the divide between British imperial history largely written from the metropole, and the nation-centred histories of the former British Dominions (Canada, New Zealand, Australia and South Africa).[33] Along with Carl Bridge, Kent Fedorowich and Douglas Francis he has edited a number of collections from these gatherings.[34]

If the British World conferences are intended as a way both beyond cringing and towards transnational history, despite the vision, the cringe has appeared at British World conferences. From personal observation, contributions at these conferences have fallen into three major groups. First were those who offered a paper based upon research about the nation hosting the conference. Such papers were indistinguishable from those presented at conferences such as the CHA, the NZHA or the AHA and represent the continuation of nation-based approaches, replete with cringeful attitudes. Second were those contributors identifying transnational themes in the historiography in the countries of the British world,

---

[33]   The first British World conference was at the Institute of Commonwealth Studies in London in June 1998, followed by Cape Town 2002, Calgary 2003, Melbourne 2004 and Bristol 2006. P. Buckner and R. D. Francis (eds.), *Canada and the British World* (Vancouver and Toronto, 2006), Introduction, pp. 1–9.

[34]   P. Buckner (ed.), *Canada and the End of Empire* (Vancouver and Toronto, 2005): a collection from a May 2001 symposium on 'Canada and the End of Empire' held at the Institute of Commonwealth Studies, School of Advanced Study of the University of London. C. Bridge and K. Fedorowich (eds.), *The British World: Diaspora, Culture and Identity* (London, 2003); from the Cape Town conference. P. Buckner and R. D. Francis (eds.), *Canada and the British World* (Vancouver and Toronto, 2006); from the Calgary conference. P. Buckner and R. D. Francis, *Rediscovering the British World* (Calgary, 2005); also from the Calgary conference. K. Darian-Smith, P. Grimshaw, K. Lindsay and S. Macintyre (eds.), *Exploring the British World* (Melbourne, 2004); from the Melbourne conference.

such as immigration, indigenous history, memory and public history, media history, and women's history. Empirical research for individual papers along these themes was also often focused on one nation and sessions were then able to involve a geographical spread. While the themes of research were transnational, the parameters of research for individual papers were restricted to national boundaries. Third were papers by those actively pursuing the study of the idea of a British world. This involved scholars having a general historical knowledge beyond national boundaries, usually focusing on networks of people and information. Ironically, but not surprisingly, it is the British-based, or British-educated, imperial historians who dominate in this area: the divide between metropole and colony may thus be reinforced, rather than bridged. And the cringe inverted remains, with 'colonials', scholars in the nations of the settler societies, feeling that they and their scholarship are separate from, and perhaps superior to, that of the 'mother country'. An example of this perpetuation of the inverted cringe was at the beginning of Veronica Strong-Boag's keynote address at the NZHA, 23 November 2007, where she began with the idea that Canada, New Zealand and Australia still bond at conferences by 'reminding the British of other ways of experiencing modernity'.[35] In spite of years of intervening historiography, the idea of scholarship being collectively ignored by Britain has echoes of Phillips' 1950 essay.

At the British World conferences there was an ideological difference between the imperial and postcolonial historians. Interestingly, it is the imperial historians who tend towards geographically transnational projects, with postcolonial scholars instead emphasising local difference. It is important to acknowledge that for postcolonialists who critique the imperial past, focusing on a British world raises issues currently considered uncomfortable and unfashionable, potentially re-opening old wounds and inflicting fresh ones. Part of the unpopularity of imperial history in an age of growing attention to recovering a diverse and dispersed Canadian past is that to reveal a British past is assumed to reassert it in the present, in the process denying French-Canadian, Aboriginal and multicultural voices. At a time when themes of transgression and hybridity are popular in history writing, tracing the end of a once dominant discourse is a potential minefield for critique. Furthermore, as history often draws its inspiration from the present, there is a clear awkwardness in arguing for the importance of a British past that is today offensive to some and irrelevant to others. These postcolonial challenges are the most important part of a fresh look at the British world.

[35] V. Strong-Boag, '"Sisters are doing it for themselves", or not: Aunts and Caregiving in Canada', Keynote address to the New Zealand Historical Association, Victoria University of Wellington, 23 November 2007.

Another forum for moving beyond national boundaries towards transnational research and overcoming the cringe is funded by the Canadian government. Indeed, if the Canadian government has promoted a culture of national scholarship, it is also responsible for supporting an international community of scholars of Canada – one that attracts scholars writing about Canadian history from outside the national borders – physically and often metaphorically. The International Council for Canadian Studies (ICCS) musters Canadianists around the globe. Who are these outsiders writing Canadian history? Some work in the rare Canadian studies programmes in Australia, Wales and until recently Edinburgh, centres allied to the United States such as the Centre for Canadian-American Studies at Western Washington University that publishes the *American Review of Canadian Studies*, and of course, the Institute for the Study of the Americas in London.

In New Zealand and Australia the Association for Canadian Studies in Australia and New Zealand (ACSANZ) provides a snapshot of those in the social sciences and humanities at large, amongst whom there are few historians. From what I have observed, scholars fall into four groups. First, Australians and New Zealanders who have undertaken graduate work in Canada, on Canadian or comparative topics, and who now work in Australasia. Their research is often about both places, and comparative or transnational. Former Commonwealth scholars are in this group. There are also postcolonial scholars who have built their careers in reaction to the cringe. Second, there are postgraduate students, often the students of the first group, who are undertaking research on Canada while based in Australia and New Zealand. Third are Canadians who are academics in New Zealand. Some may be Canadianists, but most are involved out of nostalgia for home and seem surprised that scholars from the first group can have an Australian or New Zealand accent and be experts in Canadian studies. The fourth group consists of Australian and New Zealand academics keen to learn about Canada, and incorporate aspects into their research, and who are largely starting from scratch. These enthusiastic scholars are keen to access funds. Their topics are predominantly in the areas of law, business, social policy, education and indigenous rights. Interestingly, whereas the areas of history, geography, English and political studies are central to Canadian studies, in Australasia it is professional connections and parallel policies between academics across the countries that is gaining strength. Comparative indigenous work is about professional/political connections as well as shared histories, yet considering Australia and New Zealand together often results in New Zealand as the third wheel (much like Canada as a part of studies of North America). With such a different indigenous situation between Australia and New Zealand this is particularly unsatisfactory.

Identifying Transnational Research and Teaching Difficulties

If transnational history is the latest approach for moving beyond national boundaries, or at least between them, what are the pitfalls that might be avoided? First
there are the methodological issues of geographical distance. Is it possible to
work across such distances? New information technologies are making the trans-
fer of information and individuals easier, but it still requires funding to research
on a large scale. Second, pragmatically, transnational themes take time to
research: my book *Transnational Outrage: The Death and Commemoration of Edith
Cavell* cooked for 10 years. One solution here is collaboration, and those interested in transnational projects are considering group projects. Yet this is effectively people once again sticking to their own country. Third, are nation-based
scholars prepared to renege on the cringe? This is to say that when others have
dedicated their careers to comparative research, is it offensive to add in a country as part of a sudden interest? How much is instantly knowable – I would argue
quite a lot because of parallel histories, periodisations and historiographies, but
then it takes years to immerse oneself in a national historiography and much time
and effort to keep up with new work. Are scholars prepared to overcome
parochialism, by pardoning outsiders who make 'errors' in pronunciation and
colloquial namings? An alternative way of thinking is to ask if Canadianists are
prepared, literally, to broaden their vocabularies and tolerance for different writing styles and languages.[36] For example, instead of using the term 'inferiority
complex', my use of 'cultural cringe' is an example of importing the language of
elsewhere into Canadian historiography.

A fourth danger with transnational research is that focusing on macro-level
patterns and processes can inhibit understanding of the diversity of the past, in
particular skating over the complexities identified by nationally based women's
and labour historians. For example, as I argue in *Transnational Outrage*, a 'British
world' always had porous and ever-shifting boundaries and in the case of commemoration for Cavell was intersected by an Allied world that included the
United States and continental Europe. That is, even the most typical cases of
Britishness have atypical boundaries.

Fifth, it is easy for transnational approaches to inadvertently reinforce the
nation. This occurs because research works across national boundaries, rather

---

[36]   For excellent examples of sophisticated writing beyond national, and disciplinary, boundaries
see G. Whitlock, *The Intimate Empire: Reading Women's Autobiography* (London and New York,
2000) and R. Mohanram, *Black Body: Women, Colonialism and Space* (Minneapolis, 1999, also published by Allen and Unwin in Australia). Whitlock includes Canada, and Mohanram includes New
Zealand.

than investigating the idea of nation itself. In work where networks run between nations, the nation becomes increasingly prominent. Just as for many 'post-colonial' means 'after colonialism' rather than being 'anti-colonialism' in approach, the meaning of 'transnational' can mean 'across and between nations' rather than taking a fundamentally new direction, transcending a nationalist base. Alternative approaches for anti-nation based historiographies are to focus on the movement of people and commodities, and bodily and patriarchal experiences. The historiography in question, however, is deeply involved in thinking from the nation, and not easily changed.

Phillip Buckner has written that 'One does not have to believe that the empire was a "good thing" to believe in its importance to generations of Canadians.' But are today's students interested in empire? Currently, neither Canada nor New Zealand prioritises teaching about the other, with courses virtually non-existent in either place. An added problem is that it is possible to grow up in either place with little knowledge of the other, except for old-fashioned colonial attitudes about each place persisting. Such presentism would need to be overcome. With teaching and research connected (the teaching/research nexus), the current situation of the perception of very distant, separate nations does not facilitate transnational research. If students are interested in more New Zealand and Canadian content there are plenty of common themes and events such as diaspora and immigration, royal tours, gold rushes and sport that make for engaging lectures. 'Easy' teaching beyond national boundaries, however, would be to replicate the imperial survey courses of the past and to downplay or ignore the complexities of the past 40 years. With developed national historiographies, and survey courses struggling to include a range of topics, the idea of a broader geographical base is daunting. And with undergraduate readers restricted to national boundaries, finding suitable accessible readings is a further challenge. Thematic courses are more possible at the graduate level, and so a pathway would be to start at the national level and then branch out transnationally at the postgraduate level. There are plenty of themes for framing research such as polit-ical, indigenous, women's and environmental. There are also increasing numbers of online sources, such as 'Empire Online'.

New technologies might be harnessed to have interactive teaching and learn-ing experiences between Canada and New Zealand that explore common themes. Topics are likely to be a surprise. Can New Zealand students' interest in skiing and snowboarding at Whistler and Canadian students' interest in the *Lord of the Rings* trilogy be directed into transnational histories of the environment and outdoor pursuits?

Conclusion

The issues discussed in this chapter are not particular to Canada, New Zealand and Australia. Beyond the historical community, in a global age it seems that everywhere is cringing. The former White Dominions are no longer just trying to be 'better Britons', but better than a variety of other nations.[37] As well as the Australian cringe, there is the Scottish cringe and the Welsh cringe. Placing histories on the edge is currently in vogue – indeed, everybody appears to be positioning themselves on the edge, with the language of the edge becoming a trope and inferring an ever-present centre. But where is the centre in postcolonial times when Britain has decentred itself? Hopefully, transnational intentions will necessitate addressing the politics of who can write for whom, and how, challenging cringing by stepping over previous parochial boundaries. In abandoning and/or muting the nation, however, there is a strong risk of cringing to the histories of elsewhere, of privileging the ever out-of-reach mythical metropole over the local, of going back to the future.

---

[37]   J. Belich, *Paradise Reforged: A History of the New Zealanders from the 1880s to the Year 2000* (Auckland, 2001), p. 339. Belich writes that 'In a strange way, Canada, Australia and New Zealand, and to some extent even the United States, each saw themselves as the Lone Apostle of Better Britonism, while gazing steadily past each other'.

Chapter 8
Canada in the Age of Revolutions: Rethinking Canadian Intellectual History in an Atlantic Perspective

Michel Ducharme

During the last forty years, Canadian historians, anglophone and francophone alike, have debated whether social history or political history provides a better means of understanding the human condition in a broad and all-encompassing way. This debate has grown so involved that it has dominated Canadian historiography and limited the development of many other fields, such as intellectual history. Over the past few decades, historians have acted as if ideas, prejudices, ideologies and different ways of giving meaning to one's experience were not essential elements of the human condition, or as if these intellectual forces were subject to other political or social imperatives which left them with no autonomy. When historians were interested in questions of an intellectual nature, they generally sought to justify them by social and cultural considerations, as if intellectual preoccupations did not in themselves deserve close attention. As a result, intellectual history has remained a marginalised subject within the larger field of Canadian historiography.

This marginalisation has not only prevented Canadians from better understanding their past but has also kept them isolated from some exciting international historical debates. The problem is not that Canadian and Quebec intellectual historians have been studying their history in a vacuum: over the last decades, scholars have used and adapted interpretive tools, theories, and frameworks developed elsewhere. Some have studied Canadian and Quebec experiences from a European perspective while others have privileged an American one.[1] Some have taken into consideration European as well as

---

[1] For a European perspective, see P. Resnick, *The Masks of Proteus: Canadian Reflections on the State* (Montreal and Kingston, 1990); Resnick, *The European Roots of Canadian Identity* (Peterborough, 2005); M. Bellavance, *Le Québec au siècle des nationalités (1791–1918). Essai d'histoire comparée* (Montreal, 2004); G. Stevenson, *Parallel Paths: The Development of Nationalism in Ireland and Quebec* (Montreal and Kingston, 2006). For a continental/American perspective, see A. Smith, 'Seven Narratives in North American History: Thinking the Nation in Canada, Quebec and the United States', in Stefan Berger (ed.), *Writing the Nation: A Global Perspective* (Basingstoke, 2007), pp. 63–83; Smith, *Canada: An American Nation? Essays on Continentalism, Identity and the Canadian Frame of Mind* (Montreal and

American influences on the evolution of Quebec, while others have examined its history within the context of the emergence of new societies in the Americas as well as in Oceania.[2] In the latter case, the British Empire founded two important colonies at the end of the eighteenth or beginning of the nineteenth century, Australia and New Zealand. Nonetheless, despite such efforts, Canadian and Quebec intellectual history has been and is still generally written from a Canadian perspective for a Canadian audience. As a result, not only does Canadian intellectual history remain marginal within Canadian historiography, but it seldom appears in international historiography.

The time has come to move Canadian and Quebec intellectual history out of the margins and closer to the centre of historical debate within a broad international framework. Canada's geographical position, its past political allegiances and its cultural roots – which place it at the crossroads of French, British, Irish and American influences, to name only the most important – make possible the exploration of Canadian and Quebec intellectual history within an Atlantic perspective, at least until the 1840s.

This Atlantic perspective is of course heavily influenced by British Atlantic historiography. British Atlantic intellectual historians are among the most prolific in the field and it would certainly be difficult and ill-advised for Canadians not to take into consideration their colonial past. However, this Atlantic framework, which takes the North Atlantic world (including Britain, Europe and the Americas) as its reference point, is distinct from the British imperial framework promoted by Phillip A. Buckner, and also adopted by Adele Perry, Katie Pickles and Andrew Smith, whose arguments appear elsewhere in this volume.[3]

Kingston, 1994). For the earliest expression of '*l'américanité*', see: Y. Lamonde, 'American Cultural Influence in Québec: A One-Way Mirror', in Alfred O. Hero, Jr. and Marcel Daneau (eds.), *Problems and Opportunities in US–Québec Relations* (Boulder, 1984), pp. 106–26; P. Resnick, 'Canada: A Different North American Society?', *Inroads*, 14 (2004): 98–106. See also Y. Lamonde, *Ni avec eux ni sans eux: le Québec et les États-Unis* (Montreal, 1996); G. Bouchard and Y. Lamonde (eds.), *Québécois et Américains. La culture québécoise aux XIXᵉ et XXᵉ siècles* (Montreal, 1995).

[2] For a perspective uniting European and American influences, see Y. Lamonde, *Histoire sociale du Québec* (Montreal, 2000); Lamonde, *Allégeances et dépendances. L'histoire d'une ambivalence identitaire* (Quebec, 2001). For the new societies' framework, see G. Bouchard, 'Le Québec et le Canada comme collectivités neuves: esquisse d'étude comparée', *Recherches sociographiques*, vol. 39, nos. 2–3 (1998): pp. 219–48; Bouchard, *Genèse des nations et cultures du nouveau monde. Essai d'histoire comparée* (Montreal, 2000).

[3] The British imperial perspective has been renewed over the last few years. See among others P.A. Buckner, *The Transition to Responsible Government: British Policy in British North America, 1815–1850* (Westport, 1985); P. Buckner (ed.), *Canada and the End of Empire* (Vancouver, 2005); P. Buckner and R.D. Francis (eds.), *Rediscovering the British World* (Calgary, 2005); P. Buckner and R.D. Francis (eds.), *Canada and the British world: Culture, Migration, and Identity* (Vancouver, 2006); P. Lawson, *The Imperial Challenge: Quebec and Britain in the Age of the American Revolution* (Montreal and Kingston,

The question is not which framework is inherently superior to the other. On many political, economic, social and cultural issues, the British imperial framework might provide as much if not more insight than the Atlantic one. Furthermore, Atlanticists generally assume that the Atlantic world lost its coherence after the European revolutions of the 1790s. The British perspective can therefore contribute to our understanding of Canada and Quebec in the nineteenth and early twentieth centuries in a way that the Atlantic one cannot. Nonetheless, as far as eighteenth- and early nineteenth-century Canadian intellectual history is concerned, the Atlantic perspective helps historians make sense of their past by taking into consideration intellectual developments not only in the British Empire, but also in the Americas and Europe more broadly. By interpreting Canadian and Quebec intellectual history within an Atlantic framework, historians can revisit their own history as well as participate in the larger debates of intellectual history as they currently exist on the international scene. These same historians can in turn contribute to the Atlantic framework's development by reintegrating the distinct Canadian/Quebec experience into it.

Intellectual Life in the Atlantic World in the Age of Revolutions

The idea of an 'Atlantic community' emerged during the First World War, but did not have a decisive impact before the Second World War. It was with the adoption of the Atlantic Charter (1941) and the creation of NATO (1949) that the concept of an Atlantic political community truly took shape. Although some historians, such as Carlton Hayes, Jacques Godechot, V.M. Godinho, Pierre and Huguette Chaunu, and Charles Verlinden, tried to give historical context to this emerging community in the 1940s, Atlantic history received its first comprehensive and coherent expression at the Tenth International Congress of Historical Sciences in 1955. In their paper 'Le problème de l'Atlantique', Jacques Godechot and Robert R. Palmer set the parameters of what would become the history of the Atlantic world.[4] The reception given to their paper was not very positive at first, and its impact on the historical community was not immediate. Nonetheless, more and more historians began to conceive of the Atlantic world as a coherent historical framework during the late 1950s and 1960s. Even if some

1989); A. Perry, *On the Edge of Empire: Gender, Race and the Making of British Columbia, 1849–71* (Toronto, 2001); J. McLaren, A.R. Buck, and N.E. Wright (eds.), *Despotic Dominion: Property Rights in British Settler Societies* (Vancouver, 2005).

[4] J. Godechot and R.R. Palmer, 'Le problème de l'Atlantique du XVIIIème au XXème siècle', *Relazioni del X Congresso Internazionale di Scienze Storiche*, vol. V (Florence, 1955), pp. 219–39.

Marxist historians rejected the Atlantic perspective and severely criticised its ideological orientation,[5] they did not successfully counter the development of this new historiography in the following decades.[6] Atlantic history is now a vibrant and dynamic historical field.[7]

The Atlantic framework was ambitious from its inception, trying as it did to integrate the four continents of the Atlantic Rim into a coherent historical unit founded on economic, political, cultural, and intellectual exchanges between metropoles and colonies. This framework was, and still is, complicated by the fact that the Atlantic world was not imagined as having been static, but rather as 'a world in motion'. Its history was marked by encounters between different

[5]   On the reception given to Godechot and Palmer's project, see R.R. Palmer, 'American Historians Remember Jacques Godechot', *French Historical Studies*, vol. 61, no. 4 (1990), pp. 883–4.
[6]   For an account of the development of the Atlantic framework in the context of the emergence of an Atlantic political community, see B. Bailyn, 'The Idea of Atlantic History', *Itinerario*, vol. 20, no. 1 (1996), pp. 19–44; Bailyn, *Atlantic History: Concept and Contours* (Cambridge, 2005), pp. 1–30; W. O'Reilly, 'Genealogies of Atlantic History', *Atlantic Studies*, vol. 1, no. 1 (2004), pp. 66–84.
[7]   Bernard Bailyn, Nicholas Canny and David Armitage are among the three most important figures of this historical school of thought. See B. Bailyn, *The Ideological Origins of the American Revolution* (Cambridge, 1967); Bailyn, *The Peopling of British North America: An Introduction* (New York, 1986); N. Canny and A. Pagden (eds.), *Colonial Identity in the Atlantic World, 1500–1800* (Princeton, 1987); N. Canny, *Kingdom and Colony: Ireland in the Atlantic World, 1560–1800* (Baltimore, 1988); N. Canny, 'Writing Atlantic History; or Reconfiguring the History of Colonial British America', *Journal of American History*, vol. 86 (1999), pp. 1093–1114; D. Armitage and M.J. Braddick (eds.), *British Atlantic World, 1500–1800* (New York, 2002); D. Armitage, *The Declaration of Independence: A Global History* (Cambridge, 2007). For a general overview of Atlantic history, see J.H. Elliott, *Empires of the Atlantic World: Britain and Spain in America, 1492–1830* (New Haven, 2006). For recent publications on the Portuguese and Spanish Empires in the Atlantic context, see J. Adelman, *Sovereignty and Revolution in the Iberian Atlantic* (Princeton, 2006); D. Studnicki-Gizbert, *A Nation upon the Ocean Sea: Portugal's Atlantic Diaspora and the Crisis of the Spanish Empire, 1492–1640* (New York, 2007). For recent publications on the British Empire, see among others A. Lee Hatfield, *Atlantic Virginia: Intercolonial Relations in the Seventeenth Century* (Philadelphia, 2004); E. Mancke and C. Shammas (eds.), *The Creation of the British Atlantic World*, (Baltimore, 2005); E.H. Gould and P.S. Onuf (eds.), *Empire and Nation: The American Revolution in the Atlantic World* (Baltimore, 2005); S.D. Smith, *Slavery, Family, and Gentry Capitalism in the British Atlantic: The World of the Lascelles, 1648–1834* (Cambridge, 2006). For the French Empire, see L. Choquette, *Frenchmen into Peasants: Modernity and Tradition in the Peopling of French Canada* (Cambridge, 1997); J. Pritchard, *In Search of Empire: The French in the Americas, 1670–1730* (Cambridge, 2004); J.M. Faragher, *A Great and Noble Scheme: The Tragic Story of the Expulsion of the French Acadians from their American Homeland* (New York, 2005) and the French Atlantic History Group at McGill University: http://atlantique.mcgill.ca/en. For the Dutch Empire, see J.M. Postma, *The Dutch in the Atlantic Slave Trade, 1600–1815* (Cambridge, 1990); P.C. Emmer, *The Dutch in the Atlantic Economy, 1580–1880: Trade, Slavery and Emancipation* (Aldershot, 1998); J. Postma and V. Enthoven (eds.), *Riches from Atlantic Commerce: Dutch Transatlantic Trade and Shipping, 1585–1817* (Leiden, 2003).

races, by slavery and migration, by the development of social life, by economic structures and exchanges, by imperial struggles and, finally, by the Atlantic revolutions.[8] Although critics have pointed out some limitations inherent to the framework,[9] it nonetheless remains an important one. With all its shortcomings, the Atlantic framework helps scholars move beyond regional or national history without necessarily obliterating the distinctiveness of each area within the Atlantic world.

This new framework's most important contribution was to help reinterpret the revolutions that shook the Atlantic world at the end of the eighteenth century. As early as 1955, Godechot and Palmer proposed that these revolutions had been part of one great movement that shook the Atlantic world from 1776 to 1800.[10] According to this interpretation, it was the American Revolution (1776–83) that launched the general revolutionary movement, which was then joined by the Dutch patriots (1783–7), the reformers of the Austrian Low Countries (1787–90), and the French revolutionaries after 1789. The French Revolution in turn triggered a wave of revolutions throughout Europe in the 1790s.[11] While the works of Godechot and Palmer appear extremely ambitious, their original concept of an 'Atlantic revolution' was geographically and intellectually limited.

Geographically, the framework put forth by Godechot and Palmer focused only on the United States and Europe. The unrest and revolts of Saint-Domingue in the 1790s, which eventually led to the creation of Haiti in 1804, were not even mentioned. Neither were the Latin American revolutions. From this perspective the Americas, other than the United States, did not participate in the 'Atlantic revolution'. Over the last few decades historians have worked to

---

[8] Bailyn, *Atlantic History*, pp. 31–56 (61 for quotes).

[9] For some criticisms of the Atlantic perspective, see the contributions of P.A. Coclanis, P.J. Stern, A. Games, and P. Mapp in the forum organised by the *William and Mary Quarterly* in 2006, and A. Games, 'Atlantic History: Definitions, Challenges, and Opportunities', *American Historical Review*, vol. 111, no. 3 (2006), pp. 741–57.

[10] R.R. Palmer, *The Age of the Democratic Revolution: A Political History of Europe and America, 1760–1800* (Princeton, 1959–1962); J. Godechot, *Les Révolutions (1770–1799)* (Paris, 1963). Godechot's book was translated into English as: *France and the Atlantic Revolution of the Eighteenth Century, 1770–1799* (New York, 1965).

[11] See S. Andrews, *The Rediscovery of America: Transatlantic Crosscurrents in an Age of Revolution* (London, 1998); A. Jourdan, *La Révolution, une exception française?* (Paris, 2004). For the Netherlands, see P. Geyl, *La révolution batave, 1783–1798* (Paris, 1971); S. Schama, *Patriots and Liberators: Revolution in the Netherlands, 1780–1813* (New York, 1977). For the Austrian Low Countries, see J. Polasky, *Revolution in Brussels, 1787–1793* (Hanover, 1987). For France, see K.M. Baker, *Inventing the French Revolution: Essays on French Political Culture in the Eighteenth Century* (Cambridge, 1990). For Ireland, see S. Small, *Political Thought in Ireland 1776–1798: Republicanism, Patriotism and Radicalism* (Oxford, 2002).

integrate the rest of the Atlantic world into this revolutionary framework. Even if the Haitian and Latin American revolutions were distinct from the North American and European revolutions, they are considered now as part of a greater Atlantic and/or continental revolutionary movement.[12] It is now possible to consider these Atlantic revolutions to have developed in four distinct phases: the American Revolution, the French and other European revolutions, the Haitian Revolution, and the Latin American revolutions. This historical analysis, as proposed by Godechot and Palmer and adapted and reformulated by other historians since 1955, covers most of Europe and the Americas between 1776 and 1826.

The original paradigm was also limited intellectually. Because the Atlantic revolutionaries used a 'democratic' rhetoric, Palmer initially talked about a 'democratic revolution'.[13] Since the definition of what 'democracy' means has evolved since the eighteenth century, this wording was problematic and gave a political meaning to the historical analysis. This question of the intellectual foundations of the Atlantic revolutions, at least for the first two phases (United States and Europe), was revisited by intellectual historians of the British Atlantic world such as Bernard Bailyn, J.G.A. Pocock and Gordon Wood during the 1960s and 1970s. These historians invested much time and effort in reconceptualising the intellectual history of the Atlantic world in the seventeenth and eighteenth centuries, including the ideological nature of the Atlantic revolutions. They uncovered the intellectual underpinnings of these Atlantic revolutions, at least in the northern part of the Atlantic world.

Influenced by Zera Fink and Caroline Robbins' rediscovery of the importance of republicanism in English political thought of the seventeenth and early eighteenth centuries, the Atlantic intellectual historians reassessed the nature of intellectual and political life in the Atlantic world. They contested the traditional framework that opposed liberalism to conservatism, arguing instead that the political struggles of this era could be better understood as a struggle between

---

[12] For an overview of the American revolutions, see L.D. Langley, *The Americas in the Age of Revolution: 1750–1850* (New Haven, 1996). For the revolution in Saint Domingue, see L. Dubois, *Avengers of the New World: the Story of the Haitian Revolution* (Cambridge, 2004); D.P. Geggus, *Haitian Revolutionary Studies* (Bloomington, 2002). For the impact of the Haitian Revolution in the Atlantic world, see D.P. Geggus (ed.), *The Impact of the Haitian Revolution in the Atlantic World* (Columbia, 2001); D.B. Gaspar, D.P. Geggus and D. Clark Hine (eds.), *A Turbulent Time: The French Revolution and the Greater Caribbean* (Bloomington, 2003). For the Spanish American Revolutions, see J.E. Rodríguez O. (ed.), *Mexico in the Age of Democratic Revolutions: 1750–1850* (Boulder, 1994); Rodríguez O., *The Independence of Spanish America* (New York, 1998); J. Adelman, *Sovereignty and Revolution in the Iberian Atlantic* (Princeton, 2006).

[13] R.R. Palmer, 'Notes on the Use of the Word "Democracy" 1789–1799', *Political Science Quarterly*, vol. 68, no.2 (1953), pp. 203–26.

Court and Country ideologies or, in other words, between commercialism and republicanism.[14] This new intellectual framework evolved over time to become a struggle between Lockean liberalism and republicanism. Theoretically, this opposition resembled the distinction made by Benjamin Constant in 1819 between 'la liberté des Modernes' (liberal freedom based on individual rights) and 'la liberté des Anciens' (republican freedom based on citizens' participation in the political process) as well as the distinction made by Isaiah Berlin between negative and positive liberty.[15] Although some critics have questioned the nature of republicanism and the Manichean aspect of the opposition between liberalism and republicanism, their attacks have not undermined the new framework so much as added to its complexity.[16]

[14]   Z.S. Fink, *The Classical Republicans: An Essay in the Recovery of a Pattern of Thought in Seventeenth-Century England* (Evanston, 1945); C. Robbins, *The Eighteenth-Century Commonwealthman: Studies in the Transmission, Development, and Circumstance of English Liberal Thought from the Restoration of Charles II until the War with the Thirteen Colonies* (Cambridge, 1959); Bailyn, *The Ideological Origins of the American Revolution*; J.G.A. Pocock, *Politics, Language and Time: Essays on Political Thought and History* (New York, 1971 [1960]); Pocock, *The Machiavellian Moment: Florentine Political Thought and the Atlantic Republican Tradition* (Princeton, 1975); Pocock, *Virtue, Commerce and History: Essays on Political Thought and History, Chiefly in the Eighteenth Century* (Cambridge, 1985); G.S. Wood, *The Creation of the American Republic, 1776–1789* (Chapel Hill, 1969); Wood, *The Radicalism of the American Revolution* (New York, 1992); Q. Skinner, *The Foundations of Modern Political Thought* (Cambridge, 1978); G. Bock, Q. Skinner and M. Viroli (eds.), *Machiavelli and Republicanism* (Cambridge, 1990); D. Armitage, A. Himy and Q. Skinner (eds.), *Milton and Republicanism* (Cambridge, 1995); Q. Skinner, *Liberty before Liberalism* (Cambridge, 1998); M. van Gelderen and Q. Skinner (eds.), *Republicanism: A Shared European Heritage* (Cambridge, 2002).

[15]   B. Constant, 'De la liberté des anciens comparée à celle des modernes' (1819), in Marcel Gauchet (ed.), *Écrits politiques* (Paris: 1997), pp. 589–619; I. Berlin, *Two Concepts of Liberty* (Oxford: 1958).

[16]   As early as the 1980s, historians such as Isaac Kramnick, Joyce Appleby and Lance Banning, inspired by the groundbreaking work of Bernard Bailyn, *The Ideological Origins of the American Revolution*, showed that republican and liberal values were not as antagonistic as Pocock and Wood had argued in *The Machiavellian Moment* and *The Creation of the American Republic*. See I. Kramnick, *Republicanism and Bourgeois Radicalism: Political Ideology in late Eighteenth-century England and America* (Ithaca, 1990); J. Appleby, *Liberalism and Republicanism in the Historical Imagination* (Cambridge, 1992). See also L. Banning, 'Jeffersonian Ideology Revisited: Liberal and Classical Ideas in New American Republic,' *William and Mary Quarterly*, vol. 43 (1986), pp. 3–19; Banning, *The Sacred Fire of Liberty: James Madison & the Founding of the Federal Republic* (Ithaca, 1995). Even Gordon Wood eventually agreed that Lockean (liberal) and republican values were not necessarily opposed in the eighteenth century: 'Ideology and the Origins of Liberal America', *William and Mary Quarterly*, vol. 44 (1987), p. 634. Paul A. Rahe and Vickie B. Sullivan went as far as to show the liberal nature of English republicanism in the sixteenth and seventeenth centuries. See V.B. Sullivan, *Machiavelli, Hobbes, and the Formation of a Liberal Republicanism in England* (Cambridge, 2004); P.A. Rahe (ed.), *Machiavelli's Liberal Republican Legacy* (Cambridge, 2006). Some others highlighted the differences existing between classical republicanism and the kind of republicanism promoted by the American revolutionaries, especially on the question of individual freedom. According to Thomas Pangle, Paul A. Rahe, Mark

British Atlantic intellectual historians were much more interested in the Country ideology (republicanism) than the Court ideology (commercialism/ liberalism), which was therefore understudied in the new framework. Generally, this Court ideology was presented as having been developed out of the work of Thomas Hobbes (1588–1679), David Hume (1711–76) and Adam Smith (1723–90), among others. Advocates of commercialism saw their society as being based on liberty (understood as a certain individual autonomy and some basic individual rights) and property, the most sacred of all individual rights. They encouraged commerce and the accumulation of wealth, as well as the social inequalities that go with them. For them, the only form of equality needed in a society was equality before the law. They also accepted corruption and patronage as legitimate political means. Because I am interested in the political implications of this Court ideology and because commercialists believed in the British constitution, I prefer to call it *British constitutionalism*. This ideology can be seen as the ancestor of both British liberalism and modern British conservatism. In this context, constitutionalism (or what some people have simply called liberalism) was seen as a conservative force.

In the framework of the British Atlanticists, republicanism was the reformist/ revolutionary ideology. Republicanism was based on liberty and equality; for republicans, freedom meant first and foremost participating in political life. To be able to do so, individuals needed to be socially and economically equal. This equality was essential for republicans because they thought it was impossible for individuals to be free and to participate equally in political life if there was too great a disparity between citizens, which would mean the rich having the possibility of bribing the poor and establishing a form of clientelism. In order to ensure the economic and social equality of citizens, republicans envisioned a society of small landowners, all independent of each other. This economic independence would ensure not only political independence, but also virtue. Virtue was a key concept of republicanism, as the republic rested on its citizens' virtue. Virtue had at least three meanings. First, it meant that a citizen was independent socially and economically, this being the best guarantee that he would remain

---

Hulliung and Lee Ward, to name but a few, the kind of republicanism at work during the American Revolution was not classical but modern, a balanced mixture of republican and liberal values. See T. Pangle, *The Spirit of Modern Republicanism: The Moral Vision of the American Founders and the Philosophy of Locke* (Chicago, 1988); P.A. Rahe, *Republics Ancient and Modern* (Chapel Hill, 1994); M. Hulliung, *Citizens and Citoyens: Republicans and Liberals in America and France* (Cambridge, 2002); L. Ward, *The Politics of Liberty in England and Revolutionary America* (Cambridge, 2004), pp. 325–425. See also M.N.S. Sellers, *American Republicanism: Roman Ideology in the U.S. Constitution* (New York, 1994) and Sellers, *The Sacred Fire of Liberty: Republicanism, Liberalism and the Law* (New York, 1998).

politically independent and not be corrupted. Second, virtue could be synony-mous with simplicity and frugality. Republicans despised the kind of wealth that could corrupt people and the desire for wealth that could encourage people to accept corruption. Third, virtue meant a citizen's capacity to defend the com-mon good instead of his personal interests. In this sense, virtue meant patriotism.

Republicanism was introduced in England and in the United Provinces (Dutch Republic) as early as the sixteenth century.[17] In England, the most influential republican thinker was James Harrington (1611–77). Harrington's ideas, pre-sented in his essay *Oceana* (1656), greatly influenced his contemporaries, the English Commonwealth men at the end of the seventeenth century, British radical Whigs in the eighteenth century, and the American colonists in the 1760s and 1770s. These republican ideas were adopted later by Dutch, Irish, and French revolutionaries in the 1780s and 1790s.[18] The first two chapters of Atlantic revolutions in this context were not so much 'democratic' as 'republican'.

Canadian Historians and the Atlantic Framework

For a Canadian historian, it is impossible to ignore the near total absence of Canada and Quebec from this Atlantic world historiography, as if the northern part of the Americas had not been a part of this Atlantic world in the seventeenth and eighteenth centuries. Geographically and politically, Canada has been as much a part of the Atlantic community as any other country and was heavily influenced historically by its connection to the Atlantic Ocean. It was through the Atlantic that England and France took possession of their Canadian colonies and fought to control them. For Canadians, the ocean was less a border than the

---

[17]   For a study on the influence of republicanism in England before Harrington, see M. Peltonen, *Classical Humanism and Republicanism in English Political Thought, 1570–1640* (Cambridge, 1995). For the influence of republicanism in the United Provinces in the seventeenth century, see M. van Gelderen, *The Political Thought of the Dutch Revolt 1555–1590* (Cambridge, 1992).

[18]   For England and Britain in the seventeenth and eighteenth centuries, see J. Scott, *Commonwealth Principles: Republican Writing of the English Revolution* (Cambridge, 2004); H.T. Dickinson, *Liberty and Property: Political Ideology in Eighteenth-Century Britain* (London, 1977). For the United States, see L. Banning, *The Jeffersonian Persuasion: Evolution of a Party Ideology* (Ithaca, 1978); D.R. McCoy, *The Elusive Republic: Political Economy in Jeffersonian America* (Chapel Hill, 1980); S. Elkins and E. McKitrick, *The Age of Federalism: The Early American Republic* (Oxford, 1993). For an overview of the American historiography, see R.E. Shalhope, 'Toward a Republican Synthesis: The Emergence of an Understanding of Republicanism in American Historiography', *William and Mary Quarterly*, vol. 29 (1972), pp. 49–80; Shalhope, 'Republicanism and Early American Historiography', *William and Mary Quarterly*, vol. 39 (1982), pp. 334–56. For the United Provinces in the 1780s, see N.C.F. van Sas, 'The Patriot Revolution: New Perspectives' and J.G.A. Pocock, 'The Dutch Republican

only access to Europe before the mid twentieth century. Nevertheless, very few historians have tried to integrate Canadian history into the Atlantic framework. If Atlantic historians do not normally pay much attention to Canada – with the exception of Elizabeth Mancke[19] – Canadian historians (French and English) in turn do not normally pay much attention to the Atlantic world.

As for the intellectual framework developed by the British Atlantic historians, it was adopted by only a few Canadians, and even then mainly by political scientists and sociologists rather than historians. Both in French and English Canada, these scholars argued that Canadians had participated in the struggle between Court and Country ideologies[20] or between liberalism and republicanism[21] in the eighteenth and nineteenth centuries. In Quebec, this framework often received an American spin. Louis-Georges Harvey, developing the framework of *l'américanité*, interpreted the French Canadian reformers' discourse from

Tradition,' in Margaret Jacobs and Wijnand W. Mijnhardt (eds.), *The Dutch Republic in the Eighteenth Century: Decline, Enlightenment and Revolution* (Ithaca, 1992), pp. 91–119, 188–93. For Irish patriots, see S. Small, *Political Thought in Ireland 1776–1798*. French history has been integrated into the framework developed by the Atlantic intellectual historians mainly by historians who are not French. See J. Kent Wright, *A Classical Republican in Eighteenth-Century France: The Political Thought of Mably* (Stanford, 1997); M. Kylmäkoski, *The Virtue of the Citizen: Jean-Jacques Rousseau's Republicanism in the Eighteenth-Century French Context* (Frankfurt am Main, 2001); K.M. Baker, *Inventing the French Revolution*; Baker, 'Transformations of Classical Republicanism in Eighteenth-Century France', *Journal of Modern History*, vol. 73 (2001), pp. 32–53; A. Jainchill, 'The Constitution of the Year III and the Persistence of Classical Republicanism', *French Historical Studies*, vol. 26 (2003), pp. 399–435; R. Monnier, 'Républicanisme et Révolution française', *French Historical Studies*, vol. 26 (2003), pp. 87–118.

[19] E. Mancke, 'Early Modern Imperial Governance and the Origins of Canadian Political Culture', *Canadian Journal of Political Science*, vol. 32 (1999), pp. 3–20; Mancke, *The Fault Lines of Empire: Political Differentiation in Massachusetts and Nova Scotia, ca. 1760–1830* (New York, 2005). Canada has also been integrated in this framework in G. Paquet and J.-P. Wallot, 'Nouvelle France/Québec/Canada: A World of Limited Identities', in Canny and Pagden (eds.), *Colonial Identity in the Atlantic World*, pp. 95–114; D. Delâge, 'The Fur Trade of New France' and A. Greer, 'French Colonization of New France', in Thomas Benjamin, Timothy D. Hall and David Rutherford, (eds.), *The Atlantic World in the Age of Empire* (Boston, 2001), pp. 139–44, 191–5.

[20] G.T. Stewart, *The Origins of Canadian Politics: A Comparative Approach* (Vancouver, 1986); D. Milobar, 'Quebec Reform, the British Constitution and the Atlantic Empire, 1774–1775,' *Parliamentary History*, vol. 14 (1995), pp. 65–88; Milobar, 'The Origins of British–Quebec Merchant Ideology: New France, the British Atlantic and the Constitutional Periphery, 1720–1770', *The Journal of Imperial and Commonwealth History*, vol. 24 (1996), pp. 364–90; S. Kelly, *La petite loterie* (Montreal, 1997).

[21] J. Ajzenstat and P.J. Smith (eds.), *Canada's Origins: Liberal, Tory or Republican?* (Ottawa, 1995); Ajzenstat, *The Once and Future Canadian Democracy: An Essay in Political Thought* (Montreal and Kingston, 2003); Ajzenstat, *The Canadian Founding: John Locke and Canadian Parliament* (Montreal and Kingston, 2007).

1805 to 1837 as being typically republican and American, in the sense that it had been heavily inspired by the American Revolutionaries' discourses.[22] Stéphane Kelly presented the evolution of Canadian politics after Confederation as being typically Hamiltonian (an ideology akin to commercialism, i.e. highly centralised and based on industrial capitalism) instead of Jeffersonian (a republican ideology based on a decentralised state and more egalitarian society). This was an original way to reshape the opposition between liberalism and republicanism since the middle of the nineteenth century in purely American terms.[23]

If Canadian and Quebec historians have not shown any strong interest in the Atlantic framework, their attitude towards the Atlantic revolutions has been much the same. Over the last 40 years, there has been only one conference held in Canada concerning the country's involvement in the Atlantic revolutions.[24] It was held in 1969 and the proceedings were published in 1973 in the *Annales historiques de la Révolution française*. Jean-Pierre Wallot was one of the few historians who thought about the Atlantic framework over the years.[25] Otherwise, Quebec historians interested in the period at the end of the eighteenth century mainly studied French-Canadian experience only in relation to the American and French Revolutions, which were seen as two distinct events.[26] In English Canada, it is mainly the loyalists' migration, a subject where the imperial and continental perspectives meet, that has interested historians of that

---

[22]   L.-G. Harvey, 'Importing the Revolution: The Image of America in French-Canadian Political Discourse 1805–1837', PhD diss., University of Ottawa, 1990; Harvey, *Le Printemps de l'Amérique française. Américanité, anticolonialisme et républicanisme dans le discours politique québécois, 1805–1837* (Montreal, 2005); Harvey, 'Le mouvement patriote comme projet de rupture (1805–1837)', in Bouchard and Lamonde (eds.), *Québécois et Américains*, pp. 89–112; Harvey, 'The First Distinct Society: French Canada, America and the Constitution of 1791', in Ajzenstat and Smith (eds.), *Canada's Origins*, pp. 79–108.

[23]   S. Kelly, *Les fins du Canada selon Macdonald, Laurier, Mackenzie King et Trudeau* (Montreal, 2001).

[24]   The conference was organised by the *Groupe de recherches sur les idéologies dans la société canadienne-française* of the Université de Montréal.

[25]   J.-P. Wallot, 'Révolution et réformisme dans le Bas-Canada (1773–1815),' *Annales historiques de la Révolution française*, no. 213 (1973), pp. 344–406; Wallot, 'Frontière ou fragment du système atlantique: Des idées étrangères dans l'identité bas-canadienne au début du XIXᵉ siècle', *Canadian Historical Association Historical Papers* (1983), pp. 3–14. Yvan Lamonde tried to determine the influence of the United States, Great Britain, France, the Vatican and even English Canada on Québec's development in *Histoire sociale du Québec*, vol. 1 (Montreal, 2000), pp. 19–65; Lamonde, *Allégeances et dépendances. L'histoire d'une ambivalence identitaire* (Québec, 2001).

[26]   On the American Revolution, see M. Trudel, *Louis XVI, le Congrès américain et le Canada, 1774–1789* (Québec, 1949); G. Lanctôt, *Le Canada et la Révolution américaine* (Montreal, 1965). On the influence of the American Revolution on Lower Canada, see Harvey, *Importing the Revolution*; Harvey, *Le Printemps de l'Amérique française*. On the impact of the French Revolution on Canada, see C. Galarneau, *La France devant l'opinion canadienne, 1789–1815* (Quebec, 1970); P.H. Boulle and

period.[27] It was only in 1995 that Allan Greer argued for a reinterpretation of the Lower Canadian Rebellions of 1837–8 within a real Atlantic framework (rather than a truncated version of it), returning to the ideas put forth by Wallot 20 years earlier.[28] Finally, in 1998, Jean-Pierre Boyer, a communications professor at the Université du Québec à Montréal, published a French translation of Thomas Paine's *The Rights of Man*, at the end of which he added an essay that aimed to integrate Quebec within the Atlantic framework.[29]

Even if the Atlantic framework is not popular among Canadian historians, it could revitalise Canadian intellectual history by encouraging historians to question some old interpretations and revisit the usual intellectual categories of analysis from an international perspective. For instance, it provides a solid intellectual basis for moving beyond the traditional opposition between conservatism and liberalism that has dominated Canadian history for so long. This is not to say that liberalism and conservatism have not played a significant role in shaping Canadian history. But historians have used these terms in many different ways over the last 40 years and given them so many different meanings that those two words now conceal more than they reveal. Furthermore, the liberal/ conservative framework places too much emphasis on what opposed liberals against conservatives in a Canadian context and not enough on what they had in common. For instance, both liberals and conservatives believed in a fundamentally unequal society, while defending private property, the rule of law, and the development of capitalist industries. The British Atlantic intellectual framework allows historians to conceptualise the Canadian past outside the usual

R.A Lebrun (eds.), *Le Canada et la Révolution française* (Montreal, 1989); M. Grenon (ed.), *L'image de la Révolution française au Québec 1789–1989* (Ville LaSalle, 1989); S. Simard (ed.), *La Révolution française au Canada français* (Ottawa, 1989).

[27] For important publications, see A. Gorman Condon, *The Envy of the American States: The Loyalist Dream for New Brunswick* (Fredericton, 1984); N. MacKinnon, *This Unfriendly Soil: The Loyalist Experience in Nova Scotia, 1781–1791* (Montreal and Kingston, 1986); J. Errington, *The Lion, the Eagle, and Upper Canada: A Developing Colonial Ideology* (Montreal and Kingston, 1987). On the development of the loyalist myth, see: B. Murray, 'The Loyalist Tradition in New Brunswick: The Growth and Evolution of an Historical Myth 1825–1914', *Acadiensis*, vol. 4 (1975), pp. 3–45; Norman Knowles, *Inventing the Loyalists: The Ontario Loyalist Tradition and the Creation of Usable Pasts* (Toronto, 1997). For a comparison of the emergence of French and English Canadian founding myths in the mid-nineteenth century, see M. Ducharme, 'Se souvenir de demain. Réflexion sur l'édification des mémoires collectives au Canada-Uni', *Mens. Revue d'histoire intellectuelle de l'Amérique française*, vol. VI, no. 1 (2006), pp. 1–46.

[28] A. Greer, '1837–38: Rebellion Reconsidered', *Canadian Historical Review*, vol. 76 (1995), pp. 1–18.

[29] J.-P. Boyer, 'Le Québec à l'heure des révolutions atlantiques', in Thomas Paine, *Les Droits de l'Homme*, Jean-Pierre Boyer (ed.) (Sillery, 1998), 355–424.

framework by looking at the nation's participation (or non-participation) in the Atlantic revolutions within the context of a new opposition between British constitutionalism and republicanism before 1840. The Atlantic framework also allows us to reinterpret Canadian history after 1840 by highlighting the principles that united Canadian liberals and conservatives as well as what distinguished them from the republicans. In that sense, an Atlantic framework helps us to understand the context in which the Canadian liberal state and liberal social order emerged during the 1840s.[30]

The Atlantic framework could revitalise Canadian intellectual history in another way. As Magda Fahrni notes in Chapter 1 of this volume, Canadian and Quebec historians often completely ignore each other's work.[31] It would be hardly an exaggeration to state that there has never been a truly 'Canadian' history. English Canadians do not pay much attention to Quebec, writing English Canadian history for an English Canadian audience. Conversely, Quebec historians pay no attention to English Canadian history, usually for ideological reasons (admitting that French and English Canada shared a common history would be politically unacceptable). I would argue that it is time for all Canadians to accept the fact that no matter what might happen in the future, they share a common past, and their history will never be as rich and complex as it should be without the integration of both French and English components. The Atlantic framework, imported from outside Canada, could help the historians of Canada's 'Two Solitudes' engage in dialogue on neutral ground.

---

[30]   On the emergence of a liberal order in the 1840s, see: A. Greer and I. Radforth (eds.), *Colonial Leviathan* (Toronto, 1992); I. McKay, 'The Liberal Order Framework: A Prospectus for a Reconnaissance of Canadian History', *Canadian Historical Review*, vol. 81 (2000), pp. 617–45; J.-M. Fecteau, *La liberté du pauvre: sur la régulation du crime et de la pauvreté au XIXe siècle québécois* (Montreal, 2004); J.-F. Constant and M. Ducharme (eds.), *Liberalism and Hegemony. Debating the Canadian Liberal Revolution* (Toronto, 2009).

[31]   On the necessity of taking into consideration Canada while writing Québec history, see J. Létourneau, 'L'Avenir du Canada: par rapport à quelle histoire?', *Canadian Historical Review*, p. 81 (2000), pp. 230–59; Létourneau, *Passer à l'avenir. Histoire, mémoire, identité dans le Québec d'aujourd'hui* (Montreal, 2000), pp. 15–41, 115–67; Létourneau, 'Pour un autre récit de l'aventure historique québécoise', in Damien-Claude Bélanger, Sophie Coupal and Michel Ducharme (eds.), *Les idées en mouvement: perspectives en histoire intellectuelle et culturelle du Canada* (Québec, 2004), pp. 53–73; D.-C. Bélanger, 'Les historiens révisionnistes et le rejet de la canadianité du Québec : Réflexions en marge de la *Genèse des nations et culture du Nouveau Monde* de Gérard Bouchard', *Mens. Revue d histoire intellectuelle de l'Amérique française*, vol. II, no.1 (2001), pp. 105–12; Bélanger, Coupal and Ducharme, 'Introduction' in *Les idées en mouvement*, pp. 10–11; M. Dagenais, 'S'interroger sur la nation: une autre manière d'enseigner l'histoire du Canada', *Canadian Issues* (October/November 2001), pp. 23–5.

The Province of Quebec and the first phase of the Atlantic revolutions

Revisiting the history of Quebec during the Atlantic revolutions from an Atlantic intellectual perspective promises to be beneficial for Canada and Quebec as well as for Atlantic historiography itself. It is true that the Province of Quebec did not participate directly in the Atlantic revolutions at the end of the eighteenth century. Quebec did not join the Thirteen Colonies and certain European countries in their republican revolutions or declare its independence. This was not because American and French republican ideals were not circulating throughout the colony during the first phases of the Atlantic revolutions (1776–1800). The Continental Congress sent three letters to the *Canadiens* (the French-speaking people living in the Saint Lawrence Valley), in October 1774, May 1775 and January 1776.[32] The American military commanders (including George Washington) who invaded the Province of Quebec in the fall of 1775 also wrote to the inhabitants of the Province of Quebec.[33] Fleury Mesplet's bilingual newspaper *La Gazette de Montréal/The Montreal Gazette* promoted republican ideals between 1785 and 1794,[34] as did Edmond-Charles Genêt, the French minister in Philadelphia, who sent an appeal to the *Canadiens* in 1793.[35] Nonetheless, the colonists of the Province of Quebec did not follow the lead of American and French revolutionaries at the end of the eighteenth century.

However, just because the colony failed to take the path of revolution and independence does not mean that its history should not be studied from an Atlantic perspective. In 1791, the British Parliament amended the Quebec Act (1774) and conferred upon the Province of Quebec a new constitution. The new constitution divided the colony between Upper Canada (mainly settled by refugees from the United States) and Lower Canada (comprised of French

[32] See *Journals of the Continental Congress 1774–1789* (Washington: 1904), vol. 1, p. 105–113 (1774 Address); vol. 2, pp. 68–70 (1775 Address); vol. 4, p. 85–6 (1776 Address).

[33] George Washington, 'Address to the Inhabitants of Canada', September 14, 1775 in Philander D. Chase (ed.) *The Papers of George Washington, Revolutionary War Series*, vol. 1 (Charlotteswille, 1985), pp. 461–3.

[34] For a biography of Mesplet, see J.-P. de Lagrave, *Fleury Mesplet, 1734–1794: diffuseur des Lumières au Québec* (Montreal, 1985).

[35] Genêt's text *Les Français libres à leurs frères les Canadiens* is reproduced in M. Brunet, 'La Révolution française sur les rives du St-Laurent', *Revue d'histoire de l'Amérique française*, vol. 11, no. 2 (1957), pp. 158–62. Genêt was then following the advice of Henri-Antoine de Mézière, a Canadian expatriate in the United States who had once collaborated with the *Gazette* and who wrote a brief for him entitled *Observations sur l'état actuel du Canada et sur les dispositions politiques de ses habitants*. Mézière's brief to Genêt is reproduced in M. Wade, 'Quebec and the French Revolution of 1789: The Mission of Henri Mezière', *Canadian Historical Review*, vol. XXXI, no. 4 (1950), pp. 349–51.

Canadians with an important English-speaking minority). It also granted a 'mixed' system of government to both colonies in which the legislative power belonged to the provincial legislatures, which were composed of an appointed governor, an appointed legislative council, and an elected legislative assembly. This constitution was the direct result of the Atlantic revolutions.

Because the Constitutional Act of 1791 created, even if only theoretically, 'un mouvement de participation populaire au gouvernement', Jean-Pierre Wallot argued that this constitution 's'inscrit clairement dans la ligne de la révolution démocratique de R.R. Palmer'.[36] Although representative assemblies were created, the new system did not rest on the revolutionary principles that were shaking the foundations of the Atlantic world. The Atlantic revolutions were inspired by republicanism, an ideology based on the sovereignty of the people (instead of parliamentary sovereignty), the primacy of legislative power over executive power, and the importance of the citizen's participation in the political process. It was this republican ideology that bound together all the Atlantic revolutions, at least from 1776 to 1800. The Constitutional Act did not rest on any of these principles. On the contrary, it aimed at satisfying the colonial demands for a representative assembly while preventing the dissemination of republican principles in the colonies.[37] As such, this episode cannot be interpreted as being part of the Atlantic revolutions.

Because the loyalists had fled the new republic and the British government was trying to prevent the spread of republican values in the Province of Quebec, some scholars such as S.D. Clark and Seymour Martin Lipset interpreted the policies adopted in the 1780s and 1790s as being rooted in counterrevolutionary principles and values.[38] While no one can contest that the Constitutional Act was enacted to prevent the Province of Quebec from falling into an American style of revolution and that its ideological foundations were not republican, this does not mean that the principles on which the 1791 Act rested were necessarily counterrevolutionary.

While still using the adjective 'counterrevolutionary' to depict Canadian history at the end of the eighteenth and beginning of the nineteenth century, Jerry

---

[36]   J.-P. Wallot, 'En guise de conclusion', *Annales historiques de la Révolution française*, vol. 45 (1973), p. 433.

[37]   On this question, see F. Murray Greenwood, *Legacies of Fear: Law and Politics in the Era of the French Revolution* (Toronto, 1993), p. 35–75; E. Gould, 'Revolution and Counter-Revolution', in Eliga H. Gould and Peter S. Onuf (eds.), *Empire and Nation: The American Revolution in the Atlantic World* (Baltimore, 2005), p. 211.

[38]   S.D. Clark, *The Developing Canadian Community* (Toronto, 1962), p. 190–1; S. Martin Lipset, *Revolution and Counterrevolution: Change and Persistence in Social Structures* (New York, 1968), pp. 47–63. For the same argument, see *Continental Divide: The Values and Institutions of the United States and Canada* (New York, 1990), pp. 1–18.

Bannister recently gave it a more limited meaning. He argued that Canadian history was counterrevolutionary in that Canadians rejected 'revolution' as a political instrument, and instead defended the imperial connection. He also maintained that despite this rejection of revolution as a legitimate political instrument, Canadians believed in 'liberal' principles as much as Americans. Therefore, in Bannister's view, Canadian history is distinct from American history not because of its rejection of liberalism and liberal values, but mainly because of its loyalty to the crown and the empire.[39] His argument is convincing as far as values and principles are concerned, demonstrating that 'liberal' values and loyalty to the empire were central in the development of Canada from the end of the eighteenth century onward. However, if this is so, why do Canadian historians continue to present their history as counterrevolutionary? Should it not be enough to argue that Canada was liberal in this context as well as loyal to the crown (which Bannister asserts correctly), without having to refer to counterrevolution as well? After all, if Canada did not participate in the revolutionary movements of the 1780s and 1790s, why should Canadian historians use this event as the pivotal moment of their own history? Why should we analyse our history in negative terms, looking at what it was not rather than at what it was?

An alternative way to integrate Canadian history into the Atlantic framework during the Age of Revolutions while transcending the counterrevolutionary interpretation is to study existing ideologies without defining them through the concept of revolution. After all, American, French and European revolutionaries did not promote revolution for the sake of revolution. They wanted to overthrow a political and social regime based on fundamental principles and replace it with another political and social regime based on different principles. It is therefore essential to understand what these principles were. In this context, a piece of legislation such as the Constitutional Act could be inspired by principles that were not revolutionary (i.e. republican) without necessarily being counterrevolutionary.

As the intellectual historians of the British Atlantic world have argued, the intellectual debates of the eighteenth century tended to place the supporters of the Whig settlement in England in opposition to republicans who were more susceptible to encouraging a revolution (since republicanism was essentially an opposition ideology before the American Revolution). However, this does not mean that the Whigs articulated an intrinsically counterrevolutionary ideology. In fact, their ideology – labelled as Court ideology, commercialism, or British

---

[39] J. Bannister, 'Canada as Counter-Revolution: The Loyalist Order Framework in Canadian History', in Constant and Ducharme (eds.), *Liberalism and Hegemony*.

constitutionalism – had itself been a revolutionary ideology in seventeenth-century England, inspiring the Glorious Revolution of 1688 and its settlement.[40] In the eighteenth century, it had become a source of inspiration for many influential reformers around the Atlantic world. It may not have been as corrosive as republicanism, but it did inspire many philosophers during the Enlightenment, including Voltaire, Montesquieu and Jean-Louis De Lolme. Were these counterrevolutionary philosophers? Were the French Anglophiles of the 1780s less revolutionary under the Old Regime than the Americanists? Were the principles and actions of Simon Bolivar less revolutionary than those of George Washington because Bolivar admired the British system and wanted to import sections of it to Latin America?[41]

In spite of its limitations, the system of government that the British conferred on Upper and Lower Canada in 1791 could not possibly have been considered reactionary at the time. Even if the new constitution was designed to prevent a republican revolution in the colony, it did not create an absolutist state or destroy a more progressive system of government. Rather, it created a new system which rested on British constitutionalism and aimed to strengthen the loyalty of the colonists by granting them a certain amount of political freedom. William Pitt, the British Prime Minister, was clear on this point: the new constitution 'was intended to give a free constitution to Canada, according to British ideas of freedom', insofar as this was possible given Canada's colonial status.[42] In this sense, the goal of the Constitutional Act was to fight republican freedom with British freedom, Rousseauian freedom with Voltairean or Blackstonian freedom. The geographical situation of the colony, just to the north of the new American republic, did not leave much room for the British government to manoeuvre. As Edmund Burke said during the debate leading to the adoption of the Constitutional Act, 'the people of Canada should have nothing to envy in the constitution of a country so near to their own'.[43]

---

[40]   On the revolutionary implications of the 'Glorious Revolution', and the Whig settlement, see L.G. Schwoerer, *The Declaration of Rights, 1689* (Baltimore, 1981); E.S. Morgan, *Inventing the People: The Rise of Popular Sovereignty in England and America* (New York, 1988); J.R. Jones (ed.), *Liberty Secured? Britain before and after 1688* (Stanford, 1992); T. Harris, *Revolution: The Great Crisis of the British Monarchy, 1685–1720* (London, 2006).

[41]   S. Bolivar, 'The Jamaica Letter (6 September 1815)' and 'The Angostura Address (15 February 1819)', in David Bushnell (ed.), *El Liberator: Writing of Simon Bolivar*, trans. Frederick H Fornoff (Oxford, 2003), pp. 12–30, 31–53. See also J. Marichal, 'Bolivar and the Age of Constitutions,' *Harvard Library Bulletin*, vol. 32, no. 2 (1984), pp. 176–89.

[42]   William Pitt (11 May 1791), *The Parliamentary Register* (London, 1791), vol. 29, p. 382. For the limitations of the British constitution in a colonial setting, see Buckner, *Transition to Responsible Government*, pp. 47–91.

[43]   E. Burke (6 May 1791), *The Parliamentary Register*, vol. 29, p. 319.

The British idea of freedom referred to by Pitt was in part defined by William Blackstone in his *Commentaries on the Laws of England* (1765–9). For the British constitutionalist, 'the first and primary end of human laws is to maintain and regulate these absolute rights of individuals.'[44] In theory, British freedom was based on a respect for certain fundamental individual rights. These rights could 'be reduced to three principal or primary articles: the right of personal security, the right of personal liberty, and the right of private property',[45] but also included religious toleration, habeas corpus, trial by jury, the rule of law, and the freedom of the press among others. Politically, this type of freedom referred to a regime where sovereignty and legislative power belonged to a representative institution: parliament. Following the theory of mixed government, the British Parliament included the king (monarchy), the Lords (aristocracy), and the Commons (democracy). Theoretically, the British constitution allowed (and even encouraged) competition between various interest groups within each house, and between both houses and the monarch, in order to limit the possibility of the state alienating the rights of individuals. These principles may not have been as radical as those of the Atlantic revolutions, but they were not counterrevolutionary (particularly since they had been defined prior to the American Revolution).

These British parliamentary principles were the basis of the Constitutional Act, which could therefore hardly be seen as created in reaction to the American Revolution. The principles were imported from England, where they had dominated metropolitan political life for a century. The new Canadian constitution replaced a political regime without any representative institutions so that the colony went from an almost absolutist system of local government to a representative one. The power of the elected assembly may have been more limited than under a republican regime, but at least there was now a representative institution.

This argument rejects the traditional understanding of the Constitutional Act of 1791 as counterrevolutionary, and thus rejects one aspect of the revolution/counterrevolution framework. However, if we understand a revolution as a transformation in the way state legitimacy is conceived of, the Constitutional Act can be seen as having 'revolutionary' implications in the more limited context of the Province of Quebec. For French Canadians, who formed the majority of the population in British North America in the 1790s, the new constitution brought about changes that were as important and fundamental for the British colonies as the changes that the American Revolution brought to the Thirteen Colonies. The 'new' Canadian subjects had never been able to

---

[44] W. Blackstone, *Commentaries on the Laws of England* (1765) (Chicago, 1979), vol. 1, p. 120.

[45] *Ibid.*, vol. 1, p.125.

participate in the political process through elected representatives. This is what the Constitutional Act allowed them to do, even if the influence and power of the people's representatives were limited within the context of British mixed government. Seen in this light, the adoption of the Constitutional Act was most certainly a revolution, at least in the Province of Quebec. This is how Jonathan Sewell (the son of a loyalist), Samuel Neilson (a Whig reformer), and Fleury Mesplet (a republican) saw the new constitution. They thought that Lower Canada had obtained a 'free' constitution without bloodshed.[46] Of course, this 'revolution' did not have anything to do with the Atlantic revolutions, but it was still an integral part of the development of the Atlantic world.

To summarise, the Province of Quebec, and then Lower and Upper Canada, were very much a part of the Atlantic world. The integration of the Canadian/ Quebec experience into the Atlantic and Atlantic-revolutionary frameworks highlights the fact that republicans were not the only ones who wanted 'free' institutions during the Atlantic revolutions. Thus, the main difference between Canada and the other countries that went through the Atlantic revolutions was not that the latter were based on revolution and the former on counter-revolution; rather, the difference is that certain countries went through a republican revolution (even if the 1787 constitution was a mixture of republican and constitutional ideals) while Canada went through a British constitutionalist 'revolution'. By integrating Canadian history into the Atlantic framework, Canadian historians can better understand their own history by moving beyond the revolutionary/counterrevolutionary binary. They can study the intellectual foundations of their first parliamentary institutions for what they were rather than for what they were not. Canadian historians can in turn enrich the Atlantic framework by questioning the connection between the concepts of freedom and revolution at the end of the eighteenth century, showing that it was possible to reject republicanism in the Age of Revolutions without necessarily rejecting freedom or embracing counterrevolutionary or reactionary values.

---

[46]   Samuel Neilson and Fleury Mesplet welcomed the Constitutional Act by publishing the same text promoting the new constitution in their respective newspapers: *La Gazette de Québec/The Quebec Gazette* (February 23, March 1, 8, 15, 1792) and *La Gazette de Montréal/The Montreal Gazette* (March 15, 22, 1792). Its author, Solon, was Jonathan Sewell, the future Chief Justice of Lower Canada (1808–38): John Hare, *Aux origines du parlementarisme québécois 1791–1793* (Sillery, 1993), pp. 46, 131.

The 1837–8 Rebellions as the last chapter of the Atlantic revolutions

If the Atlantic intellectual framework, with its opposition of two broad ideologies based on two different concepts of freedom, can be useful for re-evaluating the nature of the Constitutional Act and for situating the Canadian experience within a larger context, it is also useful for reinterpreting the nature of the 1837–8 Rebellions.[47] These rebellions were a complex phenomenon caused by economic, political, social, and ethnic factors. Yet, in terms of underlying ideologies, historians have generally presented the insurrections as the result of an opposition between conservatives and reformers/liberals.

But when we look at the ideological origins of the rebellions from an Atlantic perspective, we are struck by the resemblance between the Canadian debates of the 1830s and the debates that took place during the first phases of the Atlantic revolutions in both America and Europe. On one side, the colonial political and economic elite and a few moderate reformers – such as Étienne Parent and Robert Baldwin – supported the British constitutional model, as the British Whigs, French Anglophiles and American Federalists had done between 1776 and 1800. On the other side, Lower Canadian Patriots and Upper Canadian Radicals favoured republican institutions (their only hope of controlling the political agenda in the colonies), as the British Radicals, French *américanistes* and American Jeffersonians had done before. In this context, it is possible to see the 1837–8 Rebellions and the debates surrounding them as the last chapter of the Atlantic revolutions.[48]

From 1791 to 1828, Upper and Lower Canadians, conservatives and reformers alike, did not question the ideological foundations of the colonial political and social order. Even the colonial reform movements that emerged after 1806 in both colonies did not contest the basis of the Constitutional Act (except for a few individuals in Upper Canada). Canadian reformers generally did not follow the lead of Central and South American revolutionaries who had fought for their independence between 1808 and 1826. Instead, most Canadian reformers saw themselves as loyal subjects of the British Empire and defended their government and its legitimacy. They framed their demands not according to the principles of Atlantic revolutionaries, but according to Locke, Blackstone and De Lolme's analysis of the British constitution.[49]

[47] It might also be useful to revisit the Escheat Movement in Prince Edward Island in the 1830s. On this movement of protest, see R. Bittermann, *Rural Protest on Prince Edward Island: From British Colonization to the Escheat Movement* (Toronto, 2007).

[48] For a longer version of this argument, see M. Ducharme 'Closing the Last Chapter of the Atlantic Revolution: The 1837–1838 Rebellions in Upper and Lower Canada', *Proceedings of the American Antiquarian Society*, vol. 116, part 2 (2006), pp. 411–28.

[49] For the reformers, see *Le Canadien* – a reformist newspaper founded by Pierre Bédard in 1806 Between 1806 and 1810, Bédard did not mention even one republican. He always cited

Even though Canadian reformers had framed their demands within the parameters of the British constitution, by 1828 they had not managed to achieve
anything since the British government did not amend the colonial constitution.
The reformers' inability to get results forced them to look for new arguments,
and this is how they rediscovered republican principles. Republicanism, based
on the sovereignty of the people, gave them stronger arguments against the
status quo and encouraged them to question the legitimacy of the colonial constitution. After 1828, both Lower Canadian Patriots and Upper Canadian
Radicals adopted republican ideals.[50] From 1828 to 1838, Canadian colonies
went through a political process that corresponded to the criteria of the Atlantic
revolutions, a process which culminated with the 1837–8 Rebellions.

During the 1830s, Lower Canadian Patriots, led by Louis-Joseph Papineau,
and Upper Canadian Radicals, led by William Lyon Mackenzie, adopted a discourse based on freedom, equality and virtue. By freedom, the Canadian republicans did not mean individual rights or civil liberties; in fact, they seldom
mentioned such civil rights during the decade. For colonial republicans, freedom
meant first and foremost political liberty. These men believed that the right to
participate in the political process was the most fundamental right that any citizen could possess. Seen in this context, the Patriots and the Radicals cannot be
understood as liberal since they did not demand more civil freedom or autonomy from the state, but rather wanted to control the state.[51]

Like American and European revolutionaries before them, Patriots and
Radicals thought that freedom was impossible without equality of rights as well
as a certain amount of material equality. This is not to say that Canadian republicans (or most of the Atlantic republicans for that matter) were social levellers,
but they did believe that too great a disparity between citizens within one state
destroyed freedom and prevented citizens from participating equally in political
life since the rich had the means to bribe the poor. To ensure the economic and
social equality of all citizens, the republican leaders envisioned a society of independent and virtuous small landowners. In Canada, as elsewhere around the
Atlantic, virtue was a key word in republican rhetoric. It referred to the equality

---

Montesqieu, Blackstone, Locke and De Lolme. For the Tories, see J. Strachan, *A Discourse on the
Character of King George the Third: Addresses to the inhabitants of British America* (Montreal, 1810).

[50]   On the republican ideology of the Lower Canadian Patriots and Upper Canadian Radicals, see
also A. Greer, *The Patriots and the People* (Toronto: 1993); Harvey, *Le Printemps de l'Amérique française*;
J.E. Rea, 'William Lyon Mackenzie Jacksonian?', *Mid-America: An History Quarterly*, vol. 50, no. 3
(1968), pp. 223–35.

[51]   For a liberal interpretation of the Lower Canadian rebellions, see Y. Lamonde's *Histoire sociale des
idées* (vol.1, pp. 121–279) and M. Bellavance's *Le Québec au siècle des nationalités*.

and the independence of citizens, as well as to their simple way of life and their capacity to promote the common good in public life, even at personal expense.

Canadian republicans incorporated these principles into a sophisticated set of political proposals. Because they argued that the most important right of the citizen was to participate in the political process by electing representatives, the Patriots and the Radicals focused on the reform of *legislative* power. Simply put, they wanted the British government to acknowledge the sovereignty of the colonial people. In Upper Canada, the first objective of the reformers was to reform the legislative assembly which, unlike in Lower Canada, they did not control, except from 1828 to 1830, and again from 1834 to 1836. They concluded from their electoral failure that the biggest constitutional problem in the colony was the way that representation was framed.[52]

The colonial republicans also demanded that the composition of the legislative councils be reformed. In doing this, they were contesting the very foundations of the colonial constitutional order based on the British principle of mixed government. During the 1830s, colonial republicans did not see the appointed upper houses of the two Canadian legislatures as legitimate since they were unelected. In Lower Canada, 34 of the 'Ninety-Two Resolutions' (the charter of Lower Canadian republicanism) adopted by their Assembly in February 1834 concerned this reform (resolutions 9-40, 51, 54).[53] Upper Canadians also fought for such a reform, even if they were not as ardent as their counterparts from Lower Canada. The *Seventh Report on Grievances* of 1835 (the charter of Upper Canadian republicanism), submitted by a committee of the Assembly chaired by Mackenzie, presented the 'elective institutions [as] the only safeguards to prevent the Canadas from making disadvantageous comparisons between the condition of the colonists and the adjoining country.'[54]

Not only did the Patriots and the Radicals argue for republican reforms, but they also tried to connect their movement to the Atlantic revolutionary process, especially the American Revolution. In Upper Canada, William Lyon

[52] Mackenzie began to contest the state of representation in Upper Canada in 1831. An inquiry committee was created the same year, with Mackenzie as its chair. Its report was introduced in the House on 16 March 1831. Its conclusions were predictable. For the committee, 'the imperfect state of the representation in the House of Assembly is and has been the cause of much evil to the Community' [*First Report on the State of the Representation of the People of Upper Canada in the Legislature of that Province* (York, 1831), p. 4 for the quotes]. Major reforms were necessary. Notwithstanding this report, no major changes were brought to the representation in Upper Canada before the 1837 rebellion.

[53] *Journals of the House of Assembly of Lower Canada*, 4th session of the 14th Provincial Parliament (7 January – 18 March, 1834), pp. 311–35.

[54] 'Seventh Report on Grievances', *Appendix to Journal of the House of Assembly of Upper Canada*, 1st session of the 12th Provincial Parliament (15 January – 16 April 1835), vol. 1, p. 11.

Mackenzie presented the American Revolution and Republic as a great source of inspiration. In his *Sketches of Canada and the United States* (1833), he did not hide his admiration for America's independence and institutions.[55] In Lower Canada, Louis-Joseph Papineau argued that if the British Parliament tried to dominate Lower Canada as it had tried to dominate the Thirteen Colonies during the 1770s, many new Jeffersons or Washingtons would appear in the colony.[56]

By 1836, the example of the American Revolution was clearly being used to encourage Canadians to fight for their rights. In the summer of 1837, Lower Canadian Patriots organised the boycott of British products in the colony as the American Patriots had done during the 1770s. In October 1837, a militia called *Les Fils de la Liberté* (the Sons of Liberty) was organised.[57] Later that month, an important public assembly was held at Saint Charles in the Richelieu Valley: the first resolution adopted was the translation of the second paragraph of the American Declaration of Independence, beginning with 'We hold these truths to be self-evident, that all men are created equal'.[58] In Upper Canada, Mackenzie defended the right of Canadians to choose their form of government as a 'right [that] was conceded to the present United States at the close of a successful revolution'.[59] In the summer of 1837, he went so far as to reprint, in his newspaper *The Constitution*, Thomas Paine's pamphlet *Common Sense*, first published in 1776 to promote American independence.[60] Mackenzie also wrote in July 1837: 'Canadians! It has been said that we are on the verge of a revolution. We are in the midst of one; a bloodless one, I hope, but a revolution to which all those which have been will be counted mere child's play'.[61] By November, he had published a short text entitled *Independence* in which he openly promoted rebellion.

In 1836 and 1837, the republicans were challenging the very foundations of their state with the same arguments that had been used by the American, French and European revolutionaries at the end of the eighteenth century. Their opponents, who controlled the legislative councils of the colonies, defended their

---

[55] William Lyon Mackenzie, *Sketches of Canada and the United States* (London, 1833).

[56] L.-J. Papineau, 'Nécessité de nommer un délégué de la Chambre d'Assemblée à Londres' (House of Assembly, 17 November 1835), in Yvan Lamonde and Claude Larin (eds.), *Un demi-siècle de combats: Interventions publiques* (Montreal, 1998), p. 367.

[57] See the 'Adresse des Fils de la liberté de Montréal aux jeunes gens des colonies de l'Amérique du Nord' (4 October 1837), reproduced in Jean-Paul Bernard (ed.), *Assemblées publiques, résolutions et déclarations de 1837–1838* (Ville St-Laurent, 1988), p. 216.

[58] This resolution was reprinted in *La Minerve*, 30 Oct. 1837.

[59] *The Constitution*, 2 August 1837.

[60] *Ibid.*, 19 and 26 Jul., 2 and 9 Aug. 1837.

[61] *Ibid.*, 26 Jul. 1837.

constitution and form of government (and also their interests) by making references to John Locke, the great British constitutionalists and the American federalists. They denounced the republicans as traitors on the basis of Blackstonian arguments. This opposition between constitutionalists and republicans eventually paralysed the political system, at least in the lower province.

In the autumn of 1837 the Lower Canadian Patriots and the Upper Canadian Radicals launched a physical and intellectual attack against the colonial state in British North America. The rebels were not just attempting to overthrow the government; at a more fundamental level, they were trying to challenge the existing constitutional order of the colonies (based on the British principle of mixed government) and to reconfigure power relations in both Canadas according to a model of state legitimacy drawn from republican principles. In accordance with their republican ideals, they fought for the ultimate sovereignty of the people, the primacy of legislative power over executive power, and the economic and political independence of all citizens. Both groups of Canadian republicans were motivated by the same principles that had inspired American and European republicans, and although the Canadian uprisings occurred much later than these revolutions, they were ideologically similar to the upheavals that preceded them. However, unlike the other Atlantic revolutions that did succeed in overthrowing pre-existing states, the Canadian uprisings failed. Despite this failure, there is no question that the rebellions were part of the Atlantic revolutionary process.

Integrating the Canadian rebellions into the framework of the Atlantic revolutions not only gives new meaning to the uprisings, but it gives a new coherence to the framework. As the 1776 American Declaration of Independence and the British military defeat heralded the beginning of the Atlantic revolutions, so did the failure of the Canadian rebellions and the victory of the British forces and Canadian volunteers in 1837–8 herald their end.

★ ★ ★

If the general Atlantic world lost its coherence in the beginning of the nineteenth century, the intellectual framework developed by the British Atlanticists did not. Republicanism and constitutionalism continued to influence Canada's history. Republican ideals were promoted by some Clear Grits in Canada West (Ontario) up to the 1850s and by *Les Rouges* in Canada East (Quebec) well beyond Confederation. Even Louis Riel and the Métis sometimes used a republican rhetoric during the Métis rebellion of 1869–70. As for constitutionalism, it influenced both Canadian liberals and conservatives in the second half of the nineteenth century. It explains why liberals and conservatives shared many principles and values. Therefore, as far as intellectual history is concerned, the intellectual framework developed by the Anglo-American Atlanticists allows historians to better understand the intellectual roots of Canada not only for the period prior to the rebellions, but even the period after.

In sum, the Atlantic framework offers historians the possibility of reinterpreting Canadian and Quebec intellectual history, letting them place it in its original context at the crossroads of the British Empire and the Americas. The integration of the Canadian and Quebec experience within Atlantic history allows historians to revisit colonial ideological oppositions in a broader context and give new meaning to local political struggles. In the meantime, Canadian history enriches and completes the Atlantic framework. It forces historians to study commercialism/British constitutionalism – the alternative ideology to republicanism – since this ideology laid the foundations for the very creation of Canada. It also highlights the relevance of Canadian and Quebec intellectual history to the larger history of the Atlantic world.

Acknowledgements

I would like to express my gratitude to Michael Dawson, Christopher Dummitt and the conference's participants for their thoughtful comments. My thanks also go to Michael Lanthier and Robert A.J. McDonald for the assistance they offered in the preparation and writing of this article. The ideas discussed in this chapter were first developed in my PhD dissertation entitled 'Aux fondements de l'État canadien. La liberté au Canada de 1776 à 1841' (McGill University, 2005). I wish to thank the Social Sciences and Humanities Research Council of Canada (SSHRC) and the Fonds pour la Formation de Chercheurs et l'Aide à la Recherche (FCAR) for their support.

INSTITUTE FOR THE STUDY OF THE
A M E R I C A S
UNIVERSITY OF LONDON · SCHOOL OF ADVANCED STUDY

The Institute for the Study of the Americas (ISA) promotes, coordinates and provides a focus for research and postgraduate teaching on the Americas – Canada, the USA, Latin America and the Caribbean – in the University of London.

The Institute was officially established in August 2004 as a result of a merger between the Institute of Latin American Studies and the Institute of United States Studies, both of which were formed in 1965.

The Institute publishes in the disciplines of history, politics, economics, sociology, anthropology, geography and environment, development, culture and literature, and on the countries and regions of Latin America, the United States, Canada and the Caribbean.

ISA runs an active programme of events – conferences, seminars, lectures and workshops – in order to facilitate national research on the Americas in the humanities and social sciences. It also offers a range of taught master's and research degrees, allowing wide-ranging multi-disciplinary, multi-country study or a focus on disciplines such as politics or globalisation and development for specific countries or regions.

Full details about the Institute's publications, events, postgraduate courses and other activities are available on the web at www.americas.sas.ac.uk.

Institute for the Study of the Americas
School of Advanced Study, University of London
Senate House, Malet Street, London WC1E 7HU

Tel 020 7862 8870, Fax 020 7862 8886, Email americas@sas.ac.uk
Web www.americas.sas.ac.uk

Recent and forthcoming titles in the ISA series:

Democracy after Pinochet: Politics, parties and elections in Chile (2007)
by Alan Angell

Mexican Soundings: Essays in Honour of David A. Brading (2007)
edited by Susan Deans-Smith and Eric Van Young

America's Americans: Population Issues in U.S. Society and Politics (2007)
edited by Philip Davies and Iwan Morgan

Football in the Americas: Fútbol, Futebol, Soccer (2007)
edited by Rory Miller

Bolivia: Revolution and the Power of History in the Present. Essays (2007)
James Dunkerley

American Civilization (2007)
Charles A. Jones

Caribbean Literature After Independence: The Case of Earl Lovelace (2008)
edited by Bill Schwarz

The Political Economy of the Public Budget in the Americas (2008)
edited by Diego Sánchez-Ancochea and Iwan Morgan

Joaquim Nabuco, British Abolitionists and the End of Slavery in Brazil:
Correspondence 1880–1905 (2009)
edited by Leslie Bethell and José Murilo de Carvalho

The Contemporary Canadian Metropolis (forthcoming)
edited by Richard Dennis, Ceri Morgan and Stephen Shaw

Latin London: The Lives of Latin American Migrants in the Capital
(forthcoming)
by Cathy McIlwaine

CPSIA information can be obtained at www.ICGtesting.com
Printed in the USA
BVOW07s0553221214

380399BV00001B/2/P